THE ENGLISH MEDIEVAL ROOF
Crownpost to Kingpost

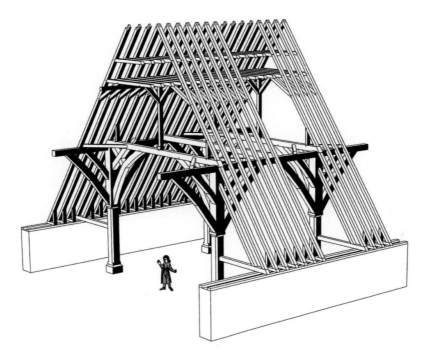

St. Mary's Hospital, Chichester, West Sussex
*c.*1290

Report of Essex Historic Buildings Group Day School 2008

Edited by John Walker

Published 2011 by Essex Historic Buildings Group
assisted by grants from
The Vernacular Architecture Group
and
The Suffolk Historic Buildings Group

ISBN
978-0-9530946-1-5

Essex Historic Buildings Group would like to thank
The Vernacular Architecture Group
and
The Suffolk Historic Buildings Group
for their generous grants towards this publication.

Printed by Gipping Press Ltd, Unit 2 Lion Barn Industrial Estate, Needham Market, Suffolk
www.gippingpress.co.uk

CONTENTS

	Authors		2
	Preface		3
	List of Figures		4
	Tree-ring Dates and Abbreviations		10
1	Introduction and Overview	*John Walker*	11
2	East Anglian Roofs: An Essex-Centric View	*David Stenning*	27
3	Early Roofs in Hampshire: 1240-1600	*Edward Roberts*	47
4	Medieval Roofs in the West Midlands: The Potential of Archaeology and Tree-Ring Dating	*Bob Meeson*	63
5	Roof Carpentry in Devon from 1250-1700	*John R. L. Thorp*	91
6	Medieval Roofs in the North of England	*Robert Hook*	115
7	Roofs in Yorkshire Timber-Framed Buildings before *c.*1560	*Barry Harrison*	125
8	Queenpost Roofs in East Anglia	*Philip Aitkens*	136
9	Glossary	*John Walker*	147
10	Bibliography		154
11	Index of Buildings Illustrated		159
	Essex Historic Buildings Group		162

AUTHORS

Philip Aitkens is an Historic Buildings Consultant based near Bury St Edmunds, Suffolk. After working on the Listed Buildings Resurvey of Suffolk in the 1980s, he became freelance. His interests include medieval carpentry, early farm buildings and the interior design of vernacular buildings.

Barry Harrison was a Lecturer in local and regional history in the Department of Continuing Education, University of Leeds from 1966 until his retirement in 1999. His main research interests lie in landscape and building history. He is the current Chair of Cleveland and Teesside Local History Society and is a leading member of the Yorkshire Vernacular Buildings Study Group.

Bob Hook is the head of training and standards at English Heritage. He was a member of the RCHME team investigating the chronology of truncated principal roof trusses in north east England.

Bob Meeson is a former President of the Vernacular Architecture Group, and was a county council archaeologist before becoming a freelance historic buildings consultant, recording and reporting on vernacular, polite and ecclesiastical buildings.

Edward Roberts has written extensively on the history of Hampshire and has promoted a tree-ring dating programme which has resulted in the publication of his recent book on Hampshire Houses 1250-1700.

David Stenning is an architect and a former head of conservation at Essex County Council, and has written numerous articles on vernacular buildings in East Anglia. He is a former President of Essex Historic Buildings Group.

John Thorp is a partner in Keystone Historic Buildings Consultants and, since 1972, has been working on aspects of the Devon vernacular tradition.

John Walker is a lecturer, writer and researcher on historic timber-framed buildings, and is a former chairman of the Essex Historic Buildings Group.

PREFACE

This publication is the result of a Day School run by the Essex Historic Buildings Group (EHBG) in the 13th century barns at Cressing Temple, Essex, on Saturday 12th July 2008.

EHBG felt it was time for a reappraisal of medieval roofs as it was 50 years since J T Smith made the first serious attempt to study these from a historical standpoint in his 1958 article 'Medieval Roofs: A Classification' in the Archaeological Journal CXV.

The first six papers published here are revised and edited versions of the those presented at the Day School. Robert Hook, the author of Chapter 6 on northern roofs, was unable to be present on the day, and sent his paper which I read to the participants. Because of this, I asked Barry Harrison, who was attending the Day School, if he could lead the discussion from the floor on northern roofs. He later agreed to write the very valuable paper on Yorkshire roofs at Chapter 7 after studying all the extensive building reports and surveys undertaken by the Yorkshire Vernacular Buildings Study Group. The eighth chapter on 'Queenpost Roofs in East Anglia' was added after Philip Aitkens gave a talk on these roofs to EHBG on 7th July 2010, again at Cressing Temple. It gives considerable insight into a roof type not very common outside East Anglia, showing how complex and varied an individual roof type could be, much as Robert Hook demonstrates for the truncated principal rafter roof in northern England in Chapter 6.

For this publication I have tried to include as many illustrations as possible. It is clear from discussion with the authors and others that historic building researchers are divided by a common language; on occasions the same description can be used for two quite different roofs. The Council for British Archaeology's illustrated glossary, 'Recording Timber-Framed Buildings' (Alcock et al 1996), has helped to create a common but limited vocabulary. Liberal use of illustrations will, I hope, resolve any such problems here.

The aim of this publication is to provide information on the development of medieval roofs on smaller non-cruck secular buildings in order to provide a framework for researchers in their own areas. It is also hoped it will be seen as a companion volume to '*Regional Variations in Timber-Framed Buildings in England and Wales Down to 1550*' (Stenning & Andrews 2002).

'*The English Medieval Roof*' is the result of a lot of hard work by many people, in particular the contribution of the authors whose papers are published here and who I thank for their patience in dealing with my many queries and questions. But none of this would have happened without the hard and willing work, and support, of members of the Essex Historic Buildings Group who organised and ran the Day School providing accommodation, seating, sound, projectors and food.

I would like to thank David Andrews, Anne Padfield and especially my wife, Pam Walker, for proof reading the final draft and for suggesting improvements. Finally I would like to thank the Vernaular Architecture Group and the Suffolk Historic Buildings Group for their grants towards this publication, without which it would have been difficult to publish this book.

John Walker
May 2011

LIST OF FIGURES

Cover
Crownpost over spear truss of Tiptofts, Wimbish,
    Essex - 1282-1327d
Kingpost in solar wing of Smithills Hall, Bolton,
    Greater Manchester, formerly Lancashire

Front Page
St. Mary's Hospital, Chichester, West Sussex - c1290

Chapter 1
1.1:   J T Smith's main roof categories
1.2:   Map of true crucks in England & Wales
1.3:   Crownpost and king strut
        a: Crownpost
        b: King strut
        c: Hybrid crownpost at Tiptofts, Wimbish, Essex
          - 1287-1329d
1.4:   Examples of clasped and butt (or tenoned)
        purlins.
1.5:   Queenpost roof over service wing - The Wood-
        lands, Brundish, Suffolk - 16th C
1.6:   Crownpost and side purlin roof 50 Stonegate,
        York - 14th or early 15th C
1.7:   Date & location of early aisled halls with pass-
        ing braces
1.8:   Centre truss of open hall with tapering passing
        braces at Westwick Cottage, St Michael, Hert-
        fordshire - 1184-1219d (VA39, 107)
1.9:   Siddington Barn, Gloucestershire with passing
        braces and side purlins - 1245-7d
1.10: Fyfield Hall, Fyfield, Essex - Building after al-
        terations of 1391-1416d when central arcade
        posts and aisles rebuilt. Roof 1167-85d
1.11: Clasped side purlin over north aisle of Wells
        Cathedral, Somerset. The brace is jointed with
        secret notched lap joints - 1212/13
1.12: Reconstruction of Royal George, Cottingham,
        Northamptonshire - 1262d.
1.13: Selection of early crownposts in England
1.14: King strut roof over Guest Hall of St
        Augustine's Abbey, Canterbury, Kent
1.15: Early crownpost with collar purlin tenoned into
        the crownpost at York Farm, West Hagbourne,
        Oxfordshire - 1284-5d
1.16: Early crownposts with continuous purlins
        a: West Bromwich Manor House, formerly Staf-
          fordshire - 1270-88d
        b: Centre crownpost Lime Tree House, Harwell,
          Oxfordshire, inserted 1294-1306d
1.17: Chapelle Saint-Laurent des Vaux, Gisors, France
        - 1224d
1.18: Outline of date ranges for roof styles in Essex
        and Suffolk
1.19: Early 15th century example of butt purlins in the
        false hammerbeam roof over the open hall of
        Bourchiers Chantry, High St, Halstead, Essex
1.20: Range of tree-ring dates for roofs in Shropshire

1.21: Example of purlins trenched onto the back of the
        principal rafters
1.22: Range of tree-ring dates for roofs in Hampshire
1.23: Percentage of roof types in each period in Kent
        houses surveyed and dated in the RCHME sur-
        vey of medieval houses in Kent
1.24: Roof of open hall of Clintons, Little Hadham,
        Hertfordshire - early 15th C
1.25: Croxton Manor House, Croxton, Cambridgeshire
        - 'H' plan house - Late 15th C
        a: Open hall centre truss
        b: Centre truss of east service wing
1.26: Range of tree-ring dates for roofs in Somerset
1.27: Roof of east end of the nave of Wells Cathedral
1.28: Base cruck with crownpost roof - The Tudor
        Tavern, Fore St, Taunton, Somerset - 1323-24d
1.29: Two-tier base cruck Glastonbury Abbey Barn
        near Wells, Somerset – 1334-44
1.30: Threaded side purlins in hall roof at Keynedon
        Barton, Sherford, Devon - late 15th/early 16th C
1.31: Arcade post with passing brace trench - Whiston
        Barn, Whiston, South Yorkshire - 1233-52d
1.32: 111 Walmgate, York - c.1400
1.33: 111 Walmgate, York - Crownpost with raked-
        purlin struts clasping side purlins - c.1400
1.34: Merchant Adventurers' Hall, York - Crownpost
        with jowled head and truncated principals clasp-
        ing side purlins - 1358-60.
1.35: Nave roof of Sainte-Croix, Liège, Belgium.
        King strut roof with truncated principal rafters
        1283-4d
1.36: Kingpost over low end crosswing of Preston
        Patrick Hall, Kendal, Cumbria – late 15th/early
        16th C
1.37: Open hall and kingpost of Smithills Hall, Bolton,
        Greater Manchester (formerly Lancashire),
        which is assigned to the early 15th C
1.38: Wealden houses
        a: Masons Court, Stratford upon Avon,
          Warwickshire
        b: Old Bell Farm, Harrietsham, Kent
        c: Bayleaf, Chiddingstone, Kent now at Weald &
          Downland
        d: Thatchers, Hundon, Suffolk

Chapter 2
2.1:   Fyfield Hall, Essex in the late 12th Century -
        1167-85d
2.2:   Abbey Barn, Snape, Suffolk - late 14th C
2.3:   Reconstruction with side purlins in the roof over
        the aisles of early 13th C Barley Barn, Cressing
        Temple, Essex - 1205-1230d
2.4:   Inserted crownpost Bradwell Hall, Bradwell,
        Essex - 13th C
2.5:   Three Blackbirds, Ely, Cambridgeshire - early
        14th C
2.6:   Crownpost in low end crosswing of Tiptofts,

Wimbish, Essex - 1287-1329d

2.7: Tweed Cottage, Stebbing, Essex - early 14th C

2.8: Ringers, Terling, Essex - 14th C

2.9: Heybridge Hall, Heybridge, Essex - 14th C

2.10: Hall centre truss of Tiptofts, Wimbish, Essex - 1287-1329d

2.11: Crosswing of Great Codham Hall, Wethersfield, Essex - 1327-70d

2.12: Crownpost over centre truss of the raised-aisled hall at The Stables, Church Farm, Fressingfield, Suffolk - mid-14th C

2.13: 15th century octagonal crownposts over centre trusses of open halls in Essex and South Suffolk
    a: River Green House, Great Sampford, Essex
    b. The George, High St, Colchester, Essex
    c. Shingle Hall, Great Dunmow, Essex
    d. Monks Barn, Newport, Essex - a wealden house
    e. Valley Farm, Flatford, Suffolk

2.14: Examples of Suffolk 'knee' braced crownposts
    a: Saxtead,
    b: Swift Manor, Preston St. Mary
    c: Bures St Mary

2.15: Cross-quadrate crownposts
    a: Cottage in grounds of Freswell House, Saffron Walden, Essex - 15th C
    b: Section of cross-quadrate crownpost
    c: Railway Terraces, Wenhaston, Suffolk - late 15th C

2.16: Arch over low end bay of open hall of the aisled hall, Normans Farmhouse, Wakes Colne, Essex - 1368d

2.17: Crownpost braces to collar purlin form an arch over hall chamber at Graves Farm, Catmere End, Littlebury, Essex - 16th C

2.18: Old Cottage, Little Chesterford, Essex - Transitional house with late crownpost roof - 16th C

2.19: Crosswing 60-64 High Street, Brentwood, Essex viewed from the rear - 15th C

2.20: Cranked crownpost in Little Waltham, Essex

2.21: Reconstruction of open hall of Gobions, Great Bardfield, Essex - late 14th C

2.22: No 3 King Street, Kings Lynn, Norfolk - 15th C

2.23: Roof of first floor hall in Thetford Priory, Norfolk now part of Abbey Farm - early 15th C

2.24: Comparison of centre trusses of Tiptofts and Baythorne Hall, Essex
    a: Tiptofts, Wimbish, Essex - Hammer beam centre truss - 1287-1329d
    b: Baythorne Hall, Birdbrook, Essex - Raised-aisled hall centre truss - 1341/2d

2.25: Queenpost roof over open hall of the White House, Wacton, Norfolk - 15th C

2.26: Two-tier queenpost roof of Warden's Hall, Merton College, Oxford built 1299-1300

2.27: Distribution of raised-aisled halls and queenpost roofs in Suffolk by parish

2.28: Centre truss of Lodge Farm, Denton, Norfolk c.1355-60d

2.29: White Hart, Coggeshall, Essex - 15th C

2.30: Queenpost roof with upper 'kingpost' at Wash Farm, Ford Street, Aldham, Essex

2.31: Clasped side purlin roof with diminished principal rafters -The Bell, Great Easton, Essex - 1527/8d

2.32: Early clasped side purlins - Monks Barn, Netteswellbury, Essex - 1439-69d

2.33: Two types of roof at Hales Hall Farmhouse, Hales, Norfolk
    a: Roof with queen struts, ridgepiece & two tiers of butt side purlins
    b: Two-tier roof of queenposts with crownpost above

2.34: Roof of service crosswing of Horham Hall, Thaxted, Essex - late 15th C

2.35: Examples of hammer beam roofs in East Anglia
    a: Ancient House, Saffron Walden, Essex
    b: Roof of two storey rear wing of Ancient House, Ipswich, Suffolk - 15th C
    c: False hammer beam truss of Bourchiers Chantry, Halstead, Essex - 15th C

2.36: Examples of arch-braced roofs in East Anglia
    a: Cellarers Hall, Stoke By Clare, Suffolk with stub tiebeams
    b: 62 Whiting Street, Bury St Edmunds, Suffolk with collar purlin & stub tiebeams- 15th C
    c: Red Lion, Billericay, Essex with butt purlins, collar purlin & crownpost - 15th C

2.37: Golden Fleece, South Weald, Essex with clasped side purlin & diminished principal rafters - early 16th C

2.38: Scissor bracing at Bretts Farm, Aveley, Essex - early 15th C

2.39: Clothiers' Hall, Ipswich, Suffolk - 16th C

2.40: The Guildhall, Bury St Edmunds, Suffolk-16th C

2.41: Spere truss of Framsden Hall, Framsden, Suffolk - late 15th C

2.42: Kingpost roof in barn at Hill Farm, Gestingthorpe, Essex - 19th C

2.43: A-frame trusses at Hosdens, Great Maplestead, Essex - 16th C

2.44: A-frame truss with extended jowls at service end of open hall at Copeland House, Fobbing, Essex - 15th C

2.45: Open hall of Copeland House, Fobbing, Essex - 15th C

2.46: Clasped side purlin roof with diminished principal rafters at 30 High Street, Maldon, Essex - 16th C

2.47: Types of clasped side purlins in East Anglia in the 16th & 17th C

2.48: Clasped side purlin roof with 'principal rafters' the same size as the common rafters - Marks Cottage, Layham, Suffolk - 18th C

2.49: Mixed construction - the third truss is an A-frame truss with butt purlins - at The Stables, Wethersfield, Essex - late 16th C

2.50: North wall of Manor Farm, Pulham Market, Norfolk, viewed internally with mixed roof construction - 1615d

2.51: Queen struts in clasped side purlin roof of Shellow Cross Farmhouse, Willingale, Essex - 17th C

2.52: Sheepcote Farmhouse, Southminster, Essex - 17th C

Chapter 3

3.1: Map of true crucks in England & Wales

3.2: A simplified geological map of Hampshire

3.3: Map of true crucks in Hampshire

3.4: Park View, Tichborne, Hampshire - A reconstruction of the hall showing the graceful Gothic arch of the hall truss and the 'fan' truss at the high end - 1448-80d

3.5: Some cruck apex types in Hampshire
   a: Type E (reused) at Water Ditch Farm, Poulner, Ringwood;
   b: Type C at Tan-y-Bryn, Hannington - 1360d
   c: Type W at Park View, Tichborne - 1448-80d
   d: Type F1 at Tan-y-Bryn, Hannington - 1360d

3.6: Cruck chronology of roofs in Hampshire

3.7: Chronology of roofs on box-framed and masonry buildings in Hampshire

3.8: Roof of the solar at Michelmersh Manor Farm, Hampshire showing the curved soulaces in the former solar - 1321/2d

3.9: Forge Sound, East Meon, Hampshire - a reconstruction of the open hall with a sans-purlin, collar rafter roof

3.10: Roof trusses from the former refectory of Romsey Abbey, Hampshire
   a: the primary roof of c.1230 with the existing second-phase purlins in solid black.
   b: a second-phase truss of 1342-47(?)d.

3.11: Wherwell Abbey, Hampshire - the roof of what was probably the infirmary - dated to 1250d and 1280d

3.12: Comparative cross-sections of early roofs in Normandy & Hampshire
   a: The church at Champagne-sur-Oise -1233/34d
   b: 15 High Street, Fareham, Hampshire - 1279-1311d
   c: Bishop's Waltham Palace stables, Hampshire - 1300-15d

3.13: Titchfield Abbey Barn, Hampshire - 1408/9d

3.14: Plain crownpost roof at The Court House, East Meon, Hampshire - 1395-7

3.15: Two basic crownpost roofs in Hampshire
   a: Lodging Range of Bishop's Waltham Palace - 1438-42
   b: Kimpton Manor - 1445d

3.16: Hall truss at No. 35 High Street, Winchester, Hampshire -1340d

3.17: Roof truss at Church Farm, West Tytherley, Hampshire -1334/5d

3.18: Hall roof at a house from Boarhunt, Hampshire now at The Weald and Downland Open Air Museum, Singleton, West Sussex - 1355-90d

3.19: Distribution of box-framed buildings with trenched side purlin roofs in Hampshire

3.20: Lilac Cottage, Burgate, Hampshire - a house in the far west of the county where the cruck tradition of ridge beams, trenched side purlins and massive rafters affected the form of roofs in box-framed buildings.

3.21: Closed trusses in principal rafter roofs in Hampshire
   a: Crown strut at No.1 King Street, Odiham - 1447d
   b: Queen struts at The Manor, Littleton - 1485d
   c: Raking queen posts at The Old Pest House, Odiham - c.1622
   d: 'Fan truss' at Tully's, Petersfield - 1442d
   e: Queen struts at Shamblehurst Manor, South Stoneham - 1547/8d

3.22: Chronology of some closed trusses in principal rafter roofs in Hampshire

3.23: Early open trusses in principal rafter roofs in Hampshire
   a: Shepherd's Cottage, North Warnborough - 1402d
   b: Manisty Cottage, Odiham -1400d
   c: The Jetty, Titchfield - 1412/13d

3.24: Later open trusses in principal rafter roofs in Hampshire
   a: No. 26-7 High Street, Lymington - 1468-1503
   b: The Angel, Andover - 1445-53
   c: The Swan, Kingsclere - 1448/9d
   d: The Manor, Littleton - 1485d

3.25: The Brethren's Hall at St. Cross Hospital, Winchester, Hampshire

3.26: The chamber over the hall and the attic above it at Priory Farm, Monk Sherborne, Hampshire - 1561d

Chapter 4

4.1: Distribution of tree-ring dated roofs in the west midlands by centuries

4.2: Tiebeams and coupled rafters as envisaged for Building AS29 at Anglo-Saxon Catholme, Staffordshire and for the roof of Odda's Chapel, Derehurst, Gloucestershire

4.3: Nave roof at Roydon Church, Essex

4.4: Nave roof of St Mary's Church, Kempley, Gloucestershire - 1128-32d

4.5: Holy Trinity Wistanstow, Shropshire - 1200-21d

4.6: Roof trusses at the Blackfriars, Gloucester
   a: over the choir, built after 1238d
   b: over the south range 1230-69d

4.7: High roof of the nave of Lincoln Cathedral - 1225-35d

4.8: Two early aisled halls –
   a: Temple Balsall, Warwickshire, shown in its second phase; 1st phase dated to 1176-1221d
   b: Bishop's Palace at Hereford, Herefordshire 1179d

4.9: Contemporary cruck and aisled barns in Worcestershire –
   a: Leigh Court Barn c.1344d
   b: Bredon Barn after 1344d

4.10: Eastington Hall, Longdon, Upton upon Severn,

Worcestershire

4.11: Four west midland base crucks -
    a: West Bromwich Manor House (formerly Staffordshire) - 1270-88d
    b: Handsacre Hall, Staffordshire - 1291-1326d
    c: Mancetter Manor House, Warwickshire - early 14th C
    d: 15 High Street, Much Wenlock, Shropshire - 1407-8d

4.12: An early base cruck truss and an early full cruck
    a: Early base cruck at Siddington Barn, Gloucestershire - 1245-7d
    b: Early full cruck at Cruck Cottage, Upton Magna, Shropshire as first interpreted - 1269d

4.13: Tree-ring date ranges of four medieval roof types in the west midlands

4.14: Tree-ring date ranges of some extant roof types in the west midlands

4.15: Three cruck-framed buildings and a small aisled hall -
    a: Stokesay Castle, Shropshire - 1289-90d
    b: Hill Top, Longdon, Staffordshire
    c: Bedstone Manor, Shropshire - 1448d
    d: Anne Hathaway's Cottage, Stratford upon Avon, Warwickshire -1462/3d

4.16: Some west midland crownpost roofs, all with coupled rafters with collars -
    a: Rushton Spencer Church, Staffordshire - 1293-1318d
    b: Mancetter Manor crosswing, Warwickshire - c.1325d
    c: Heritage Centre, Henley-in-Arden, Warwickshire - 1345d
    d: Horninglow Street, Burton upon Trent, Staffordshire - 1345d
    e: Mavesyn Ridware Gatehouse, Staffordshire - 1391/2d
    f: 169 Spon Street, Coventry, Warwickshire - 1391-1404d

4.17: 81-82 Barton St, Tewkesbury, Gloucestershire - sections of main & intermediate trusses in hall

4.18: Arch-braced collar roof trusses in the west midlands -
    a: Guesten Hall roof (originally at Worcester) 1320
    b: Moat House, Longnor, Shropshire -1467d
    c: Padmore, Onibury, Shropshire
    d: Newport Guildhall, Shropshire -1487d
    e: Colemore Farm, Astley Abbotts, Shropshire

4.19: Truss at Great Binnal, Astley Abbotts, Shropshire - 1460d

4.20: Four principal rafter, tiebeam and collar trusses with four types of side purlins
    a: Clasped side purlins with diminished principal rafters at 8 Vicars' Close, Lichfield, Staffordshire - 1450-75d
    b: Tenoned/butt purlins in the east range at Baddesley Clinton, Warwickshire - c.1579-85
    c: Trenched side purlins at 88 Main Street, Alrewas, Staffordshire - 17th century
    d: Threaded side purlins in east range roof at Baddesley Clinton, Warwickshire - c.1703d

4.21: The difference between a tenoned or butt purlin and a threaded purlin

4.22: Simplified section of a double hammer beam roof based on that over the nave of Donington Church, Shropshire - attributed to 1635

4.23: Kingpost roofs
    a: 44-45 Church Street, Tamworth, Staffordshire - 16th C?
    b: Baddesley Clinton, Warwickshire - c.1790

4.24: The nave and chancel roofs of Ingestre Church, Staffordshire

4.25: Solar wing of Abbot's House, Burton Abbey, Burton upon Trent, Staffordshire

4.26: Rigg's Hall, Shrewsbury, Shropshire

Chapter 5

5.1: Smoke blackened thatch in Devon
5.2: Mass wall construction
    a: Cob built house, Hayne, Zeal Monachorum, Devon
    b: Stone built South Wood, Cotleigh, Devon
5.3: Fragment of aisle post in Bishop's Palace, Exeter, Devon - 1225-45
5.4: Domestic chapel at Fardel, Cornwood, Devon
5.5: Oldest part of Fishleigh Barton, Tawstock, Devon
5.6: Reused timber dated to 1258-63d in Townsend, Stockland, Devon
5.7: Old Rectory, Bridford, Devon - 1279d
5.8: Mirror-dovetail at Old Rectory, Bridford, Devon - 1279d
5.9: Roof with yoke and square-set ridge at Old Rectory, Bridford, Devon - 1279d
5.10: Barn, Shamlands, Abbotsham, Devon
5.11: Scarfed crucks
    a: Face-pegged jointed cruck with slip tenon - Langford Court, Cullompton, Devon
    b: Side-pegged jointed cruck - South Yarde, Rose Ash, Devon
    c: Post scarf - East Liddaton, Brentor, Devon
5.12: Old Cheriton Rectory, Cheriton Bishop, Devon - 1299-1300d
5.13: A king stud acting as a false kingpost - Old Cheriton Rectory, Cheriton Bishop, Devon - 1299-1300d
5.14: St Mary, Luppit, Devon
5.15: Pilliven, Witheridge, Devon
5.16: Chimsworthy, Bratton Clovelly, Devon - 1305-6d
5.17: Higher Horselake, Chagford, Devon
5.18: Leigh Barton, Coldridge, Devon
5.19: Gatehouse of Dartington Hall, Totnes, Devon
5.20: Base cruck truss over hall of Moorstone Barton, Halberton, Devon - 1304-29d
5.21: Truss at end of open hall of Moorstone Barton, Halberton, Devon - 1304-29d
5.22: Uplowman Court, Uplowman, Devon - c.1310
    a: Base cruck truss in open hall

b: South end wall of open hall

5.23: Base cruck truss over hall at Woodbarton, Kentisbeare, Devon - *c.*1336

5.24: Roof of the nave of Exeter Cathedral early 14th C

5.25: Rudge, Morchard Bishop, Devon - 1316d

5.26: Bury Barton, Lapford, Devon - 1328-39d

5.27: Truss 3 of Rudge, Morchard Bishop, Devon - 1316d

5.28: Truss 3 of Bury Barton, Lapford, Devon - 1328-39d

5.29: Cleavanger, Nymet Rowland, Devon - 1396-1400d

5.30: Hall centre truss, South Wood, Cotleigh, Devon

5.31: Prowse, Sandford, Devon

5.32: Hall roof of Cullacott, Werrington, Cornwall - 1472d

5.33: Chamfered purlins, Lower Chilverton, Coldridge, Devon - 1488-1518d

5.34: South Yarde, Rose Ash, Devon - 1447-8d

5.35: Old Rectory, Lustleigh, Devon

5.36: Three of the "Exeter Group" roofs
a: Archdeacon of Exeter's House, Exeter, Devon - 1414-40d
b: The Law Library, The Close, Exeter, Devon
c: Cadhay, Ottery St Mary, Devon

5.37: Archdeacon of Exeter's House, Exeter, Devon

5.38: Exeter Guildhall, Exeter, Devon - *c.*1467-9

5.39: The Law Library, The Close, Exeter, Devon

5.40: Solar crosswing of Prowse, Sandford, Devon

5.41: Detached chamber block, Elley, Colebrooke, Devon

5.42: Hall truss, 38 North St, Exeter, Devon

5.43: Dovetail-shaped lap-jointed collar - Parlour chamber, Cullacott, Werrington, Cornwall - 1579

5.44: Manor House, Cullompton, Devon - 1603

5.45: Pound Farm, Luppit, Devon - house & barn both built 1675-80s d
a: House - A-frames
b: Barn - jointed crucks

5.46: Roof of disused farmhouse at East Week, South Tawton, Devon

5.47: Higher Bonehill, Widecombe, Devon - early 18th C

5.48: 28 South Street, Great Torrington, Devon - 1701

Chapter 6

6.1: Reconstruction and possible interpretation of Foulbridge Hall, Snainton, North Yorkshire - 1288d

6.2: Foulbridge Hall today looking west - The aisles have been removed and the crownpost roof has been lowered, converting the crownposts to kingposts with the collar purlin becoming a ridgepiece

6.3: One bay of Lady Row, 60-72 Goodramgate, York - 1316

6.4: Jowled crownpost in the Merchant Adventurers' Hall, York - 1358-60

6.5: Crownpost with expanded head clasping the collar purlin in north crosswing of Carlisle Guildhall, Cumbria. The roof has been lowered as at Foulbridge Hall, converting the crownposts to kingposts. - 1392-7d

6.6: 16-22 Coney Street, York

6.7: Late 13th century roof over nave of Chichester Cathedral, Sussex. A crown stud rises to a collar which carries a collar purlin and raked-purlin struts to side purlins - *c.*1272-1307d

6.8: 12-15 Newgate, York - 1337

6.9: Open truss of rear range of 28-32 Coppergate, York

6.10: Types of truncated principal rafter trusses
1a: Type 1 - Merchant Adventurers' Hall, York - 1358-60
2a: Type 2 - 79 Low Petergate, York
3a: Type 3 - 23 Stonegate, York - late 16th C
3b: Type 3 - 49 Goodramgate, York - mid 16th C
4a: Type 4 - 7 Eastgate, Lincoln, Lincolnshire - *c.*1500
5a: Type 5 - 2 The College, Durham, County Durham - 1531-2d
5b: Type 5 - Pockerley Farm, Beamish, Northumberland - 1441-2d

6.11: Roof of Merchant Adventurers' Hall, York with alternating type 1 & 2 trusses - 1358-60
a: Main truss - Type 1 truncated principal rafter truss
b: Intermediate truss - Type 2 truncated principal rafter truss

6.12: Type 2 truncated principal rafter truss, Barley Hall, Coffee Yard, York - 15th/early 16th C

6.13: Type 4 truncated principal rafter roof truss at Church Farm, West Tytherley, Hampshire - 1334/5d

6.14: Type 4 truncated principal rafter roof over Choir of Durham Cathedral, County Durham

6.15: Type 4 truncated principal rafter roof at Crook Hall, Durham, County Durham - 1467-8d

6.16: Type 4 truncated principal rafter roof truss in Street Range of 11 Minster Yard, Lincoln, Lincolnshire

6.17: Type 5 truncated principal rafter roof of Pockerley Farm, Beamish, County Durham - 1441-2d

6.18: Type 5 with kingpost 1-2 The College, Durham, County Durham - 1531-2d

6.19: Reconstruction of open hall of Canons' Garth, Helmsley, North Yorkshire - early 14th C

Chapter 7

7.1: Baxby Manor, Husthwaite, Thirsk, North Yorkshire - 1308d

7.2: Regions of Yorkshire showing the number of box-framed buildings in each region

7.3: Yorkshire: Cruck, box-frame and mixed zones

7.4: Development of crownpost roofs in York
a: Lady Row - 1316
b: 12-15 Newgate - 1337
c: 28-32 Coppergate

7.5: Scotton Old Hall, Scotton, near Knaresborough, North Yorkshire

7.6: Example of "flying braces" at 41-43 Goodramgate, York – late 15th/early 16th C

7.7: Common rafters with collars & later inserted side purlins at Rose Cottage, Clint, near Harrogate, North Yorkshire

7.8: Kirkness Cottage, Briggate, Knaresborough, North Yorkshire

7.9: Examples of truncated principal rafter roofs in Yorkshire
   a: Sexhow Hall, Sexhow, North Yorkshire
   b: Girlington Hall, Wycliffe with Thorpe, County Durham (formerly Yorkshire N.R.)

7.10: Double roof over the Merchant Adventurers' Hall, York – 1358-60

7.11: Sexhow Hall, Sexhow, North Yorkshire

7.12: St Agnes House, Ripon, North Yorkshire - c.1542-1573d

7.13: Clasped side purlins with raked-purlin struts - Longley Old Hall, near Huddersfield, West Yorkshire

7.14: Tithe Barn, Easington in Holderness, East Yorkshire

7.15: Kingposts at Low Hollin, Hebden Bridge, near Halifax, West Yorkshire
   a: centre truss of open hall
   b: closed truss at high end of hall

7.16: Example of 'V' strutting - 176 Leeds Road, Lofthouse, West Yorkshire

7.17: Solar wing of Smithills Hall, Bolton, Greater Manchester (formerly Lancashire)

7.18: Weston Hall Barn, Lower Wharfedale, North Yorkshire

7.19: Arch-braced truss Bedern Hall, York - mid-14th C

7.20: Great Hall of St. Anthony's Hall, York
   a: Arch-braced trusses in the foreground with three bays of truncated principals beyond, looking west - both roofs 1435-59d
   b: Arch-braced truss

7.21: Rear Hall of 35 The Shambles, York

7.22: Arch-braced truss Fold Farm, Kettlewell, Wharfedale, North Yorkshire

7.23: Example of large triangular block between the top of the principals in the false hammer beam roof of the Chapel at Calverley Hall, Leeds - 1485-95d

7.24: Manor Farm, Morton-on-Swale, near Thirsk, North Yorkshire - late 16th C

7.25: Nether Poppleton Barn, near York - 1542/3d

7.26: Through-purlin roof over Watton Priory near Beverley, East Riding of Yorkshire - early/mid 16th C

Chapter 8

8.1: Single-tier queenpost roof - Wisteria Cottage, Hacheston, Suffolk - a transitional high end stack house of 1541

8.2: A two-tier queenpost roof at Park Farm, Somerleyton, Suffolk

8.3: Distribution of raised-aisled halls and queenpost roofs in Suffolk and types of historic fields

8.4: Location of some of Norfolk's queenpost roofs

8.5: Centre truss of open hall of Mill Farm Cottage, Bedfield, Suffolk - 15th C

8.6: Decorated queenpost on centre truss of open hall at Messuage Farmhouse, Kenton, Suffolk - early 15th C

8.7: Decorated queenpost on centre truss of two storey house 'The Guildhall', Wrentham, Suffolk - 16th C

8.8: Choppins Hill, Coddenham, Suffolk - A raised-aisled hall built about 1390

8.9: Low Barn Cottage, Thorndon, Suffolk - An aisled hall converted to a raised-aisled hall in the 15th C

8.10: Reconstruction of the raised-aisled hall - The Hermitage, Frostenden, Suffolk - 14th C

8.11: Reconstruction of Hilltop Farmhouse, Baylham, Suffolk.

8.12: Types of single-tier queenposts
   a: No upper collars or ridgepiece - Wisteria Cottage, Hacheston, Suffolk - 1541
   b: With ridgepiece - King's Head Cottage, Banham, Norfolk - 15th C
   c: An upper collar on each rafter couple - Moat Farmhouse, Kenton, Suffolk - 15th C

8.13: Coupled rafter roof over Upper Spring Cottage, Coddenham, Suffolk - an open hall house-15th C

8.14: Nave roof of St Mary Magdalen, Pulham St. Mary, Norfolk - 15th C

8.15: Queenpost roof of barn at Crows Hall, Debenham, Suffolk - 1478d

8.16: Types of two-tier queenpost roofs
   a: Two-tier queenpost roof with crownpost - Buck's Hall, Rishangles, Suffolk - 15th C
   b: Two-tier queenpost roof with kingpost and ridgepiece at Poplar Farmhouse, Oakley, Suffolk - late 15th C
   c: Two-tier queenpost roof with clasped side purlins in barn at Eye, Suffolk - mid 16th C
   d: Two tiers of queenposts over Dairy Farm Barn, Newton Flotman, Norfolk - 15th C

8.17: No 22 Castle Street, Eye, Suffolk - a town house combining queenposts and full height crownposts - early 16th C

8.18: Barn with queenposts and ridgepiece at Wingfield College, Wingfield, Suffolk - 1527d

8.19: Centre truss of Lewknor Church Farm, Oxfordshire - 1350/1d

8.20: Roof of Lewknor Church Farm, Oxfordshire - 1350/1d

Chapter 9

9.1: Aisled buildings

9.2: Normal & reverse assembly tiebeams at Brick House, Debden, Essex, a wealden house

9.3: Base Crucks
   a: Base cruck with double tiebeams - Eastington Hall, Upton upon Severn, Worcestershire
   b: Base cruck with single tiebeam in reverse as-

sembly - Siddington Barn, Gloucestershire - 1245-47d

    c: Base cruck with single tiebeam in normal assembly - York Farm, West Hagbourne, Oxfordshire - 1284-5d

    d: Hybrid base cruck - Chennelsbrook Farm, Horsham, Sussex - 1296d

9.4:   Box-framing

    a: Box-framed building with crownpost roof - Valley Farm, Flatford, Suffolk - 15th C

    b: Box-framed building with side purlin roof - also called post & truss construction (not recommended) - Wynters Cottage, Magdalen Laver, Essex - 16th C

9.5:   Example of crown strut - 1 King Street, Odiham, Hampshire - 1485d

9.6:   Crownpost

9.7:   True cruck - Leigh Court Barn, Worcestershire - *c.*1344d

9.8:   Jointed cruck - Cleavanger, Nymet Rowland, Devon - 1396-1400d

9.9:   Example of gablet, gable and crosswing on Valley Farm, Flatford, Suffolk

9.10: King strut

9.11: Kingposts

    a: Kingpost northern style

    b: Early kingpost - 15 High Street, Fareham, Hampshire 1279-1311d

9.12: Types of notched lap joints

9.13: Examples of queen struts

    a: Clasped side purlin roof with queen struts - 30 High Street, Maldon, Essex

    b: Trenched purlin roof with queen struts - 88 Main Street, Alrewas, Staffordshire

9.14: Single-tier 'East Anglian' queenposts

    a: Jowled queenposts with no ridgepiece - Wisteria Cottage, Hacheston, Suffolk - 1541

    b: Jowled queenposts with ridgepiece - King's Head Cottage, Banham, Norfolk - 15th C

9.15: Two-tier 'East Anglian' style queenpost roofs

    a: Buck's Hall, Risangles, Suffolk

    b: Church Farm, Lewknor, Oxfordshire - 1350/1d

9.16: Queenposts with no collar and unjowled

    a: Queenposts over service crosswing - Gainsborough Old Hall, Lincolnshire - 15th C

    b: Queenposts over barn - Greenhill, Chebsey, Staffordshire - 1857

9.17: Raised-aisled hall

    a: Centre truss of raised-aisled hall with dropped tiebeam well below wall plates - Baythorne Hall, Birdbrook, Essex - 1341/2d

    b: Raised-aisled hall with centre truss having a dropped tiebeam in reverse assembly (that is immediately under the wall plates), with full arcade posts in the closed trusses at Wymondleybury, Little Wymondley, Hertfordshire - 1378/9d

9.18: Raked-purlin strut

9.19: Raking struts at Tully's, Petersfield, Hampshire - 1442d

9.20: Sans purlins roofs

9.21: Butt/tenoned and threaded side purlin roof

    a: butt & threaded purlins

    b: Butt or threaded purlin roof

9.22: Collar clasped side purlins

    a: Collar clasped side purlin with diminished principal rafter

    b: Collar clasped side purlin with soffit trench

9.23: Exploded drawing of trenched side purlin roof

9.24: Tension brace - also called down brace or foot brace

9.25: Truncated principal rafter roofs

    a: Merchant Adventurers' Hall, York 1358-60

    b: 23 Stonegate, York

9.26: Apex methods for crucks

Back Cover

Base cruck hall with crownposts in Old Deanery, 62 The Close, Salisbury, Wiltshire - 1258-74

Clasped side purlin - Place House Cottage, Titchfield, Hampshire - 1447/8d

Butt side purlins in 1st floor chamber at Leigh Barton, Churchstow, Devon - *c.*1494-1514d

Tree-ring Dates and Abbreviations

Dates

Dates for a building followed by 'd', indicates that these dates were obtained by dendrochronology. When the date is followed by '+d', it indicates that the timber was felled sometime after the latest date obtained by the dendrochronologists. Where these dates are published in *Vernacular Architecture*, the date is also followed by (VA *X, Y*), where '*X*' is the volume of VA in which it is published and '*Y*' is the page number in that volume. In the text the authors have referred such dates as 'obtained by dendrochronology', 'dendro-dated', and 'tree-ring dated'.

Abbreviations

Antiq. J	Antiquaries Journal
Archaeol. J.	Archaeological Journal
BAR	British Archaeological Report
CBA	Council for British Archaeology
EHBG	Essex Historic Buildings Group
Med. Arch	Medieval Archaeology
RCHME	Royal Commission on Historical Monuments England

1   INTRODUCTION AND OVERVIEW

By John Walker

(Unless stated otherwise, all drawings are by the author)

Over fifty years ago J T Smith published the first serious attempt to study medieval roofs from a historical standpoint (Smith J T 1958). Using mainly pictures in the National Monuments Record and the limited published information, he identified the main regional roof types, all of which are represented in this publication. Much of his paper has stood the test of time but since 1958 much more detail of individual buildings has been published, our understanding has improved and, most importantly, dendrochronology has enabled us to start to observe the chronological development of roofs in the main areas of the country.

The main roof categories J T Smith considered are shown in Figure 1.1.

The information available today suggests it is possible in broad terms to fit the development of these various medieval roof types into a historical time and regional pattern, but one for which additional data and analysis is still required.

Overview

The regions and counties covered in the following papers were chosen to give a broad coverage of the main regional roof types identified by J T Smith. The authors were asked to concentrate on the development of roofs in their areas after 1300 and up to around 1600. The purpose of this introductory paper is twofold: first to provide an overview of developments between the late 12th century and 1300, and sec-

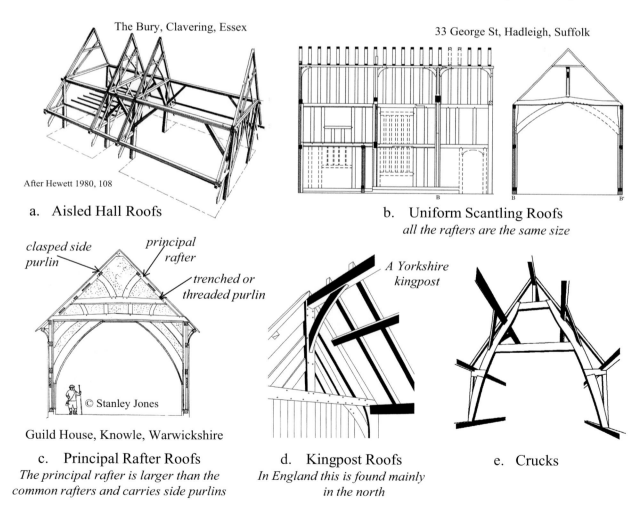

The Bury, Clavering, Essex

After Hewett 1980, 108

a. Aisled Hall Roofs

33 George St, Hadleigh, Suffolk

b. Uniform Scantling Roofs
all the rafters are the same size

clasped side purlin *principal rafter* *trenched or threaded purlin*

© Stanley Jones

Guild House, Knowle, Warwickshire

c. Principal Rafter Roofs
The principal rafter is larger than the common rafters and carries side purlins

A Yorkshire kingpost

d. Kingpost Roofs
In England this is found mainly in the north

e. Crucks

Fig 1.1: J T Smith's main roof categories

ond to provide a brief summary of the developments in roofs in the main regions up to the end of the 16th century, thus providing a wider context for the developments presented in the subsequent papers.

This overview is concerned with the development of secular roofs on box-framed timber and mass-walled buildings (Fig 1.1a-d), as are most of the following papers. It is not concerned with the development of cruck framed buildings, though crucks must have had an effect on non-cruck buildings as it was those areas with crucks that were the first to adopt side purlins for their non-cruck buildings (Fig 1.2). However crucks do raise questions, particularly in the west of England, on the status of the buildings being discussed and whether box-framed roofs were used mainly by higher levels of society, with crucks mainly for the lower levels. This question is less marked in the east where, with some exceptions, all levels use the same roof types, the main difference being in the quality and finish of the carpentry.

The earliest secular roofs surviving in England date from the late 12th century and they employ common rafters of uniform scantling constructed in bays with passing braces on the main trusses (Fig 1.1a). Versions of these roofs are found across the whole country in the 12th and 13th centuries. With the occasional exception, none of these roofs had any longitudinal support until the in-

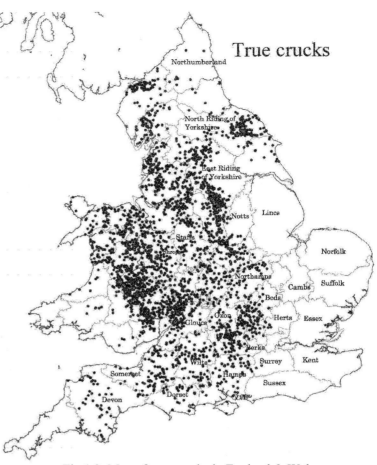

Fig 1.2: Map of true crucks in England & Wales
(after N W Alcock)

(Mapping by N W Alcock from the VAG database of crucks. 1910 county boundaries based on data provided through EDINA UKBORDERS with the support of the ESRC & JISC and uses boundary material which is copyright of the Great Britain Historic GIS Project, Portsmouth University.)

troduction in the late 13th century of the collar purlin carried by crownposts or king struts (Fig 1.3). Crownposts appear to have been adopted across the whole of England in the late 13th or the first half of the 14th century.

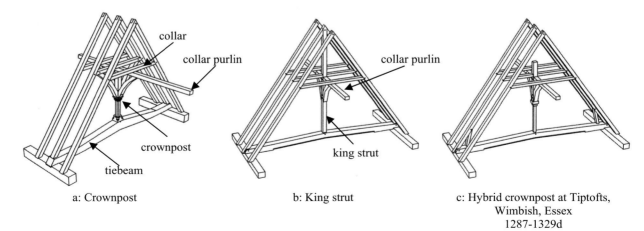

a: Crownpost

b: King strut

c: Hybrid crownpost at Tiptofts, Wimbish, Essex 1287-1329d

Fig 1.3: Crownpost and king strut

By about 1400, or shortly after, the crownpost had been replaced by side purlins in the Midlands and in most of those parts of southern England where crucks are found. As mentioned above, the use of side purlins on crucks seems to have influenced their development and use on non-cruck buildings. However within the cruck region the speed of change var-

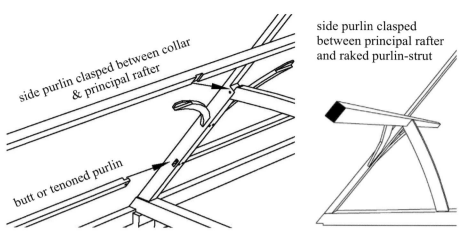

Fig 1.4: Examples of clasped and butt (or tenoned) purlins.

ied as did the type of side purlin roof adopted. In the east, in Essex and Kent, the crownpost remained the main roof form until the 16th century when, as the open hall declined, it was replaced by side purlins, mainly clasped (usually with the purlin clasped between the principal rafter and a collar but occasionally by a raking strut) though many buildings had butt purlins (also called tenoned purlins as the purlin is tenoned into the principal rafter) (Fig 1.4). Suffolk and Norfolk also kept the crownpost into the 16th century but from around 1400 also built houses and barns with queenpost roofs with square-set side purlins (Fig 1.5).

In those counties between eastern England and the cruck area, side purlin roofs were adopted to varying degrees during the 15th century but probably did not fully replace the crownpost until the 16th century. On the eastern side of the

north of England crownpost roofs continued into the 16th century but were being built alongside the various types of side purlin roof which appeared in the early 14th century. Also roofs combining crownposts and side purlins appeared in York in the second quarter of the 14th century (Fig 1.6). In West and South Yorkshire the crownpost was replaced by kingposts (Fig 1.1d) during the 15th century, while further north the truncated principal rafter roof became a major roof type (Fig 1.34). In the West Country, where the main vernacular buildings were crucks, the side purlin seems to have been adopted slightly earlier. Crownposts made a brief appearance in the late 13th and first half of the 14th century over a few base cruck halls, but butt side purlins were used on other contemporary base crucks, and thereafter the butt purlin seems to have become the favoured type of side purlin on non-cruck buildings in this region.

Fig 1.5: Queenpost roof over service wing
The Woodlands, Brundish, Suffolk
16th C

Fig 1.6: Crownpost and side purlin roof
50 Stonegate, York
14th or early 15th C (RCHME 1981, 224)

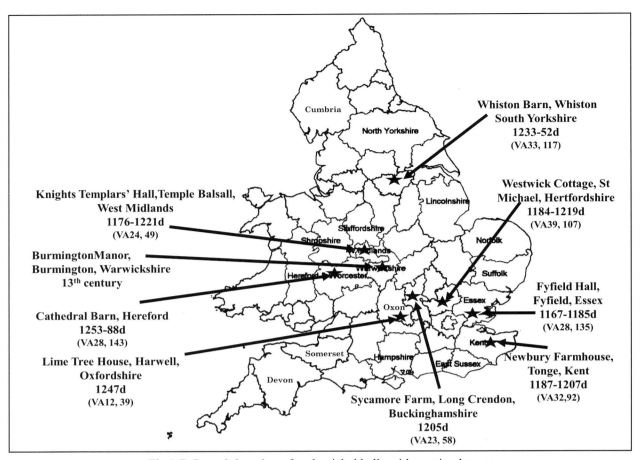

Fig 1.7: Date & location of early aisled halls with passing braces

Whiston Barn, Whiston
South Yorkshire
1233-52d
(VA33, 117)

Westwick Cottage, St
Michael, Hertfordshire
1184-1219d
(VA39, 107)

Knights Templars' Hall, Temple Balsall,
West Midlands
1176-1221d
(VA24, 49)

BurmingtonManor,
Burmington, Warwickshire
13th century

Cathedral Barn, Hereford
1253-88d
(VA28, 143)

Lime Tree House, Harwell,
Oxfordshire
1247d
(VA12, 39)

Fyfield Hall,
Fyfield, Essex
1167-1185d
(VA28, 135)

Newbury Farmhouse,
Tonge, Kent
1187-1207d
(VA32,92)

Sycamore Farm, Long Crendon,
Buckinghamshire
1205d
(VA23, 58)

The Early Roofs: the development of roofs in the 12th and 13th centuries

The earliest surviving secular timber buildings in England date from the late 12th and 13th centuries and, with a few exceptions, all are aisled halls or aisled barns, and are spread widely across the country, as shown by Fig 1.7. They had uniform scantling collar rafter roofs with passing braces on the principal trusses and did not have purlins.

There are some regional variations in that, for some regions, the passing braces rise from the aisle up to the rafters, while for others they rise only from the arcade posts, and some, for example in Hertfordshire, have the braces tapering towards the top (Fig 1.8). But these variations are minor; the point is that a similar roof technology was being used across the whole country in the 12th and first half of the 13th centuries; that is one where the roof is stabilised by locking the rafter couple over each main truss into place using passing braces, with the rafters between the trusses held in place by the battens for the roof covering. South west England is

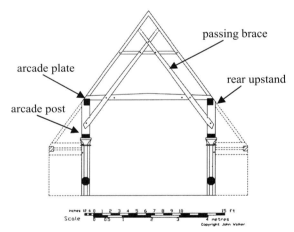

Fig 1.8: Centre truss of open hall with tapering passing braces at
Westwick Cottage, St Michael, Hertfordshire
1184-1219d (VA39, 107)
(partly based on drawings by Alan Greening)

not included in the examples in Figure 1.7, but the earliest dated base cruck building, the 1245-7d (VA23, 44) barn at Siddington in Gloucestershire, has passing braces, indicating that passing brace technology was in use in this part of the country in the 13th century (Fig 1.9).

14

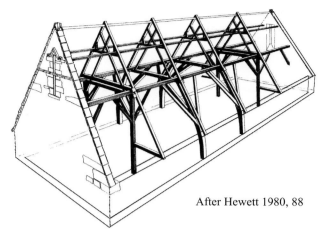

After Hewett 1980, 88

Fig 1.9: Siddington Barn, Gloucestershire
with passing braces and side purlins.
Common rafters did not have a collar.
1245-7d (VA23, 44)

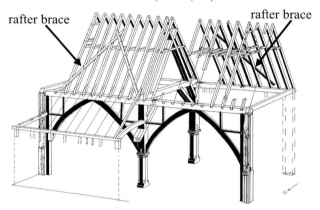

rafter brace

rafter brace

Fig 1.10: Fyfield Hall, Fyfield, Essex
Building after alterations of 1391-1416d when central
arcade posts and aisles rebuilt (Walker 1999).
Roof 1167-85d (VA28, 135)

clasped side purlin

secret notched
lap joint

Fig 1.11: Clasped side purlin over north aisle of
Wells Cathedral, Somerset. The brace is jointed
with secret notched lap joints.
1212/13

With the exception of this last building, none of the late 12th and early 13th century buildings had purlins, though Fyfield Hall, Essex and the Knights Templars' Hall at Temple Balsall in the West Midlands (formerly Warwickshire) had rafter bracing, where a timber runs obliquely across a group of common rafters, showing that medieval carpenters were aware of the need to brace rafters to prevent racking (Fig 1.10). During the course of the 13th century there were moves to develop purlins to give longitudinal support. The Siddington Barn (1245-7d) and the Wheat Barn, Cressing Temple, Essex (1257-80d, VA24, 51) both have square-set side purlins clasped between the collar, the rafter and an 'ashlar' piece. Also there is an early 13th century clasped side purlin roof – where a side purlin runs down the side of the roof and is clasped between a collar and the rafter – over the north aisle of Wells Cathedral, Somerset, assuming it is contemporary with the nave roof of 1212/13d (VA29, 125) (Fig 1.11).

It is important to note that our earliest dated cruck, built in 1262d (VA32, 77) – the Royal George, Cottingham, Northamptonshire – apparently came fully developed with a ridgepiece and side purlins trenched onto the backs of the cruck blades (Fig 1.12) (Hill & Miles 2001), though it is possible the purlins are a later insertion (personal communication from Nick Hill). If original, this indicates that the concept of side purlins had been fully developed by then, though probably not the methods to incorporate them on non-cruck roofs.

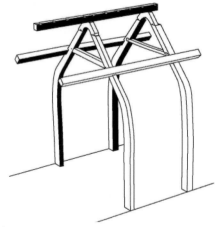

Fig 1.12: Reconstruction of Royal George,
Cottingham, Northamptonshire
1262d
Side purlins do not survive and lower part of
cruck blades are encased in a later stone wall.
(Based on drawings by Hill & Miles 2001)

15

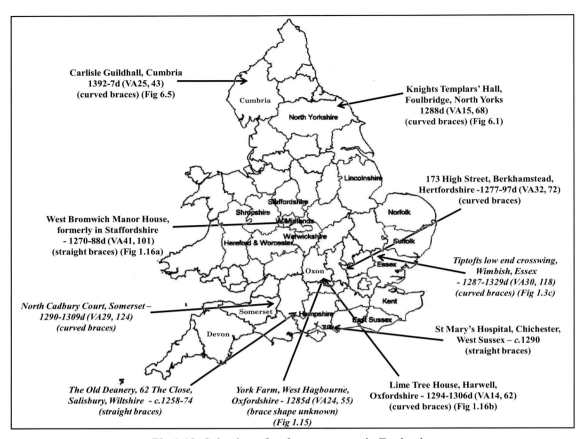

Fig 1.13: Selection of early crownposts in England

Those in italics have the collar purlin tenoned into the crownpost: those not in italics have a continuous collar purlin

Crownpost and King Strut Roofs

In the 1270s/1280s crownpost roofs appeared across most of England (Fig 1.13). Here each rafter couple is joined by a collar and there is an upright timber, the crownpost, standing on each tiebeam supporting a central purlin – called a collar purlin – running under the collars (Fig 1.3a). Around the same time, or perhaps a little later, king strut roofs with collar purlins also appeared; this roof type has common rafters, each pair joined with a collar as on crownpost roofs, a king strut rising from each tiebeam to the apex of the roof, and a collar purlin tenoned into the king struts, with the collar purlin running under the collars of the common rafters as on a crownpost roof (Fig 1.3b). There are small concentrations of these king strut and collar purlin roofs in and around Canterbury and in the South Hams district of Devon, most dating to the early 14th century (Pearson 1994, 52; VAG 2008). Munby, Sparks and Tatton-Brown suggested that two of the Canterbury roofs, both on stone buildings, dated to the third quarter of the 13th century - one over the Guest Hall of St Augustine's Abbey, which they dated to the late 1260s (Fig 1.14), and another over the

Table Hall, Christ Church which they thought was pre *c.*1285, though Sarah Pearson has suggested both could be either late 13th or early 14th century (Munby et al 1983; Pearson 1994, 52).

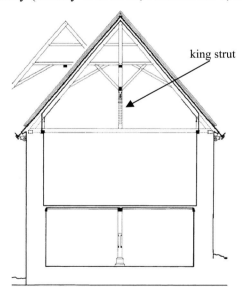

king strut

Fig 1.14: King strut roof over Guest Hall of St Augustine's Abbey, Canterbury, Kent

(After Munby, Sparks & Tatton-Brown 1983)

16

Because of their proposed early date for king struts, Munby, Sparks and Tatton-Brown have suggested that the crownpost developed from king strut roofs. This is difficult to prove or disprove. They are likely to be related as some of the early crownpost roofs have their collar purlin tenoned into the crownpost, rather than being a continuous timber, similar to the king strut roof which, as mentioned above, has a truncated collar purlin tenoned into the king struts (Figs 1.13 & 1.15). The low end cross-wing of Tiptofts, a manor house in Wimbish, Essex built 1287-1329d (VA30, 118), is a classic example (Fig 1.3c) where the 'crownpost' is cut off above the purlin, rather like a truncated king strut. However other contemporary late 13th century crownposts have continuous purlins (Figs 1.13 & 1.16). Probably king struts and crownposts both appeared in England around the same time, the late 13th century, and were simultaneous developments of similar ideas.

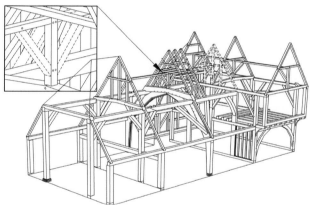

Fig 1.15: Early crownpost with collar purlin tenoned into the crownpost at York Farm, West Hagbourne, Oxfordshire 1284-5d

(Based on survey by Chris Currie 1992)

| a: West Bromwich Manor House, formerly Staffordshire 1270-88d | b: Centre crownpost Lime Tree House, Harwell, Oxfordshire inserted 1294-1306d |

Fig 1.16: Early crownposts with continuous purlins

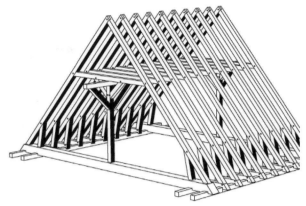

Fig 1.17: Chapelle Saint-Laurent des Vaux, Gisors, France 1224d

(Based on drawings in Epaud 2007, 185)

It is possible both the king strut and crownpost developed in France or Belgium and were imported into England, where we made crownposts our own. Early crownposts published in 'De la Charpente Romane à la Charpente Gothique en Normandie' by Frédéric Épaud (2007) include:

Chapelle Saint-Laurent des Vaux, Gisors, France - 1224d (Fig 1.17) (Epaud p185)
nef de l`abbatiale, Floreffe, Belgium - 1227-37d (p186)
prieuré Saint-Martin-des-Champs, Paris, France - 1215-20d (p186)
Cathédrale d`Auxerre, Auxerre, France - 1234-36d (p189)

Early king struts published by Épaud include:
église Notre-Dame, Étampes, Essonne, France - c.1177-87d (p185)
nef de Cathédrale de Rouen, France - 1227-32d (p188)

One feature that is noticeable about our late 13th century crownposts is that curved braces were contemporary with straight braces, as shown by Fig 1.13 which indicates the shape of the braces on the crownpost. It is often suggested that curved braces replaced straight braces, but that was not the case. Both were used from the late 13th century and into the 14th, with curved braces becoming the dominant style in the second half of the 14th century.

Although crownpost roofs are found in the 14th century all over England on box-framed buildings (Fig 1.13), from the early 14th century we start to see much greater regional variation.

Introduction of Side Purlins and Regional Variation

East Anglia

In Essex, roof development is fairly clear after 1300 and is summarized in Fig 1.18. In broad terms, the crownpost became the main roof type until the 16th century when, during the middle quarters of the century, it was replaced by the side purlin roof, either the clasped side purlin (mainly with the purlin clasped between the principal rafter and a collar) or butt purlins (Fig 1.19). However the developments are more complex than this, as David Stenning's paper shows. It has been suggested that the adoption of side purlins in Essex was due to the change in the 16th century from open halls to two storey buildings, and the need to create head room in first floor chambers and attics. But it is unlikely to be this simple, as the change to side purlins further west occurred long before the decline of the open hall.

Medieval roof development in south Suffolk is broadly similar to Essex but in north Suffolk and south Norfolk, from at least the beginning of the 15th century, many medieval open halls and other buildings were constructed with a side purlin roof in the form of jowled queen-posts with square set purlins (Fig 1.5), looking like an aisled hall raised onto the tiebeams. As Philip Aitkens shows in his paper, this roof type has a surprising number of variations, including the use of a ridgepiece. It never fully replaced the crownpost in north Suffolk and south Norfolk, both forms being used through the 15th century. These queenpost roofs continued into at least the late 16th or early 17th century in north Suffolk and south Norfolk, co-existing with the butt and clasped side purlin roofs which replaced the crownpost.

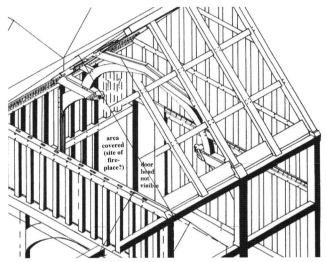

Fig 1.19: Early 15th century example of butt purlins in the false hammerbeam roof over the open hall of Bourchiers Chantry, High St, Halstead, Essex

Essex & Suffolk: Estimated Date Range for Types of Roofs (all box-framed)
(for definitions of the roofs and types of building see the Glossary)

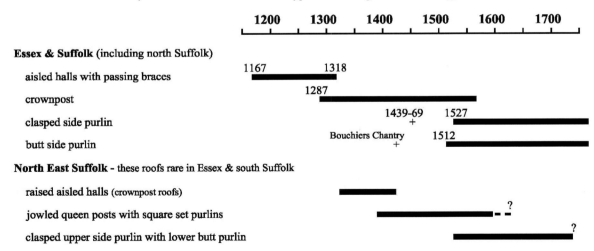

Fig 1.18: Outline of date ranges for roof styles in Essex and Suffolk

Only the range for aisled halls with passing braces is based on tree-ring dates

1167 is Fyfield Hall, Fyfield, Essex - 1167-1185d (VA28, 135)
1318 is Brockley Hall, Brockley, Suffolk - d (VA 36, 34)
1287 is Tiptofts, Wimbish, Essex - 1287-1329d (VA30, 118)
1439-69 is Monks Barn, Netteswellbury, Essex - d (VA 28, 141)

1512 is Otley Hall, Otley, Suffolk - d (VA32, 73)
1527 is The Bell, Great Easton, Essex - 1527/8d (VA32, 71)
Bourchiers Chantry is early 15th century based on documentary
   evidence (Fig 1.19)

West Midlands

As we move west towards the Midlands where crucks are the main vernacular building type, a very different pattern of development emerges for non-cruck roofs, as shown for Shropshire by Madge Moran's dendrochronological study of her county's buildings (Moran 2003). An analysis of the data in her book (Fig 1.20) shows that crownposts were the county's dominant roof form on box-framed buildings through the 14th century and into the first decades of the 15th century. These were then replaced by side purlins, first by mainly butt purlin roofs and then, from around the middle of the 16th century, by trenched purlins – that is where the purlins are trenched onto the backs of the principal rafters, as in most cruck roofs (Fig 1.21). In this analysis butt purlins include threaded purlins because Madge Moran did not distinguish between the two in her book - something that can be difficult to do, particularly when one cannot get close to the purlins. Threaded purlins are those which pass through a hole in the principal rafter. These purlins are also usually scarfed at this point (Fig 1.30).

This pattern of development for non-cruck buildings is likely to be broadly representative of the west midlands in general except that the clasped side purlin is probably under-represented in these figures. In his paper, Bob Meeson suggests the clasped side purlin was in use in the west midlands from at least the second half of the 14th century to the late 16th century and even later, with a probable peak use in the 15th century. It was used for Manor Farm, Tredington, Gloucestershire, built around 1366-95d (VA34, 99) and found as late as 1582d on the Polesworth Abbey Gatehouse annexe,

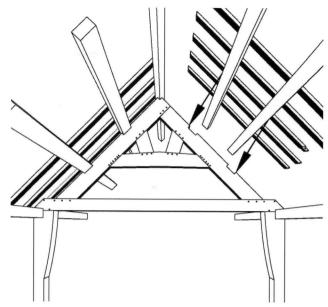

Fig 1.21: Example of purlins trenched onto the back of the principal rafters

Polesworth, Warwickshire (VA38, 113). Bob Meeson also notes that kingpost roofs were used in the west midlands from the second half of the 15th century through into the 19th century, the earlier ones having the kingpost in compression supporting a ridgepiece, whereas from the 17th century they tended to be in tension giving support to the tiebeam.

The type of roof over and under these various types of side purlins varied in the west midlands, as Bob Meeson's paper shows. The clasped side purlin tends to be on tiebeam trusses of various types, but the butt and trenched purlins are found over tiebeam trusses, arch-braced trusses and hammerbeams, while most of the kingpost roofs have trenched purlins.

Shropshire: Tree-ring Date Range for Types of Roofs on Box-framed Buildings
(for definitions of the roofs and types of building see the Glossary)

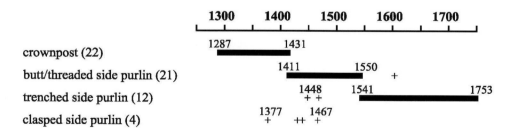

Fig 1.20: Range of tree-ring dates for roofs in Shropshire

(figures in brackets are number of buildings dated)
(derived from dates and information in Moran 2003)

Central, South and South East England

For those counties in central and southern England which are within the cruck region, the crownpost seems to have been the main roof form for box-framed buildings by at least the first half of the 14th century, with side purlin roofs of various types becoming the main form from around 1400. For the counties between the cruck region and the eastern counties of Kent and East Sussex, and of East Anglia, the change to side purlin roofs occurred during the 15th century, but did not fully replace the crownpost until the 16th century.

In Hampshire which, apart from the very east of the county, lies in the cruck region, Edward Roberts' study of Hampshire vernacular houses has shown a similar pattern to that in the west midlands for box-framed buildings (Fig 1.22), except that for much of his county it is the clasped side purlin which became the dominant roof type on box-framed buildings from the first half of the 15th century and through into the 17th century (Roberts 2003). Crownposts dominated through the 14th century as his paper shows, and while the latest dated crownpost had its timber felled around 1440, side purlin roofs took over in the first half of the 15th century and became the standard roof form. The clasped side purlin was the most common type in central and eastern Hampshire, while in the west of the county trenched side purlins with ridgepieces were the favoured form. Butt purlin roofs tended to be confined to the larger or higher status box-framed buildings.

In Surrey, which has two crucks on its western border with Hampshire, Joan Harding has suggested that sans purlin roofs, mostly with collars, were probably the earliest roof form along with two roofs in the county with passing braces (Harding 1980 & 1993). Sans purlin roofs are common rafter roofs of uniform scantling without any purlins. Both crownposts and side purlins are found over open halls, suggesting that side purlins were introduced into Surrey by the 15th century at the latest. Peter Gray has suggested they appeared in the west of the county around 1400, 100 years earlier than in the east (Gray 1990, 55). However the side purlin probably did not fully replace the crownpost until the second half of the 16th century, with both roof types being used through the 15th and the first half of the 16th century. In 1980 Joan Harding wrote, that before the end of the 16th century 'a stage had been reached when all roofs were being built with clasped side purlins, and this form of roof construction, together with the butt form, continued into the seventeenth century' (Harding 1980, 11.39).

In Kent the RCHME survey of medieval houses found that crownposts were the predominant roof form in the late medieval period, accounting for 85% of the roofs surveyed and dated to 1370-1475, with collar rafter roofs (common rafter roofs with collars and no purlins) accounting for the rest. The side purlin appeared in the late 15th century over a small number of houses, the numbers growing in the first half of the 16th century, but still only accounting for 20% of dated roofs between 1511-40. They were being built alongside crownposts, which still accounted for 54%, while collar rafter roofs took 26% (Fig 1.23) (Pearson 1994, 83-89). Side purlins did occur, in conjunction with crownposts, in the roof of Penshurst Place built in 1340s but this was built by Sir John de Pulteney, a London merchant and financier, and had no successors in the county. Interestingly there is no evidence that side purlins first appeared in the west of county (ibid 87). Simi-

Hampshire: Tree-ring Date Range for Types of Roofs on Box-framed Buildings

(for definitions of the roofs and types of building see the Glossary)

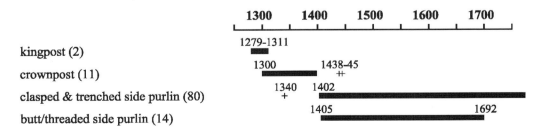

Fig 1.22: Range of tree-ring dates for roofs in Hampshire
figures in brackets are number of buildings dated
(derived from dates and information in Roberts 2003)

larly in the Rape of Hastings in East Sussex, crownposts and collar-rafter roofs were progressively superseded by clasped side purlins in the period *c.*1490-1540 (Martin & Martin 2006, 85).

In the Vale of White Horse in south Oxfordshire, which is in the cruck region, Chris Currie has suggested that side purlin roofs on box-framed buildings were an alternative to crownposts between 1280 and 1350, and that crownposts were relatively scarce after 1350 until they finally disappeared around 1410 (Currie 1992, 98-99).

In Bedfordshire, most of which is outside the cruck region, John Bailey said the crownpost was replaced by the clasped side purlin in the early 15th century (Bailey 2002, 55).

In Hertfordshire, most of which, apart from its western edge, also lies outside the cruck area, there are many crownpost roofs. However Adrian Gibson felt that side purlin roofs, butt and clasped, were the main roof forms over open halls by the middle of the 15th century in at least the western half of the county (personal correspondence) (Fig 1.24).

Similarly Cambridgeshire, which has no crucks, has many 15th century open halls with side purlin roofs as well as some with crownposts. The RCHME volume for West Cambridgeshire records a number of open hall houses which they attribute to the 15th or early 16th century, some of which have crownposts, while others have clasped side purlins or butt purlins (RCHME 1968, crownposts pp116, 205; clasped side purlin pp15, 69, 95, 124, 166; butt purlin pp155, 156). Beth Davis notes that 'there are a number of lesser manor houses and farmhouses where crownposts were used in the crosswing and a windbraced side purlin roof in the hall range in what were contemporary structures', an example being the 'H' shaped Croxton Manor House (Fig 1.25) (Davis 2002, 33 & 35). It seems probable that, like Suffolk, side purlin roofs did not fully replace the crownpost in Cambridgeshire until the 16th century.

We need a major study of these counties to determine the dates and progression of the decline in the crownpost and the rise of side purlins and their associated roof forms.

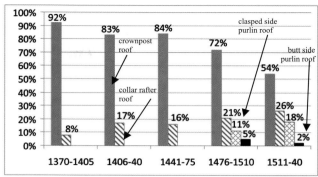

Fig 1.23: Percentage of roof types in each period in Kent houses surveyed and dated in the RCHME survey of medieval houses in Kent
(Pearson 1994, 83)

Fig 1.24: Roof of open hall of Clintons, Little Hadham, Hertfordshire early 15th C
(Smith J T 1992, 24-25)

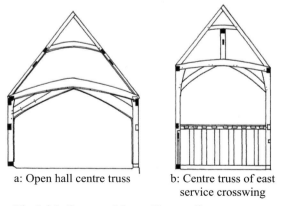

a: Open hall centre truss

b: Centre truss of east service crosswing

Fig 1.25: Croxton Manor House, Croxton, Cambridgeshire - 'H' plan house Late 15th C
(After Davis 2002, 35)

21

South-West England

The south-west is different again. This is a region of mass walling of cob or stone. There is no timber framing except in the larger towns where the houses were of mixed construction with the front and rear walls being of timber and the side walls of stone. In common with the rest of the country, crownpost roofs were used in the late 13th and first half of the 14th century. These appeared on a relatively small proportion of the region's surviving base crucks, all of which are supra-vernacular or polite buildings. Thereafter, through the 14th to the 17th centuries, the main roof type on non-cruck roofs was butt purlins of various types. Outside the towns, vernacular buildings were crucks. The earliest tree-ring dated cruck in Somerset is 1263/4d (VA28, 172) for a re-used cruck blade, while in Devon the earliest dated is 1279d. The earliest crucks in both counties are true crucks, with these being replaced by jointed crucks around 1400.

In Somerset, the Somerset Dendrochronology Project by the Somerset Vernacular Building Research Group has tree-ring dated a substantial number of buildings with extant roofs, the earliest dating to the last quarters of the 13th century as shown in Fig 1.26 (McDermott 2006, 79). The earliest dated Somerset roof is the 1212/3d collar rafter sans purlin roof with notched lap joints over the east end of the nave

After Hewett 1974, 17

Fig 1.27: Roof of east end of the
nave of Wells Cathedral
1212/3d

of Wells Cathedral (VA29, 125) (Fig 1.27). Apart from this, the earliest dated buildings are all crucks; the earliest a re-used cruck blade of 1263/4d at Bridge Farm, Butleigh (VA28, 172), followed by Higher Broughton Farmhouse, Stoke St Mary of 1267-99d (VA28, 173) and West End Farmhouse, Barton of 1278/9 (VA30, 111), each with a ridgepiece and with a single side purlin trenched on to the back of the blades on each side of the roof (Penoyre 2005, 44 & 94).

Somerset: Tree-ring Date Range for Types of Roofs
(for definitions of the roofs and types of building see the Glossary)

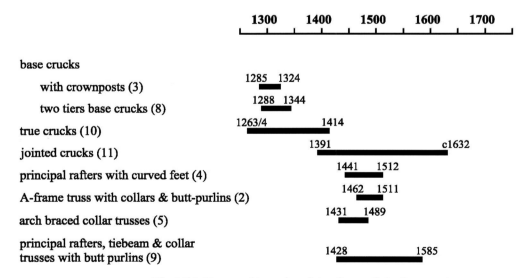

Fig 1.26: Range of tree-ring dates for roofs in Somerset

(figures in brackets are number of buildings dated)
(derived from dates and information in Penoyre 2005 and McDermott 2006)

Fig 1.28: Base cruck with crownpost roof
The Tudor Tavern, Fore St, Taunton, Somerset
1323-24d (VA34, 117)

Fig 1.29: Two-tier base cruck
Glastonbury Abbey Barn near Wells, Somerset
1334-44 (McDermott 2006, 79)

Then came a group of base crucks, three of which have crownpost roofs built between 1290 and 1324 (Fig 1.28). However, contemporary with these are a series of two tier base crucks which have butt purlins above the tiebeam/ collar (Fig 1.29). From around the mid 14th century butt purlins seem to have been the preferred type of purlin over non-cruck buildings, being used in the 15th century on roofs with principal rafters with curved feet, on A-frame principal rafters, on arch-braced collar trusses and on trusses consisting of principal rafters, tiebeam and collar.

Devon roofs, as John Thorp shows in his paper, had a similar development to Somerset. There is evidence of some early collar rafter sans purlin roofs, and crownposts were used over base crucks in the first half of the 14th century. Also, in the South Hams area around Dartmouth, a number of stone buildings dating to the late 13th/early 14th century have king strut roofs with collar purlins (VAG 2008, section 1), similar in date to those found around Canterbury in Kent. As in Somerset, Devon's vernacular buildings were crucks, usually with the purlins carried on the backs of the blades. However in some high-class crucks, butt purlins were being used from the early 14th century, along with threaded purlins (Fig 1.30). Butt purlins were also the main type of purlin used in non-cruck 'polite' roofs until their use virtually died out around 1600, while trenched purlins continued in widespread use.

Fig 1.30: Threaded side purlins in arch braced hall roof at Keynedon Barton, Sherford, Devon
late 15th /early 16th C

Northern England

Another pattern of roofs developed in northern England, as the papers by Robert Hook and Barry Harrison illustrate. Fewer early buildings survive here, but those that do suggest a similar pattern of development to other parts of the country in the 13th and early 14th centuries; passing brace structures in the 13th century followed by crownpost roofs in its last decades. The earliest dated building is a barn at Whiston, near Rotherham, South Yorkshire of 1233-52d (VA33, 117) which had a common collar rafter roof with passing braces (Fig 1.31), while in *c.*1288d (VA15, 68) the Knights Templar built their Preceptory at Foulbridge Hall, Snainton, North Yorkshire with a crownpost roof (Fig 6.1). Two early 14th century base crucks survive in North Yorkshire, both with crownpost roofs. Crownpost roofs appear to have been erected across most of the north in the 14th century, being found as far north as Carlisle, Cumbria over their Guildhall dated to 1392-7d (VA25, 43), whilst side purlin roofs on box-framed buildings appeared in Yorkshire from at least the second quarter of the 14th century, often in combination with crownposts (Fig 1.6).

The early 14th century crownposts in the region were thin and plain, but by the middle of the 14th century they had developed jowled or expanded heads to clasp the collar purlin, creating their own regional style (Fig 1.32). These continued to be built in York and to the east into the 16th century, after which side purlin roofs of various types became the city's dominant roof form (RCHME 1981, lxviii-lxxii). However, most Yorkshire crownposts were in towns; the few rural ones being in the larger houses. Combined crownpost and side purlin roofs were developed in York. One type, which appeared by the second quarter of the 14th century, combined side purlins and crownpost where the purlins were clasped against the rafter by raking struts with jowled/expanded heads (Fig 1.33). These combined crownpost and side purlin roofs with raked-purlin struts were common in York townhouses in the 15th century. Probably evolving from these were the roofs with raked-purlin struts without crownposts, a form originally used on the eastern flanks of the southern Pennines. As Barry Harrison indicates, these were the dominant roof form for smaller houses in both town and country throughout the Central and Northern Vale of York in the late 16th

Fig 1.31: Arcade post with passing brace trench Whiston Barn, Whiston, South Yorkshire 1233-52d (VA33, 117)

Fig 1.32: 111 Walmgate, York *c.*1400 (RCHME 1981, 241)

raked-purlin strut

Fig 1.33: 111 Walmgate, York Crownpost with raked-purlin struts clasping side purlins *c.*1400 (RCHME 1981, 241)

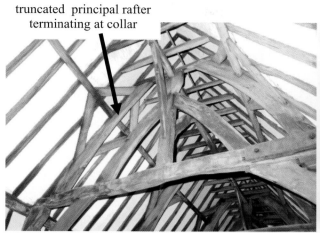

truncated principal rafter
terminating at collar

Fig 1.34: Merchant Adventurers' Hall, York
Crownpost with jowled head and truncated principals
clasping side purlins
1358-60

principal rafter   common rafter

Fig 1.36: Kingpost over low end crosswing of
Preston Patrick Hall, Kendal, Cumbria
– late 15th/early 16th C

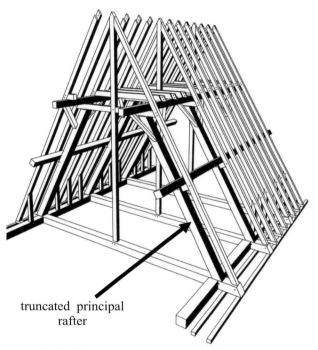

truncated principal
rafter

Fig 1.35: Nave roof of Sainte-Croix, Liège, Belgium
King strut roof with truncated principal rafters
1283-4d
(Based on drawings by Hoffsummer 2009, 194)

and early 17th centuries.

A second combination of crownpost with side purlins was in use just after the middle of the 14th century when the roof over the Merchant Adventurers' Hall in York combined a crownpost with truncated principal rafters clasping side purlins - that is where the principal rafter terminates at the collar (Fig 1.34) - as discussed more fully by Robert Hook. Truncated princi-

pal rafter roofs with and without crownposts were a relatively common form in the North-East, with a number of them tree-ring dated to between c.1440 to 1570. This roof form spread southwards down to at least Lincoln, but the earliest dated version found so far is in Hampshire at Church Farm, West Tytherley, tree-ring dated to 1334/5d (VA38, 128) (Fig 3.17), while a possible proto-type was used in 1283-4d over the nave of Sainte-Croix collegiate church in Liège, Belgium (Fig 1.35) (Hoffsummer 2009, 194 & 269).

Various forms of arched braced roofs are found in Yorkshire, mainly in the 15th century, usually with butt purlins. Kingposts are the most common roof form on non-cruck buildings in West and South Yorkshire, Cheshire, Lancashire and Cumbria and these seem to date from around the middle of the 15th century to the 17th century (Fig 1.36). These have a ridgepiece and carry their side purlins trenched on the backs of the principal rafters. Colum Giles has suggested that in West Yorkshire crownposts were used in gentry houses up to 1450 when they were superseded by kingpost roofs (Giles 1986, 21). Peter Ryder has suggested the change to kingposts in South Yorkshire was slightly earlier in the 15th century (Ryder 2002, 127), and one occurs over the open hall of Smithills Hall, Bolton, Greater Manchester (formerly part of Lancashire), which is assigned to the early 15th century (Fig 1.37). The kingpost in the north appears to have emerged suddenly and at a relatively late date on secular buildings, and continued into at least the 17th century.

Fig 1.37: Open hall and kingpost of Smithills Hall, Bolton, Greater Manchester (formerly Lancashire) which is assigned to the early 15th C

Summary

This introduction has tried to identify some underlying trends across England in roof development for mainly box-framed buildings, showing that roofs with passing braces were used across the country in the 13th century, followed by crownposts appearing in all regions in the late 13th or early 14th century, with these being replaced by side purlins of various types much earlier in the cruck region in the west than in eastern England. However for many areas of the country which are not covered by the following papers the picture is far from clear and there is a need for more studies before a complete picture will emerge of the development of roof types in England. Also for a fuller understanding of the development of English roofs, future studies should consider church and cathedral roofs as well as secular roofs, something that, in the main, it has not been possible to cover in the papers in this publication.

One aspect that would benefit from further research is why roofs across the country were all pretty similar up to the early 14th century and then became regionally more diverse after that. Part of the reason for the similarity of the early buildings could be because most are generally higher status buildings whose builders were interconnected. However not all the surviving early buildings are higher status – Westwick Cottage, Hertfordshire (1205d) and Sycamore Farm, Buckinghamshire (1205d) are much smaller than the other surviving early houses and well below manorial status (Fig 1.7) – and there is already evidence of some regional variation between these early buildings (Walker 1999). This limited variation clearly developed strongly in the 14th century giving rise to very marked regional differences. Was this driven by regional bands of carpenters, or by the clients, or were there other forces at work? The wealden house is a symbol of these entrenched differences (Fig 1.38). These houses, with their two jettied ends and recessed open hall all under an inline roof, are found across a large area of England with a concentration in the south east (Alcock 2010, 40). However each one uses the framing traditions of its region – close studding, Kentish framing, large or small panels etc. – and the roof type common in that region at the time. The only thing that seems to have travelled between regions is the concept of the jettied ends with a recessed hall all under an inline roof. Some areas even invented their own way of supporting the flying wall plate across the front of the open hall.

a: Masons Court, Stratford upon Avon, Warwickshire   b: Old Bell Farm, Harrietsham, Kent

c: Bayleaf, Chiddingstone, Kent now at Weald & Downland   d: Thatchers, Hundon, Suffolk

Fig 1.38: Wealden houses

Acknowledgements

Thanks to all the authors in this publication for their discussion, advice and comments on this paper. David Andrews, Nick Hill, Anne Padfield and Pam Walker are acknowledged for their advice and comments on a draft of this paper. My wife, Pam, is also thanked for proof reading and correcting it.

2 EAST ANGLIAN ROOFS: AN ESSEX-CENTRIC VIEW

by David Stenning
(Unless stated otherwise, all drawings are by the author)

This paper considers the timber-framed roofs of East Anglia, including the counties of Essex, Suffolk and Norfolk. I take as my starting point the year 1300. Before this date, there appears to be fairly widespread standardisation, but after it the various areas of Britain begin to evolve their more pronounced local distinctiveness.

There are clearly problems in understanding and relating the rich variety of medieval roof forms, but with time and study, some aspects start to fall into place. Truly *vernacular* buildings were remarkably conservative and the most obvious place to find local differences. Where patrons, either as individuals or as institutions, wished to reflect greater status, then carpentry could be noticeably more varied. Parish church roofs are more varied again and could draw on a geographically wider source of influence. We still have little understanding as to why this should be, but there were clearly imposed restraints beyond the limitations of a particular carpenter's knowledge. There are two important factors which need to be untangled. One is the concept of independent invention which could result in similar-seeming structures appearing in widely distant locations.

The other is simply a matter of lines of communication, by which carpentry ideas could spread from one area to another.

The pre-1300 roof tended to involve long straight timbers of relatively uniform size, lap-jointed to ease assembly. Overall stability was achieved with passing or scissor bracing, which ensured triangulation in the lateral plane. Some high status buildings sought to achieve a more masonry-like effect with segmental curved braces to copy the Romanesque style, such as Fyfield Hall in Essex built in 1167-85d (VA28, 135) (Fig 2.1). I suggest this straight-timber style may reflect a wider north-east European tradition which could have originated with the exploitation of mast-like pine or other softwood trunks. Viewed nationally, the cruck building tradition had also been established with naturally curved timbers that were more readily available in hardwoods.

The alternative box-frame tradition, with which we are familiar in East Anglia, superseded vertical earth-fast posts, possibly with a forked head and requiring only the simplest of jointing techniques. While the subject remains controversial, it seems probable that the utilisation of natural curvature (as in crucks), would form a part of any primitive technology.

By 1300 East Anglia had adopted the crownpost and this was to remain its main domestic roof type until the middle of the 16th century when it was superseded by side purlins, except in north Suffolk and Norfolk where, alongside the crownpost, they also used a queenpost roof with square-set side purlins and jowled queenposts (see Chapter 8).

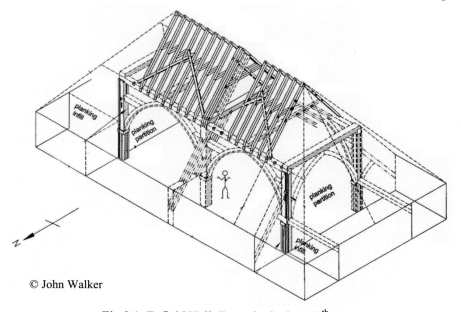

© John Walker

Fig 2.1: Fyfield Hall, Essex in the late 12th C
1167-85d

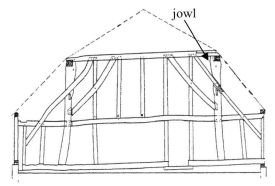

Fig 2.2: Abbey Barn, Snape, Suffolk
late 14th C
(© Hussey 2003)

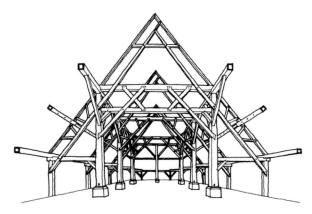

Fig 2.3: Reconstruction with side purlins
in the roof over the aisles of early 13th C
Barley Barn, Cressing Temple, Essex
1205-1230d

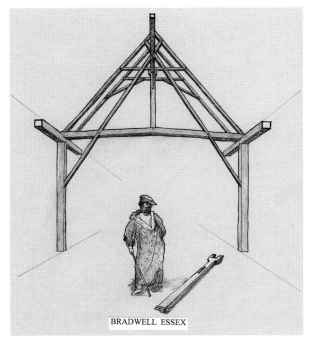

BRADWELL ESSEX

Fig 2.4: Inserted crownpost
Bradwell Hall, Bradwell, Essex
13th C

Crownposts

In the late 13th century, a number of technical advances began to appear. The root-bole jowl started to replace the vertical up-stands hewn into the top of the post. Having arrived, probably from France, this feature enjoyed a short period of immense popularity and jowls were used in some unlikely locations, such as in side girths or aisle ties where they seem to have had relatively little practical benefit beyond gaining a little more bearing surface. Tension braces, triangulating a frame between a post and a lower member (sometimes called 'foot braces'), began to be utilised. This may be connected to the increased popularity of jettying, where the tension brace would stabilise the overhanging upper floor. In Essex, this form of bracing made rapid headway and soon became a feature of most closed trusses. Further north in East Anglia and to the south near London the arch brace retained its popularity and, from at least the late 14th century, arch braces with reversed curvature spread throughout north Suffolk, Norfolk and Lincolnshire. Possibly one of the earliest examples of such bracing is in the aisled barn at Abbey Farm, Snape, Suffolk (Fig 2.2) (Hussey 2003).

Carpentry of the pre-1300 period suffered one noticeable shortcoming. The lack of an effective form of longitudinal bracing in roofs led to a tendency for them to 'rack' in this direction. In high status work various devices, including purlins in the roof plane, had been somewhat experimentally employed such as in the Tithe Barn at Siddington, Gloucestershire (1245-7d, VA23, 44) (Fig 1.9) and the two 13th century barns at Cressing Temple, Essex - the Barley Barn (1205-30d, VA24, 50) (Fig 2.3) and the Wheat Barn (1257-80d, VA24, 51) - but no vernacular solution had yet emerged.

The first major solution to solve the racking problem was the introduction of crownposts. This also had the big advantage of its ability to be inserted into most of the preceding roof forms without modifications. The crownpost, with its collar purlin, may well be another continental import and is, in effect, a small arcade transported into the roof space. Some of our earliest crownposts were added to give longitudinal stability to a pre-existing roof, such as in Bradwell Hall, Bradwell, Essex (Fig 2.4) (Walker J 1996). We have yet to explore objec-

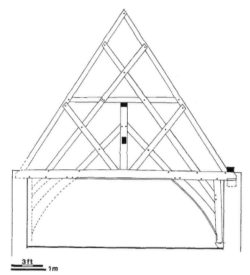

Fig 2.5: Three Blackbirds, Ely, Cambridgeshire early 14th C

(© Davis 2002)

The crownpost and collar purlin roof requires triangulation in the form of longitudinal arch braces rising from the crownpost to the collar purlin. Lateral braces are structurally less necessary and were frequently omitted both early and late in the evolution of the crownpost in Essex.

For most roofs with crownposts the collar purlin is continuous through the whole roof, continuing across the tops of the crownposts. However we retain two examples in Essex where, in open trusses, the crownpost continues a short distance vertically above the collar purlin, and the collar purlin is tenoned into each side of the post. One is over the service wing of Tiptofts, Wimbish dated to 1287-1329d (VA30, 118) (Fig 2.6) and the other Tweed Cottage, High Street, Stebbing, Essex (Fig 2.7). This is clearly an interim type where roof assembly took place one bay at a time, an advantage soon thought unimportant. As discussed in Chapter 1, purlins tenoned into crownposts do exist elsewhere. Devon is an example, such as in the base cruck gatehouse range of Dartington Hall, Totnes, where the base crucks have a strong bay system (Fig 5.19). These roofs are also probably related to, and may even have been derived from, the late 13th century king strut roofs with tenoned collar purlins found around Canterbury and discussed in Chapter 1.

tively which of these roofs were retrospectively strengthened with crownposts. Where the crownposts and the lateral stiffening were contemporary, the crownpost bracing could be integrated into an orderly pattern such as in the roof of The Three Blackbirds in Ely, Cambridgeshire (Fig 2.5). This shows 'hybridisation' where the past and future systems are seen to overlap and briefly cohere to form a distinctive idiom. Once curved braces were introduced, this temporary unity of design was lost.

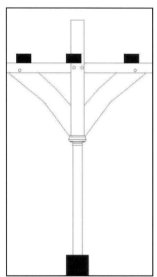

Fig 2.6: Crownpost in low end crosswing of Tiptofts, Wimbish, Essex 1287-1329d

(© John Walker)

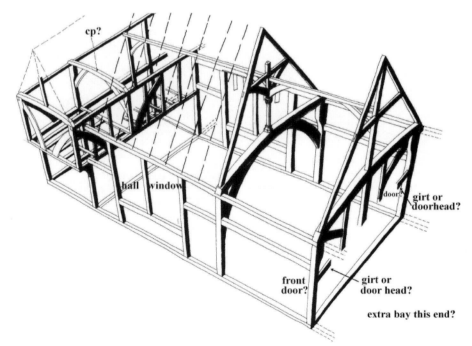

Fig 2.7: Tweed Cottage, Stebbing, Essex early 14th C

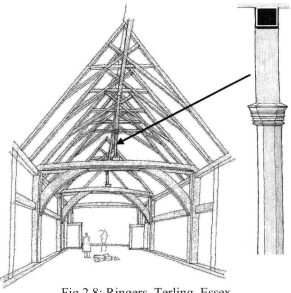

Fig 2.8: Ringers, Terling, Essex
14th C

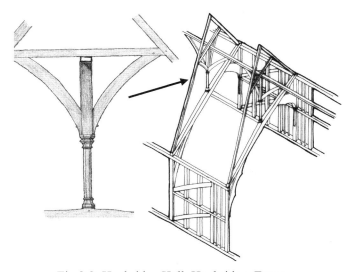

Fig 2.9: Heybridge Hall, Heybridge, Essex
14th C

Fig 2.10: Hall centre truss of Tiptofts, Wimbish, Essex
1287-1329d

Crownposts with octagonal posts and moulded caps and bases appeared in Essex from the early 14th century. Early examples include Ringers in Terling and Heybridge Hall, Heybridge (Figs 2.8 & 2.9); both are clearly 14th century, and both are over large span buildings. The crownpost, particularly in open trusses, quickly began to have aesthetic and perhaps symbolic attributes in addition to its structural role. Frequently the decorated part is about half the total height, which secures an elegant effect as at Tiptofts, Wimbish where the crownpost over the hall's centre truss, tree-ring dated to 1287-1329d (VA30, 118), has a capital and base of 'late decorated' type (Fig 2.10). The jowled head, as at Tiptofts, was popular in the early 14th century and resembles a naturally-grown fork. At Great Codham Hall, Wethersfield, Essex (Fig 2.11), the high-status crosswing, tree-ring dated to 1327-70d, has no lateral braces to the collar, partially to take account of the soulace pieces. Many early crownposts however, are simple square posts devoid of decoration or merely chamfered on each corner.

The crownpost over the central truss of the open hall of The Stables, Church Farm, Fressingfield, Suffolk, a mid-14th century raised-aisled hall, is slightly reminiscent of Tiptofts and illustrates some commonality of development (Fig 2.12). The device sometimes used of tenoning the crownpost braces to the rafters rather than the collar, lengthens these members allowing a relatively slightly longer crownpost (Figs 2.13c & 2.15a).

In the 14th and 15th centuries the East Anglian crownposts with octagonal posts (Fig 2.13) show the move from 'late decorated to perpendicular' decoration, with the 'bell' part of the capital becoming more pronounced (sometimes doubled), and the more frequent use of crenellations (Fig 2.13b & e).

Early crownposts had thick braces, usually as thick as the post itself. The braces were steeply angled, sometimes straight, but more usually gently curved. One Bedfordshire crownpost roof, that over 2 Bunyans Mead, Elstow, a two-bay long-jettied building dated to the early 14th century (Bailey 2002, 64), retains lap-jointed collar purlin braces, indicating that old techniques could linger. In Suffolk, braces could be almost solid 'knees' (Fig 2.14).

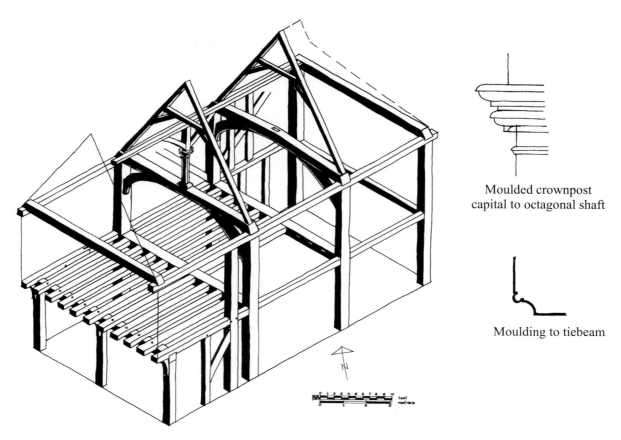

Moulded crownpost
capital to octagonal shaft

Moulding to tiebeam

Fig 2.11: Crosswing of Great Codham Hall, Wethersfield, Essex
1327-70d

(© Brenda Watkin)

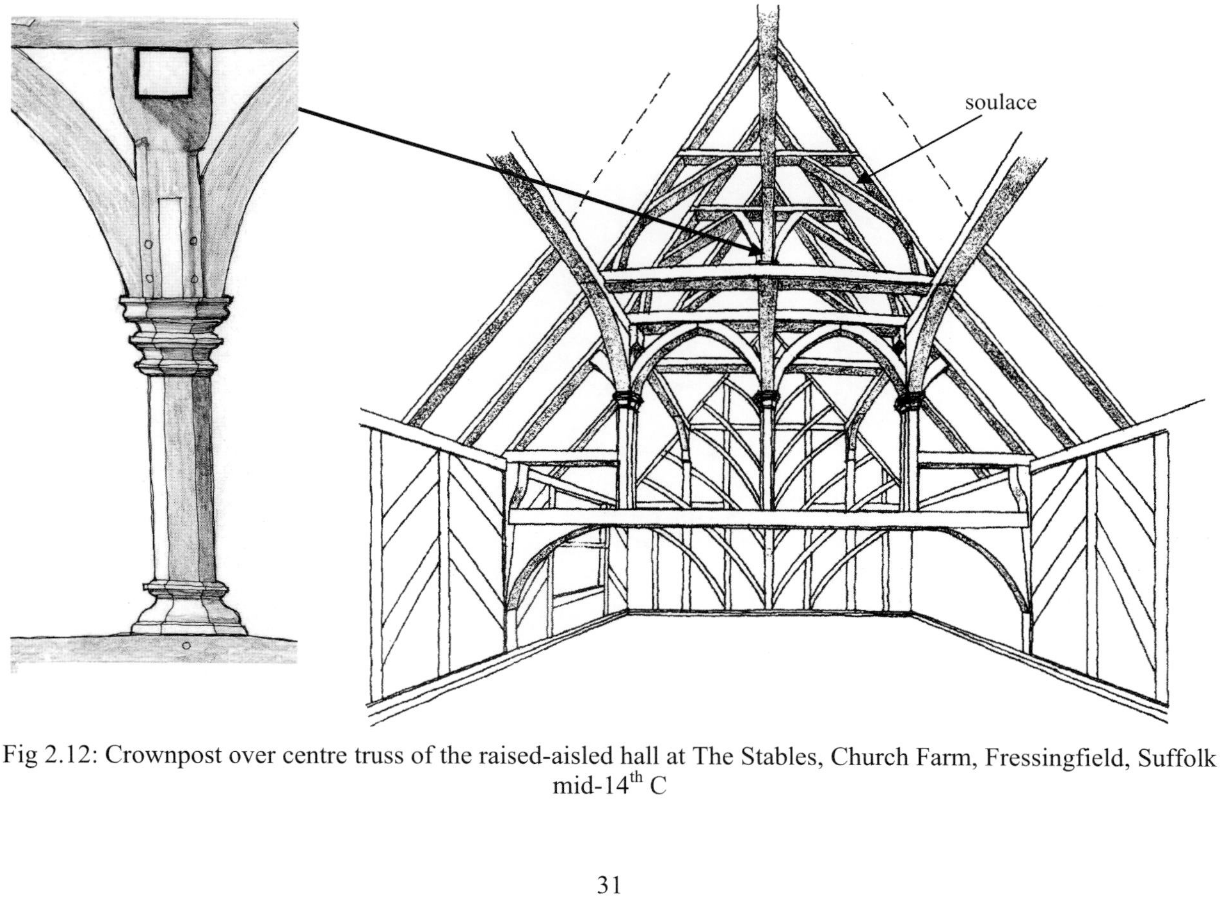

soulace

Fig 2.12: Crownpost over centre truss of the raised-aisled hall at The Stables, Church Farm, Fressingfield, Suffolk
mid-14th C

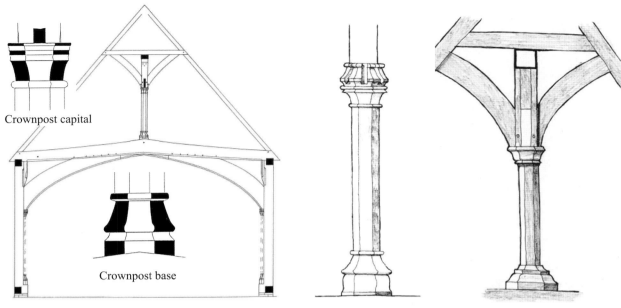

Crownpost capital

Crownpost base

a.   River Green House, Great Sampford, Essex
© John Walker

b. The George, High St,
Colchester, Essex

c. Shingle Hall, Great Dunmow,
Essex

d.   Monks Barn, Newport, Essex - a wealden house

e. Valley Farm, Flatford, Suffolk

Fig 2.13: 15th century octagonal crownposts over centre trusses of open halls in Essex and South Suffolk

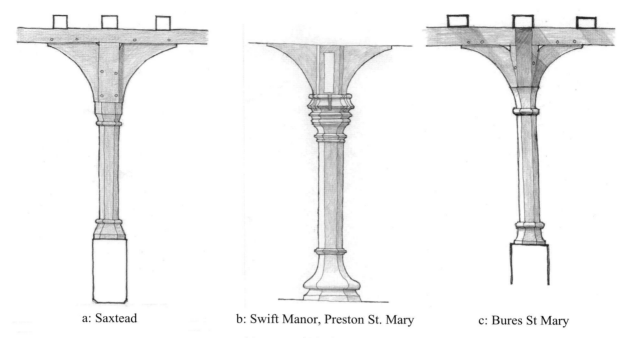

a: Saxtead   b: Swift Manor, Preston St. Mary   c: Bures St Mary

Fig 2.14: Examples of Suffolk 'knee' braced crownposts

Later in the 14th century, the cross-quadrate type of crownpost began to find favour (Fig 2.15). Both simple and elegant, it may well have been first employed in parish church roofs, as there remain a number of early Essex examples, such as Chipping Ongar and Panfield Churches. With the cross-quadrate form, the braces become inevitably thinner, so as to merge with the shaft on the post itself.

On occasions crownpost bracing, such as at Normans Farmhouse, Wakes Colne (early) and Graves Farm, Catmere End, Littlebury (late), is located so as to form an arch profile over a bay. At Normans Farmhouse, an aisled hall built *c.*1368d (VA34, 102), the arch is over the low end bay of the open hall (Fig 2.16) (Stenning 1997), while at Graves Farm, a 16th century two-storey transitional long-jettied house, the arch is over the hall chamber (Fig 2.17).

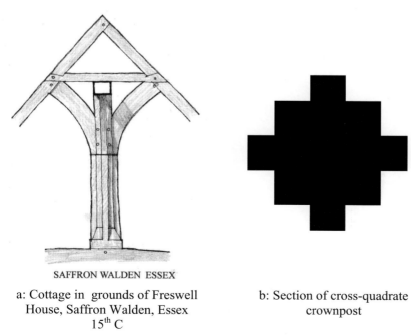

SAFFRON WALDEN ESSEX

a: Cottage in grounds of Freswell House, Saffron Walden, Essex 15th C

b: Section of cross-quadrate crownpost

c: Railway Terraces, Wenhaston, Suffolk late 15th C

Fig 2.15: Cross-quadrate crownposts

Fig 2.16: Arch over low-end bay of open hall of the aisled hall, Normans Farmhouse, Wakes Colne, Essex 1368d

Fig 2.18: Old Cottage, Little Chesterford, Essex Transitional house with late crownpost roof 16th C

As time went on, braces gradually became thinner, with very late (1550) examples looking more like thin plywood (Fig 2.18). However in north Suffolk and Norfolk some carpenters continued making crownposts in the early 14th century style with heavy thick braces on into the late 15th century, as at the Ancient House, King William Street, Needham Market, Suffolk.

Where the roof was not visible from the ground floor, the crownpost braces were occasionally omitted altogether. 60-64 High Street, Brentwood - a crosswing of the 15th century - has an

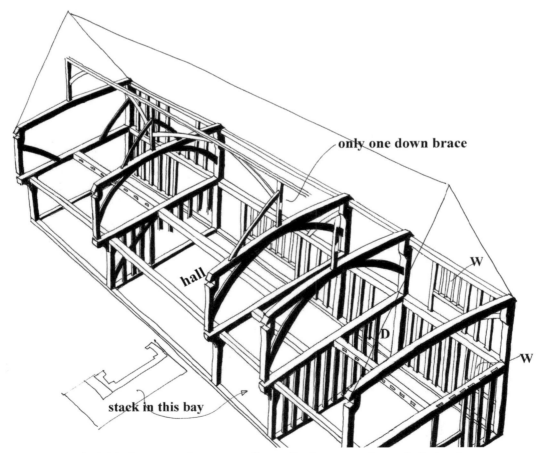

only one down brace

hall

W

D

W

stack in this bay

Fig 2.17: Crownpost braces to collar purlin form an arch over hall chamber at Graves Farm, Catmere End, Littlebury, Essex 16th C

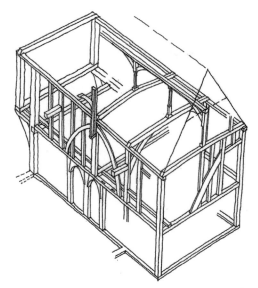

Fig 2.19: Crosswing 60-64 High Street, Brentwood, Essex viewed from the rear
15th C

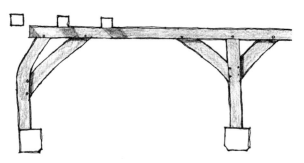

Fig 2.20: Cranked crownpost in Little Waltham, Essex

Fig 2.21: Reconstruction of open hall of Gobions, Great Bardfield, Essex
late 14th C

intermediate decorative crownpost without braces (Fig 2.19). At a house in Little Waltham one crownpost is strangely cranked, for no apparent reason (Fig 2.20), although deliberately cranked thin braces were a fashionable device in Essex around 1500.

The tension (or foot) brace from the crownpost down to the tiebeam was a ubiquitous feature of gables and closed trusses throughout Essex and Suffolk. However, they are rarely found in the open trusses of domestic buildings except in north-west Essex, as in the second and third trusses from the left at Graves Farm, Catmere End, Littlebury (Fig 2.17). They were however used in big agricultural buildings where presumably a long file of open trusses was thought to require extra stabilising. Gobions, Great Bardfield, Essex has a rare tension braced central truss, but the awkwardness of the composition suggests the reason it was not commonly emulated (Fig 2.21).

Local diversity does not necessarily respect county boundaries. The roofs of Kings Lynn in north-west Norfolk seem more attached to the North, rather than to Essex and the South-East. For example, the 15th century No 3 King Street, Kings Lynn has straight collar braces with attached cranked, tension braces (Fig 2.22). Integral raking struts can be seen in the city of York, where they were adapted to locate and carry side purlins. The truss over the early 15th century first floor hall at Thetford Priory, Norfolk, now a barn at Abbey Farm, Thetford, is similar, but without the raking struts (Fig 2.23).

Some developments seem curiously isolated, both temporally and geographically, such as the impressive hammer beam central truss of Tip-

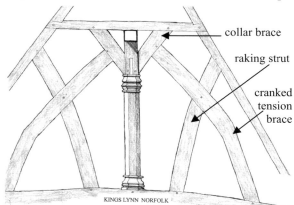

collar brace

raking strut

cranked tension brace

Fig 2.22: No 3 King Street, Kings Lynn, Norfolk
15th C

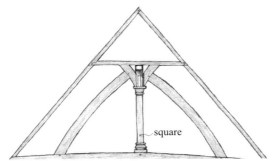

Fig 2.23: Roof of first floor hall in Thetford Priory, Norfolk now part of Abbey Farm early 15th C

tofts at Wimbish, Essex built in 1287-1329d (Fig 2.24a). There is a relatively long time-period between Tiptoft's mature hammer beam roof and the abundant later 15th and 16th century examples of this intriguing roof type. Excluding churches, the only other early hammer beam roof is over the Pilgrims' Hall in Winchester, tree-ring dated to 1310/11d (VA32, 80). However this is a public building; the second earliest known domestic hammer beam hall is the now-destroyed Balle's Place, Salisbury, dated to 1370-85 (Bonney 1964). At Tiptofts, the slightly precarious looking assembly is locked into massive buttress-like wall posts which consist of two separate large vertical timbers joined together. A virtually identical arrangement, including having the wall posts constructed out of two separate vertical timbers, can be seen in the raised-aisled hall of Baythorne Hall at Birdbrook, Essex (1341/2d, VA forthcoming), suggesting some connection between these two structural types (Fig 2.24b). Both were probably built by Sir John de Walton, Sheriff of Essex and Hertfordshire in 1331, and who died in 1347.

Queenposts

The crownpost remained the main roof type in Essex and south Suffolk until the mid-1500s when it was replaced by side purlin roofs. However in north Suffolk and south Norfolk a distinctive type of side purlin roof appeared towards the end of the 14th or early in the 15th century – a queenpost roof with jowled queenposts carrying square-set side purlins with a collar on top of the purlins, looking somewhat like an aisled hall on top of the tiebeams (Fig 2.25).

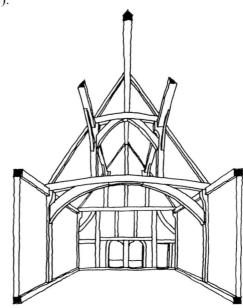

Fig 2.25: Queenpost roof over open hall of the White House, Wacton, Norfolk 15th C

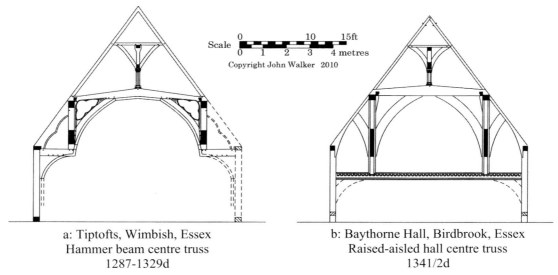

Scale

| 0 | 10 | 15ft |

| 0 | 1 | 2 | 3 | 4 metres |

Copyright John Walker 2010

a: Tiptofts, Wimbish, Essex
Hammer beam centre truss
1287-1329d

b: Baythorne Hall, Birdbrook, Essex
Raised-aisled hall centre truss
1341/2d

Fig 2.24 Comparison of centre trusses of Tiptofts and Baythorne Hall, Essex

Fig 2.26: Two-tier queenpost roof of
Warden's Hall, Merton College, Oxford
built 1299-1300

Probably the earliest prototype of this roof is not in Suffolk or Norfolk but over the Warden's Hall, Merton College, Oxford, dated to 1299-1300, except that this also has a crownpost on top of the collar (Fig 2.26). However in Suffolk

this roof type must have developed from raised-aisled halls as both are highly concentrated in north Suffolk (as shown in the map in Fig 2.27) and south Norfolk. It seems likely that the first (and remarkably influential) prototype raised-aisled hall in Suffolk would have had masonry walls like the Warden's Hall, as in the surviving example at Ashe Abbey, Campsey Ash, near Wickham Market, Suffolk. Without the heavy wall support, spectacular versions like Lodge Farm, Denton, Norfolk, built *c.*1355-60d (VA25, 25), required noticeably substantial timbers (Fig 2.28).

It seems perfectly natural that this potent, high-status concept should provoke the queenpost roof for use in humbler, more vernacular, buildings such as the White House, Wacton, Norfolk (Fig 2.25). Here, the 'purlins' retain their horizontal arcade plate-like disposition, though angled on their back against the rafters, producing a triangular shaped purlin. Many of these

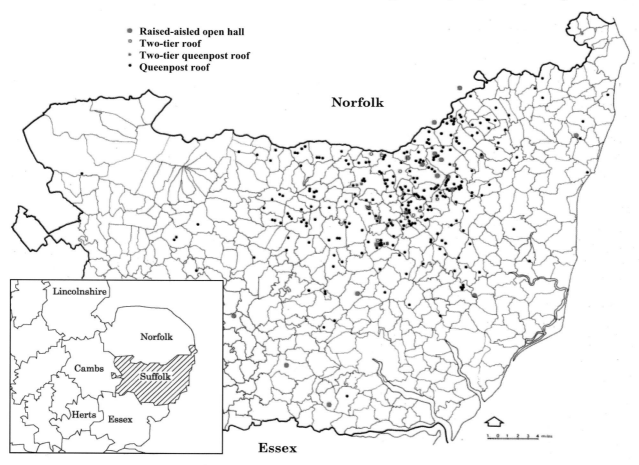

Fig 2.27: Distribution of raised-aisled halls and queenpost roofs in Suffolk by parish
(from Colman & Barnard 1999)

Fig 2.28: Centre truss of Lodge Farm, Denton, Norfolk
*c.*1355-60d

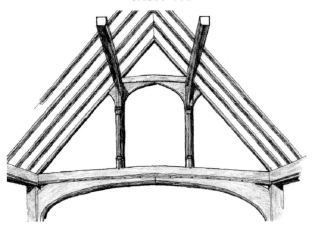

Fig 2.29: White Hart, Coggeshall, Essex
15th C

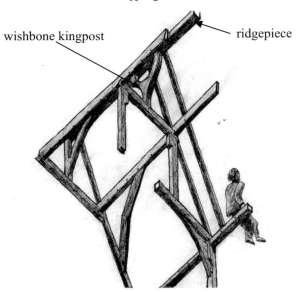

wishbone kingpost   ridgepiece

Fig 2.30: Queenpost roof with upper 'kingpost' at
Wash Farm, Ford Street, Aldham, Essex

queenpost roofs also have ridgepieces as at the White House, Wacton (Fig 2.25), usually triangular in shape, possibly derived from the fact that the intermediate rafters lack collars. The ridgepiece can be seen as an alternative arrangement to locate the rafter ends. Ridgepieces in general do not appear in East Anglia, other than on these roofs, until the 18th century. Evidently, this was a completely different mind-set than that which employed the roof-plane purlin in other parts of England. If true crucks had ever been popular in the south-east, a completely different picture might well have emerged.

This queenpost system seems to have evolved as a powerful roof type that partially over-rode the conventional crownpost in the northern part of East Anglia, although its use seems to have expanded down into the northern part of Essex, particularly in higher status buildings. The White Hart, Coggeshall, has a pair of wafer-thin queenpost trusses abutting tall crosswings, enclosing a fine single-bay open hall (Fig 2.29). A building in Trinity Street, Colchester has a simpler version with the collar tenoned into the triangular shaped 'purlins'.

We occasionally encounter extraordinary buildings that contradict our usual expectations. Aldham in Essex lies just north-west of Colchester, and is an unlikely location to find a vernacular farmhouse with a pair of Suffolk/Norfolk-like queenposts. Above the collar is a nature-formed wishbone acting as a one-piece 'forked' kingpost, supporting a substantial ridgepiece (Fig 2.30). Is this the work of an untutored carpenter (it is well made), or is it a last flowering of an unknown tradition? Alas, we will probably never know. With such prevalence of routine 'standard' roof-types, this particular exception seems quite bewildering.

Although by the third quarter of the 16th century the crownpost roof had been almost completely replaced by side purlin roofs, the queenpost roof with its jowled posts and square-set purlins continued in use over vernacular buildings in north Suffolk and south Norfolk throughout the second half of the 16th century, and possibly into the early 17th century, appearing over many transitional houses, usually those without attics, until it was itself superseded by side purlins, usually clasped side purlins.

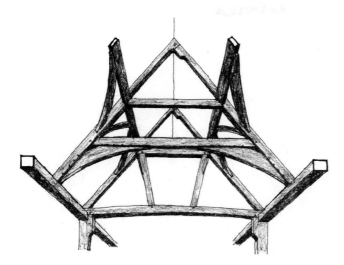

Fig 2.31: Clasped side purlin roof with
diminished principal rafters
The Bell, Great Easton, Essex
1527/8d

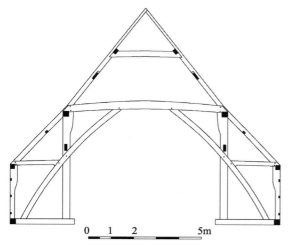

Fig 2.32: Early clasped side purlins
Monks Barn, Netteswellbury, Essex
1439-69d
© John Walker

Side-Purlin Roofs

Side-purlin roofs with the purlin set in the roof plane became the standard roof form in East Anglia in the 16th century replacing the crownpost, and eventually the queenposts. Two types of side purlin were used in the area; butt purlins (also called tenoned purlins) and clasped side purlins, the latter being the main type for vernacular buildings. Butt purlins were probably the first to be more widely adopted in East Anglia but both were being used from the 16th century. The monastic owned manor house, St Aylotts, Saffron Walden, Essex, built in 1501d (VA28, 142), has two tiers of butt purlins as does the hall range of the gentry house, Otley Hall, Otley, Suffolk, built in 1512d (VA32, 89). However two long-jettied transitional houses with chimneys built around the same time still had crownpost roofs - the manor house Cann Hall, Clacton, Essex built 1512d (VA30, 117) and Moone Hall, Stambourne, Essex built 1488 -1515d (VA31, 122). The earliest tree-ring dated house in Essex with a clasped side purlin is The Bell, Great Easton of 1527/8d (VA32, 71) (Fig 2.31), though the earliest known use was in 1439-69d (VA28, 141) when the monks of Waltham Abbey built the Monks Barn at Netteswellbury, Harlow, an aisled barn with clasped side purlins and diminished principal rafters (Fig 2.32) (Andrews et al. 1997).

Many of the earlier examples of side purlins were combined with crown or queenposts as shown by the large brick courtyard house, Hales Hall Farmhouse in Hales, Norfolk (Fig 2.33). Over the utility areas, the roofs have twin collars, queen struts, ridgepiece and two tiers of butt side purlins, the purlins set in the roof plane (Fig 2.23a). However, over the main

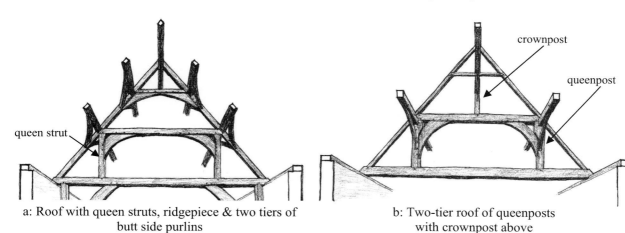

a: Roof with queen struts, ridgepiece & two tiers of butt side purlins

b: Two-tier roof of queenposts with crownpost above

Fig 2.33: Two types of roof at Hales Hall Farmhouse, Hales, Norfolk

Fig 2.34: Roof of service crosswing of Horham Hall, Thaxted, Essex
late 15th C

domestic part (servants hall?), it has queenposts with square-set purlins, over which are crownposts, providing a more dignified effect (Fig 2.23b). The long reign of the crownpost/ queenpost in East Anglia, seems to be more than a purely functional issue. I would suggest that the visual image of these linked types was symbolically important at this time.

The sophisticated late 15th/early 16th century service crosswing of the gentry house, Horham Hall, Thaxted, Essex, has a crownpost combined with butt purlins; the latter probably being all that is necessary to achieve a stable roof

(Fig 2.34). The decorative square crownpost is set diagonally (of which only a few examples are known in Essex), and was provided principally for effect. With hybrid side purlin/ crownpost roofs it is sometimes difficult to determine whether the crownpost is incorporated for structural reasons or just for decoration. Perhaps their authors were unsure.

In the late 15th and early 16th centuries, many decades after the Tiptofts hammer beam was built, this structural type (in debased form) became popular, particularly for public buildings (Fig 2.35). These tended to have butt side

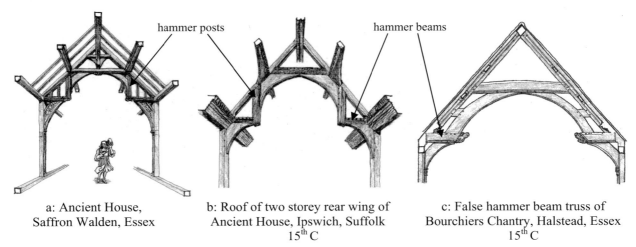

a: Ancient House,
Saffron Walden, Essex

b: Roof of two storey rear wing of
Ancient House, Ipswich, Suffolk
15th C

c: False hammer beam truss of
Bourchiers Chantry, Halstead, Essex
15th C

Fig 2.35: Examples of hammer beam roofs in East Anglia

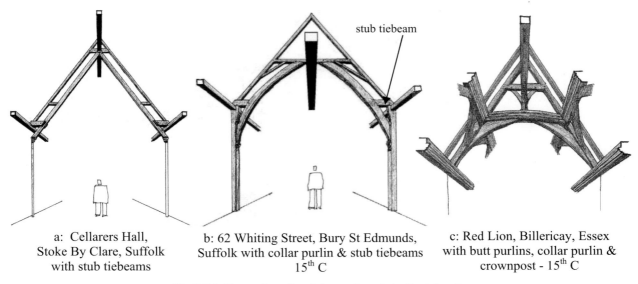

a: Cellarers Hall,
Stoke By Clare, Suffolk
with stub tiebeams

b: 62 Whiting Street, Bury St Edmunds,
Suffolk with collar purlin & stub tiebeams
15th C

c: Red Lion, Billericay, Essex
with butt purlins, collar purlin &
crownpost - 15th C

Fig 2.36: Examples of arch-braced roofs in East Anglia

purlins. Church porches, such as that at South
Benfleet, Essex can be instructive, being fully
timber framed and equally comparable as the
embodiment of high status. Colchester Guildhall, which has been re-erected in Colchester
Museum, has two tiers of butt purlins, and hammer beams tenoned into the uprights; these
somewhat resemble queenposts. Other examples include the Ancient House, Saffron Walden, Essex (a probable guildhall and known
only from an engraving) (Fig 2.35a), which had
tiny high mounted crownposts; the roof over the
late 15th century two-storey two-bay rear wing
of The Ancient House, 30 Buttermarket, Ipswich (Fig 2.35b); and the centre truss of the
open hall of the 15th century Bourchiers Chantry, built for a College of Canons, in Halstead,
Essex, the braces forming a visual bridge - another sub-type (Fig 2.35c).

East Anglia has a number of buildings with
arch-braced collars and stub tiebeams (Fig
2.36). Most of them seem to be 15th or early
16th century, but this is a fairly early truss type
appearing for example in Kent in the early 14th
century at Hurst Farm, Chilham (Pearson et al.
1994, 35). The wide arches, thus formed, have
a strong gothic feel, which must have been the
basis for their popularity. The type of purlins
used with these roofs vary from clasped side
purlins to butt purlins to collar purlins. Clasped
side purlins were used in the early 16th century
open hall and contemporary high end crosswing
of the Golden Fleece, Brook Street, South
Weald, Essex (Fig 2.37). It has a series of

trusses, alternating between tiebeam and arch
braces with a single clasped side purlin each
side, the principal rafter diminishing above the
purlin. The hall is of four equal bays, an unusual form in Essex, and the roof is not smoke
blackened (Gilman 1991). It is unlikely to have
been a domestic building; possibly it was a
guildhall. A collar purlin was used in the arch-
braced trusses over the domestic open hall of 62
Whiting Street, Bury St Edmunds, Suffolk
where the collar purlin was clasped by the arch
braces to the soffit of the collar. Here all the
common rafters had collars which were pegged
to the collar purlin (Fig 2.36b). A number of
arch-braced roofs have been found clustered
around Bury St Edmunds.

Fig 2.37: Golden Fleece, South Weald, Essex
with clasped side purlin & diminished principal rafters
early 16th C

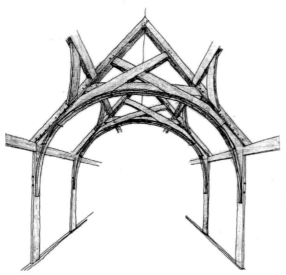

Fig 2.38: Scissor bracing at
Bretts Farm, Aveley, Essex
early 15th C

Fig 2.39: Clothiers' Hall, Ipswich, Suffolk
16th C

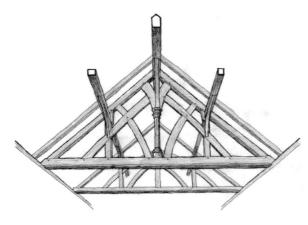

Fig 2.40: The Guildhall, Bury St Edmunds, Suffolk
16th C

Another variation of the arch-braced roof is the scissor-braced roof. This has a long history dating back at least to the 13th century. Its advantages continued to be enjoyed, on rare occasions, over a wide part of eastern England. Like the arch-braced stub tiebeam roof, it provided wide arches over an impressive hall as at the early 15th century Bretts Farm, Aveley, Essex (Fig 2.38).

By the 15th century, the carpenter of a high-status building had the choice of a variety of different components, all of which will seem suitably impressive. A popular arrangement was to have alternating trusses with a tiebeam at every other truss such as outlined above at the Golden Fleece, Brook Street, South Weald, Essex (Fig 2.37) and the 16th century Clothiers' Hall in Ipswich, Suffolk (Fig 2.39). The intention was to articulate the space with a dramatic sequence of silhouettes. The Guildhall roof at Bury St. Edmunds, is a wonderful collection of East Anglian features all happily combined (Fig 2.40).

One might expect that a high-status domestic building would employ an alien collection of techniques. While, in fact, this is rarely the case, Framsden Hall, Framsden, Suffolk is an extreme example. This manor house was built in the late 15th century and has an open hall between two crosswings. The hall is remarkable for its structural complexity and rich ornamentation and consists of a cross-entry half bay, partitioned from the two bay hall by a spere truss (an uncommon feature in Suffolk but more common in Essex). The roof consists of king-posts carrying a ridgepiece and two tiers of moulded butt purlins with cusped windbraces forming quatrefoil patterns between the purlins (Fig 2.41). Roofs with foliate panels can be found in parish churches and there are domestic examples in Shropshire and elsewhere, but they are rare in East Anglia. However, the curiously shaped short raking struts from the tiebeam to the rafters are virtually unknown in any context. Kingpost roofs are rare in East Anglia, but some are found in the 17th century after which they become a little more common, particularly over farm buildings, probably derived from the many carpenters' manuals then in print (Fig 2.42).

Fig 2.41: Spere truss of Framsden Hall,
Framsden, Suffolk
late 15th C

Fig 2.42: Kingpost roof in barn at Hill Farm,
Gestingthorpe, Essex
19th C

Another side-purlin roof form used in the 16th and 17th centuries was the A-frame where the tiebeam is replaced by a collar as at Hosdens, Great Maplestead, Essex (Fig 2.43). This type was mainly used in buildings with an upper storey and low side walls where a conventional tiebeam would block access between the bays on the first floor. Usually it is combined with side purlins but occasionally crownposts were

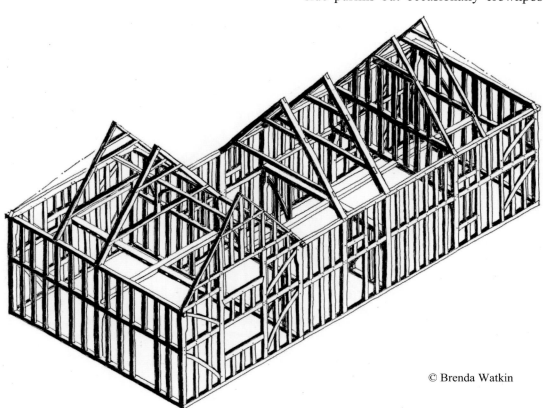

© Brenda Watkin

Fig 2.43: A-frame trusses at
Hosdens, Great Maplestead, Essex
16th C

43

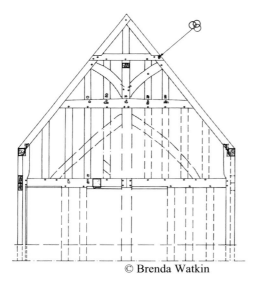

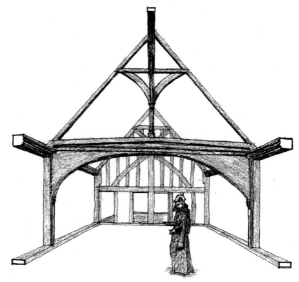

Fig 2.44: A-frame truss with extended jowls at service end of open hall at Copeland House, Fobbing, Essex 15th C

Fig 2.45: Open hall of Copeland House, Fobbing, Essex 15th C

© Brenda Watkin

used sitting on the collar as in the crosswing at Hosdens. The rafters are usually dovetailed or birdmouthed over the wall plate, but sometimes the principal post has a jowl extending up to the principal rafter (Fig 2.44). It was sometimes used in medieval houses, such as Copeland House, Fobbing, Essex, a small in-line hall house (Fig 2.45). This and a nearby identical house, 6-10 Norsey Road, Billericay, share this unusual feature of extended jowls and raised collar/tiebeams in their end partitions. This seems to have offered the limited advantage of providing plenty of space in otherwise low walls for the display of decorative wall bracing. Low overall height is a characteristic feature of many late in-line hall houses in Essex. A number have crownposts over the hall and side purlins over the upper chambers, a practical solution that follows from the limitations of the space.

The clasped purlin roof is one where the side purlin is clasped between

the rafter and a collar (Fig 2.46) and was a real innovation that seems to have percolated into East Anglia from the west. The crownpost was at last abandoned in favour of an efficient and economical substitute. Early examples, such as the Bell at Great Easton (West Essex) can retain some of the flavour of the earlier butt purlin types (Fig 2.31). In the 16th and first half of the 17th century, clasped side purlin roofs came with windbraces and in two main types, those

Fig 2.46: Clasped side purlin roof with diminished principal rafters at 30 High Street, Maldon, Essex 16th C

44

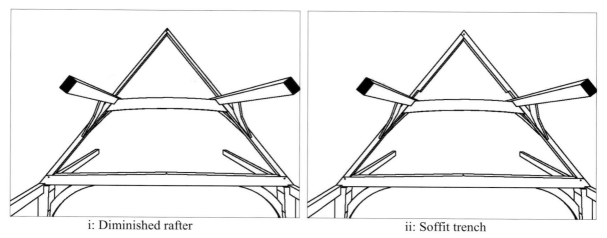

i: Diminished rafter   ii: Soffit trench

a: Clasped side purlin with single purlin

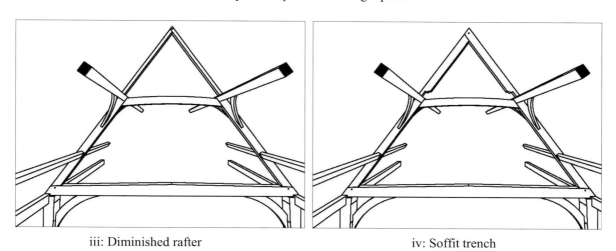

iii: Diminished rafter   iv: Soffit trench

b: Clasped side purlin with lower butt purlin

Fig 2.47: Types of clasped side purlins in East Anglia in the 16th & 17th C

(© John Walker)

with principal rafters which diminished above the purlin to the thickness of the common rafters and those with a trench cut out of the soffit of the principal rafter above the purlin so as to allow the purlin to be fitted to the roof (Fig 2.47a). These were used throughout East Anglia but alongside these in north Suffolk and Norfolk another variant was also used with a second lower butt purlin, again with diminished principal rafters or soffit trenches (Fig 2.47b). Refinements such as windbraces and reduced rafters tend to disappear in the later 17th century. In these later clasped side purlin roofs the principal rafter was often the same size as the common rafters (Fig 2.48).

Some roofs have bays of both clasped purlins and butt purlins, indicating the carpenter's choice was dependant on location. An example

Fig 2.48: Clasped side purlin roof with 'principal rafters' the same size as the common rafters
Marks Cottage, Layham, Suffolk
18th C

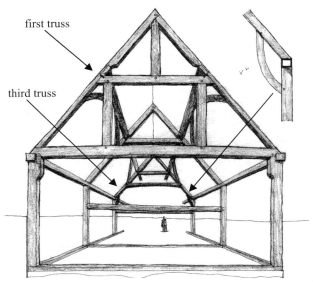

first truss

third truss

Fig 2.49: Mixed construction - the third truss is
an A-frame truss with butt purlins - at
The Stables, Wethersfield, Essex
late 16th C

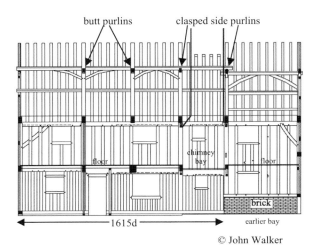

butt purlins   clasped side purlins

floor   chimney
bay   floor

brick

← 1615d →   earlier bay

© John Walker

Fig 2.50: North wall of Manor Farm, Pulham Market,
Norfolk, viewed internally with mixed roof construction
1615d

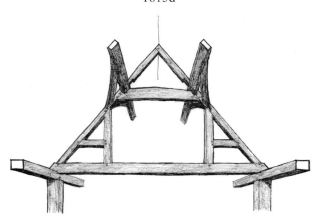

Fig 2.51: Queen struts in clasped side purlin roof of
Shellow Cross Farmhouse, Willingale, Essex
17th C

is The Stables, Wethersfield, Essex probably built in the third quarter of the 16th century (Fig 2.49), though roofs of this type are more common in the 17th century such as at Manor Farm, Pulham Market, Norfolk (1615d, Brown S & M & Tyers I 2010) (Fig 2.50). Some clasped side purlin roofs have queen struts rising to the collar as in the first truss at The Stables in Wethersfield, Essex in Fig 2.49. At Shellow Cross Farmhouse, Willingale, Essex the queen struts are set further to the edge of the roof and rise to the rafter rather than the collar (Fig 2.51), a national roof type associated with an attic floor. A variant of this uses butt purlins enabling the collar to be set higher, allowing easier movement within the attic. Roofs were now free to be relatively utilitarian as they were no longer visible from important rooms. Sheepcote Farmhouse in Southminster, Essex, is an in-line, floored 17th century building which is ingeniously constructed to provide a well-proportioned attic (Fig 2.52). The framing is unusual in a way that suggests continental influences. Its coastal location probably bears this out.

The East Anglian common rafter roofing tradition endured long, particularly at the vernacular level. This particular box-frame approach first spread out widely, and then became technically outdated by developments elsewhere. There were, clearly, reasons for this resistance to change, which may have had a cultural dimension.

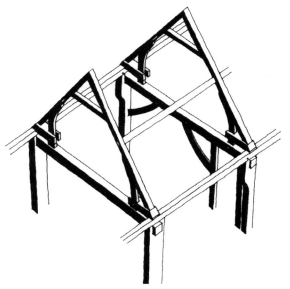

Fig 2.52: Sheepcote Farmhouse, Southminster, Essex
17th C

3   EARLY ROOFS IN HAMPSHIRE: 1240-1600

by Edward Roberts

(Unless stated otherwise, all illustrations are by Bill Fergie after the author)

Introduction

Hampshire cannot claim to have extraordinarily early roofs, like those found in some eastern counties of England, nor can it match the highly decorative roofs of Shropshire and the Welsh Marches. Hampshire roofs are no more than moderately early and are, on the whole, moderately plain. What, then, might be their interest to people outside the county?

Firstly, an extensive campaign of dendrochronology, in which over 150 buildings have been dated, has allowed us to trace the chronological development of regional building types.[1] Thus, we now know not only the date-range of a given roof type, but also its evolution in relation to other forms. For example, we have come to realise that the crownpost roof, which is common in the counties to the east as late as the 16th century, was superseded in Hampshire at a much earlier date by the principal rafter roof; a development which may have been partly influenced by the cruck tradition which was common in Hampshire but not in counties to the east.

Secondly, Hampshire lies astride the boundary between eastern and western carpentry traditions. Many of its historic roofs, like those in counties to the east, lack ridge beams and are of clasped side purlin form above a box-framed building. However, the county lies on the south-eastern border of cruck distribution. To the west are counties where cruck frames are common (Fig 3.1) and where, even in box-framed buildings, there was a tradition of trenched side purlins, ridge beams and massive principal rafters. Finally, some early roofs in Hampshire share a carpentry tradition with northern France (Epaud 2007; Munby *et al.* 1983). How this mixture of carpentry traditions affected the historic development of roofs in Hampshire will be explored below.

'True' Cruck Roof Trusses

A cruck has been defined as 'a single piece of timber, straight or curved, serving as a principal [rafter] of a roof, and stretching from a point at,

or close to, the apex of the roof to a point substantially down the side walls' (Alcock 1981, 3). Most crucks have some form of side purlin roof.

The geographical distribution of true crucks[2] reveals a clearly defined boundary running north-east to south-west across England and approximately along the Weald edge in east Hampshire (Figs 3.1, 3.2 & 3.3). To the southeast of this line, true crucks are unknown, to the north and west they are locally common throughout England and Wales.

On the chalklands of central and parts of southern Hampshire, crucks are mainly found in the ancient nucleated villages that are strung out along the river valleys. They are noticeably more numerous in the River Avon valley in the far west than in river valleys in the east which are on the very border of national cruck distribution. In the north, and especially in the clay lands, cruck distribution is more scattered and this may reflect more dispersed medieval settlement in small hamlets.

Hampshire's crucks are of superior quality to those of many other areas in the country. They generally exhibit good carpentry and were made from fine timbers with a smooth, even curve. Thus, even though the county was on the fringe of the area of cruck distribution, its cruck houses may not in their day have been socially marginal or low-status buildings. Certainly the truncated crucks which form the hall truss at Park View, Tichborne (1448-80d) have finely shaped and moulded timbers that seem to proclaim their owner's relative wealth (Fig 3.4).

A national survey of cruck buildings by Alcock established a classification of crucks according to the form of their apexes and gave them 'type' names (Fig 3.5) (Alcock 1981, 7 and 96). Following this, an analysis of cruck apexes in Hampshire showed that, of 58 cruck buildings, Alcock's type C – in which the tops of the cruck blades are held together by a saddle that

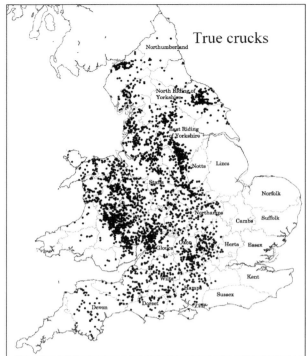

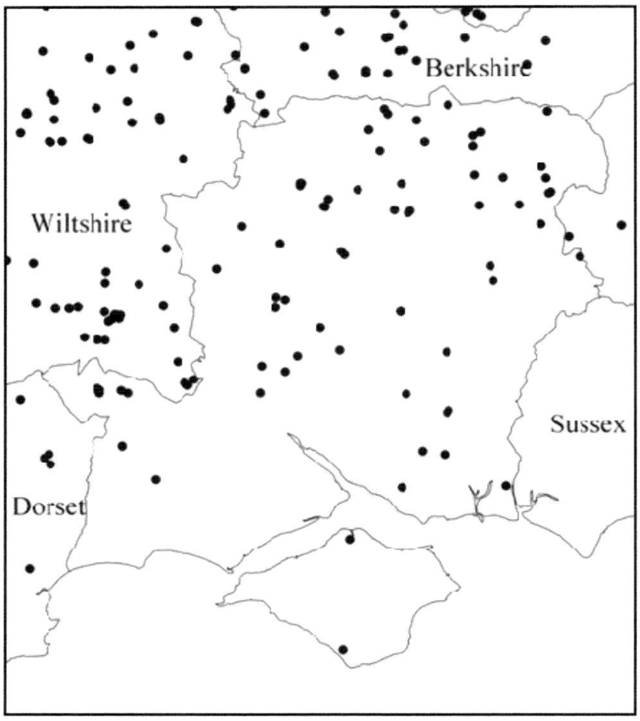

Fig 3.1: Map of true crucks in England & Wales
(after N W Alcock)

(Mapping by N W Alcock from the VAG database of crucks.
1910 county boundaries based on data provided through EDINA
UKBORDERS with the support of the ESRC & JISC and uses
boundary material which is copyright of the Great Britain Historic GIS Project, Portsmouth University.)

Fig 3.3: Map of true crucks in Hampshire
(after N W Alcock)

(Mapping by N W Alcock from the VAG database of crucks. 1910
county boundaries based on data provided through EDINA UKBOR-
DERS with the support of the ESRC & JISC and uses boundary material which is copyright of the Great Britain Historic GIS Project,
Portsmouth University.)

Fig 3.2: A simplified geological map of Hampshire showing sources of upper greensand stone
which mark the Weald edge and the lower greensand beds in the Weald

(Bob Edwards, Hampshire County Council)

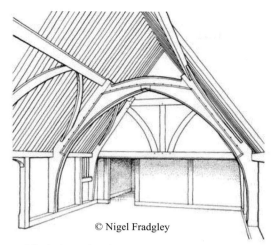

© Nigel Fradgley

Fig 3.4: Park View, Tichborne, Hampshire
A reconstruction of the hall showing the graceful
Gothic arch of the hall truss and the 'fan' truss at
the high end
1448-80d

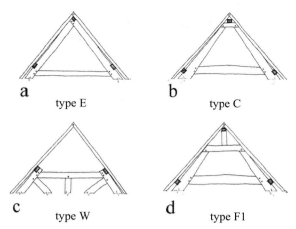

a   type E   b   type C

c   type W   d   type F1

Fig 3.5: Some cruck apex types in Hampshire
a: Type E (reused) at Water Ditch Farm,
Poulner, Ringwood
b: Type C at Tan-y-Bryn, Hannington - 1360d
c: Type W at Park View, Tichborne - 1448-80d
d: Type F1 at Tan-y-Bryn, Hannington - 1360d

carries the ridge beam (or ridge purlin) – was the commonest with nineteen examples: type W - sometimes called a truncated cruck because the crucks barely rise above purlin height, as at Park View, Tichborne (see Fig 3.4) – had twelve examples; type F1, with a short post above the collar to support the ridge beam, had seven examples, and type E – in which the cruck blades join diagonally to support the ridge beam at the apex of the roof – had four examples (Lewis *et al.* 1988, 17).

At a national level, it is still unclear how far cruck apex types represent chronological stages of cruck development. Type W seems in general to be a late type and this national trend is, to some extent, borne out in Hampshire (Roberts 2003, 22). However, it is not at all uncommon for Hampshire's cruck houses to have more than one apex type and type F1 is generally present in these combinations, suggesting that it was used as a levelling device where crucks were of uneven height. Moreover, where there is more than one apex type present, it is the hall truss which often has the longest, and presumably best, crucks with a type C apex, whereas the closed trusses have shorter crucks necessitating other apex types. It thus would appear that the medieval carpenter's selection of apex type could be a matter of convenience and local tradition rather than of chronological period. However, it may be that the age of Hampshire's cruck houses can be more accurately assessed by features other than

apex types (see the discussion below).

The date at which cruck-framed houses were first built is a matter of dispute, although no true cruck in England and Wales has so far been dated by dendrochronology earlier than the mid 13th century. There is documentary evidence for crucks (called 'forks' or *furci* in Latin) in Hampshire as early as 1254/55 when a carpenter built the Town Mill at Alresford with ten forks (Roberts 2003, 20). However, the earliest known cruck framed building that survives within the county – dated to 1282-4d (VA26, 63) - is at The Manor, Rockbourne. This building, now used as a barn, seems to have been intended for some other non-domestic function. The earliest dated cruck house in the county, dated to 1311/12d (VA39, 135), is No. 1 Somerset's Cottages at Bentley (Miles *et al.* 2008, 35) and the latest is Hatch Cottage, Tadley (1496-1528d, VA41, 107), a house which, nonetheless, was built some 200 years before the last dated cruck house in Britain - Hall Farm, Moorhouse, a clay-lump cruck house in Cumbria built in 1742 (VA30, 91). Rye Cottage, Mapledurwell is a cruck house dated to 1487d (VA30, 107) but when an extra bay was added in 1525/6d, it was made in box-framed form with straight, upright posts supporting the roof truss. While too much weight should not be put on one example, this would seem to be a neat illustration of the demise of the cruck tradition in the county (Fig 3.6).

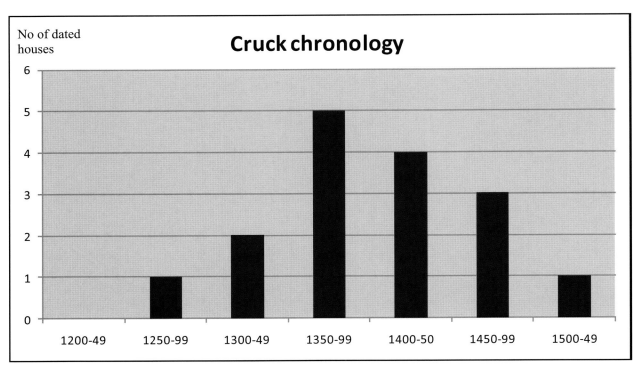

Fig 3.6: Cruck chronology of roofs in Hampshire

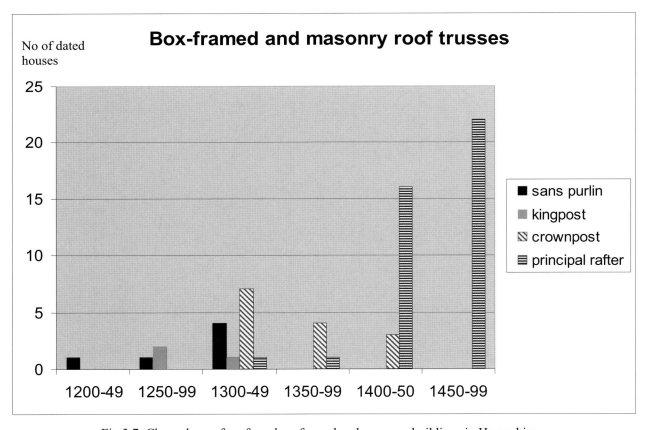

Fig 3.7: Chronology of roofs on box-framed and masonry buildings in Hampshire

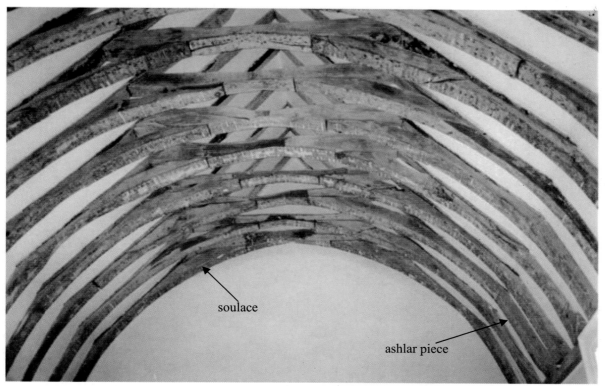

soulace

ashlar piece

Fig 3.8: Roof of the solar at Michelmersh Manor Farm, Hampshire
showing the curved soulaces in the former solar
1321/2d

(photo –Richard Haddesley)

Collar Rafter, Sans Purlin Roofs

The chronology of the roof trusses associated with box-frame buildings has been broadly established in Hampshire (Fig 3.7). The earliest roofs of this type have two notable features. First, they lack principal rafters so that all rafters are of uniform scantling, each rafter couple being linked by a collar beam. Second, they lack purlins to give longitudinal stability.

The earliest dated example of this form of roof in Hampshire is over the nave of Winchester Cathedral (1246-1250d, VA29, 120) and the latest is at Michelmersh Manor (1321/2d, VA33, 92), a former country house of the Prior of St Swithun's in Winchester. Here, above what was almost certainly the Prior's solar, curved soulaces and ashlar pieces bear rows of broken nails which were damaged when a probably original ceiling was removed (Fig 3.8). However, in what was either a small closet or garderobe, the soulaces and ashlar pieces are straight and bear no evidence of a ceiling .

Although collar rafter roofs of timber-framed

buildings derive some stability from full hips at both ends, greater stability is afforded to collar rafter roofs on stone buildings by masonry gable ends. It is probably for this reason that collar rafter roofs have rarely survived in Hampshire on timber-framed buildings. One such roof on a timber-framed aisled barn at West Court, Binsted (1296-1304d, VA39, 136) is in a fragmentary state (Miles *et al.* 2008, 136; Smith C 2008). The most complete example within the county is Forge Sound at East Meon, a house which unfortunately failed to date by dendrochronology, but which may be assigned to the early 14th century (Fig 3.9). Its roof has probably survived intact because it is fully hipped at both ends and because the battens that are nailed across the rafters appear to be original and have thus always given some longitudinal stability.

In eastern England early roofs of this sort that began to fail were given longitudinal support by the insertion of a collar purlin supported by and braced from a crownpost. The Barley Barn at Cressing Temple, Essex, whose roof has been dated to 1205-30d (VA24, 50), was later modi-

Fig 3.9: Forge Sound, East Meon, Hampshire -
a reconstruction of the open hall with a sans
purlin, collar rafter roof

(© *Nigel Fradgley*)

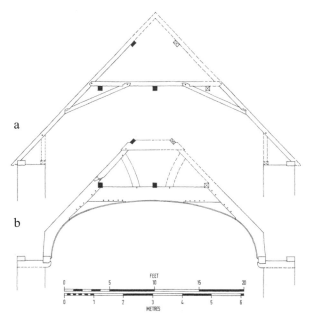

Fig 3.10: Roof trusses from the former refectory
of Romsey Abbey, Hampshire
a: the primary roof of *c.*1230 with the existing
second-phase purlins in solid black.
b: a second-phase truss of 1342-47(?)d.

(Courtesy Vernacular Architecture Group).

fied with the insertion of crownposts after 1510. Another aisled barn at Littlebourne, near Canterbury, Kent built in 1307-27d (VA35, 92) has an inserted crownpost roof of 1525. At Thorley Hall, Bishop's Stortford, Hertfordshire, an aisled hall dated to 1253/4d (VA33, 108) has an inserted crownpost roof of *c.*1397d (VA33, 108) and several more examples of this process could be given from eastern and south-east England (Roberts 2005).

At the so-called King John's House, Romsey, Hampshire, a collar rafter roof dated to 1256d (VA27, 99) was also stabilised with crownposts, probably in the 14th century. However, at the former refectory of Romsey Abbey this kind of repair work was handled differently. Here, the collar rafter roof, which may have been built *c.*1230, had begun to fail by 1342-74?d (VA35, 105). The original roof, had ashlar pieces, and soulaces with notched lap joints to both the collars and rafters (*ibid*). What is especially interesting, however, is the way that a carpenter chose to support this roof. He inserted five purlins beneath the earlier timbers and supported the whole construction on cruck-like principals (Fig 3.10); an expedient clearly suggestive of the influence of the western,

cruck tradition.

It is noteworthy that cruck roofs are generally associated with side purlins, usually carried on the backs of the cruck blades, but at the former refectory of Romsey Abbey four of the purlins resemble extraordinarily early examples of clasped side purlins; that is, the purlins are clasped between the principals and either the upper or lower collars. It is possible that the influence of the cruck tradition of side purlins accounts for the early emergence of side purlin roofs in box-framed houses in Hampshire. I will revisit this question later.

Finally, the remarkable roof at the probable infirmary of the former Wherwell Abbey is almost *sui generis* in an English context. This roof, dated to 1250d and with a repair and extension of 1280d (VA27, 99) (Fig 3.11), has great tiebeams supporting an aisled construction rising from the tiebeams. Technically it is a queen strut roof where the struts support a collar which carries a square-set purlin, though the struts are effectively like arcade posts supporting an upper tiebeam with passing braces topped by a collar rafter roof (Roberts 1998).

52

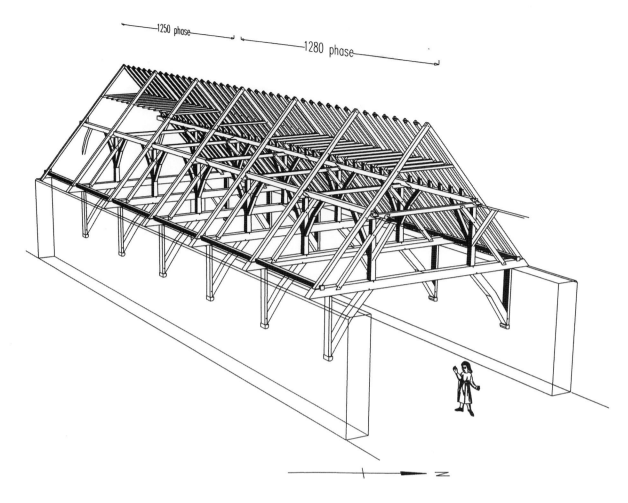

Fig 3.11: Wherwell Abbey, Hampshire
the roof of what was probably the infirmary
dated to 1250d and 1280d

(© John Walker)

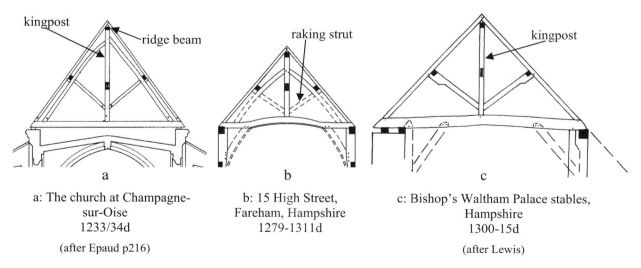

a: The church at Champagne-
sur-Oise
1233/34d

(after Epaud p216)

b: 15 High Street,
Fareham, Hampshire
1279-1311d

c: Bishop's Waltham Palace stables,
Hampshire
1300-15d

(after Lewis)

Fig 3.12: Comparative cross-sections of early roofs in Normandy & Hampshire

Uniform Scantling Roofs with Kingposts and Clasped Side Purlins

A few roofs in Hampshire were part of an early carpentry tradition that spanned the English Channel, examples being found in several south eastern counties and in Normandy (Munby *et al.* 1983; Epaud 2007, 241). The roof at Wherwell Abbey, discussed above, appears to have been part of this tradition and is comparable to the early 13th century roof of Abbeye de Vauclaire, Boueconville-Vauclaire (Epaud 2007, 208). Both roofs have braces that rise from tiebeams and pass queenposts/queen struts to meet lower collar beams, above which are collar rafters.

Similar parallels with early French carpentry are found in a small group of early kingpost roofs in Hampshire. Perhaps the most striking similarity is between the church at Champagne-sur-Oise dated 1233/34d (Fig 3.12a) (Epaud 2007, 216) and two almost identical roofs at Chesil Street, Winchester (1292/93d, VA27, 99) and No. 15 High Street, Fareham (1279–1311d, VA29, 117) (Fig 3.12b) (Roberts 2003, 28; Roberts et al. 1996, 66-68). In all three cases a kingpost supports raking struts and braces that rise to a ridge beam, while side purlins are clasped between under and outer rafters. The main difference seems to be that whereas the raking struts in the English examples pass the under rafters to support the side purlins, in the French example – as at Titchfield Abbey (see below and Fig 3.13) - the purlins are supported by small blocks.

A similar roof at a mainly timber-framed building associated with the bishop's palace at Bishop's Waltham (1300-15d, VA40, 125) has been compared with early roofs in both France and south-east England (Fig 3.12c) (Epaud 2007, 241; Munby et al. 1983, 129). This roof has kingposts supporting braces that rise to a ridge beam, but lacks under rafters. Instead, raking struts from the kingpost have spade-shaped ends that alone serve to clasp the purlins to the rafters. Indeed, this roof form could also be seen as an early attempt to dispense with the collar rafter roof in box-framed buildings and to transfer the weight of the roof to ridge beams and side purlins and thence to the kingposts and down to the tiebeams.

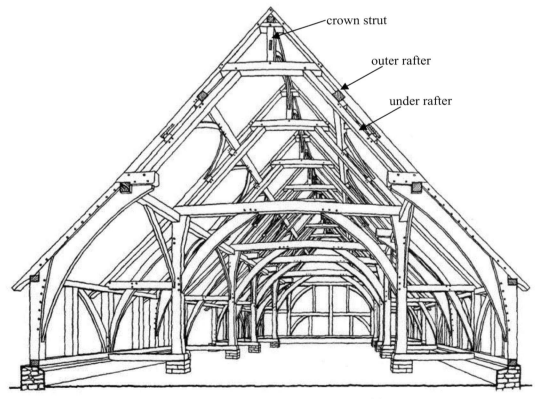

Fig 3.13: Titchfield Abbey Barn, Hampshire
common rafters have been omitted for the sake of clarity
1408/9d

(© Jonathan Snowdon)

54

Peter Smith has pointed out that whereas there are many hundreds of such kingpost roofs in northern France, dating from the Middle Ages and later, yet there is only a handful in southern England and these are all medieval. He asked whether the Hampshire examples represent strays from the main concentration and origin of the form in France or whether they were relics of an early Anglo-Norman scatter before the main French concentration developed. Given the early date of the Hampshire roofs, he argued for the latter explanation: namely, an Anglo-Norman tradition of roof carpentry of which the Hampshire examples are important relics (Smith in Roberts *et al.*1996).

A surprisingly late example related to this tradition is Titchfield Abbey barn (1408/9d VA29, 119) where under-rafters still clasp the side purlins to the outer rafters with the help of small blocks (Fig 3.13). Here, however, there are only short crown struts rising to a short collar carrying a ridgepiece. Raking struts were absent from the original design, only to be added at a later date when the under rafters began to fail. This roof is so unlike any other that survives in Hampshire from the early 14th century that one might wonder, given that Titchfield was a Premonstratensian Abbey, whether it was still within a lingering Anglo-French tradition.

Fig 3.14: Plain crownpost roof at
The Court House, East Meon, Hampshire
1395-7

(photo John Crook)

Crownpost Roofs

Greater stability was given to the collar rafter roof by the introduction of crownposts which held collar purlins beneath the collars, thus reducing the possibility of racking. In south-eastern counties, many crownposts are elegantly moulded with carved capitals and bases. In Hampshire, elegant crownposts are occasionally found on the Surrey border in the far east of the county, as at Bramshott Manor, but in most of the county crownposts are neither elegant nor decorative. A typical example is the stubby, undecorated and simple crownpost at Monks Cottage, Odiham (1300d, VA27, 98) but even at William of Wykeham's Court House at East Meon (1395-97, document) the crownpost roof in his great chamber is exceptionally plain (Fig 3.14). William of Wykeham was the wealthiest bishop in Britain and could easily have afforded something more extravagant.

Unlike neighbouring Surrey and Sussex where the crownpost is common, less than three dozen are known in the whole of Hampshire and these are mainly in the east of the county. For long we were puzzled as to why this should be. Did Hampshire carpenters or their clients find crownpost roofs unappealing? Dendrochronology has made it clear that the small number was due to their restricted and early time-span (Fig 3.7 Box-frame chronology) - quite unlike Sussex where the crownpost persisted as the main roof form until the 16th century.

In only three aristocratic buildings did the use of the crownpost linger on into the mid 15th century and it is a strangely spare and generally unbraced form. All three are connected with the Beaufort family. The Lodgings at Bishop's Waltham Palace (1438-42, document) (Fig 3.15a) and at St Cross Hospital, Winchester (*c.*1445) were both built by Cardinal Beaufort, while Kimpton Manor (1445d, VA33, 91) was built by an associate of the Beaufort family (Fig 3.15b). The persistence of the crownpost in these cases would seem to be an accident of high-status patronage but hardly a desire for elaborate or aesthetically-pleasing carpentry.

a: Lodging Range of Bishop's Waltham Palace
1438-42

b: Kimpton Manor
1445d

Fig 3.15: Two basic crownpost roofs in Hampshire

Principal Rafter Roofs

Side purlin roofs in box-framed buildings, in which the weight of the roof is transferred by purlins to principal rafters, do not become almost universal in Hampshire until the early 15th century although a few mid 14th century precursors seem to show carpenters feeling their way towards this roof form (Fig 3.7).

The roof at No. 35 High Street, Winchester (1340d, VA27, 99) is not easy to categorise (Fig 3.16) in that it has crownposts with integral clasped side purlins. In this respect it is comparable with the roof at Penshurst Place, Kent which is also datable to the 1340s (Pearson 1994, 87). By contrast, the roof at Church Farm, West Tytherley (1334/5d, VA38, 128) represents a clear and fascinating attempt to create a principal rafter roof by a carpenter who was still working and thinking within the uniform-scantling tradition (Fig 3.17). Instead of making principal rafters that diminished in width above the clasped purlins, he took a rafter of uniform scantling with the common rafters

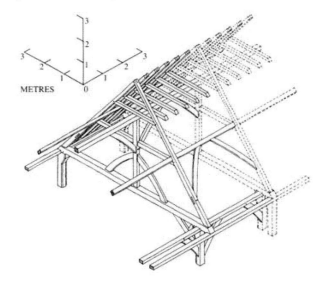

METRES

Fig 3.16: Hall truss at
No. 35 High Street, Winchester, Hampshire
1340d
(© Jonathan Snowdon)

and added an extra timber along its length between the tie and collar beams. This timber is technically called 'a short principal'.

56

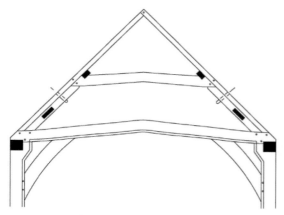

Fig 3.17: Roof truss at
Church Farm, West Tytherley, Hampshire
1334/5d

Fig 3.18: Hall roof at a house from Boarhunt,
Hampshire, now at The Weald & Downland
Open Air Museum, Singleton, West Sussex
1355-90d

(photo – Steve Taylor)

Why Hampshire carpenters were experimenting with principal rafter roofs at this early date is hard to tell, but it is possible that it may be connected with their exposure to the cruck tradition in which side purlins are common features. This exposure has already been noted with regard to the repair to the collar rafter roof of the former refectory of Romsey Abbey (1342-74?d, VA35, 105), by the insertion of clasped side purlins supported by cruck-like principal rafters. It is even more apparent at the house from Boarhunt in south-east Hampshire (1355-90d), now erected at the Open Air Museum at Singleton, West Sussex (Harris 2007) (Fig 3.18). This is essentially a box-framed house with a pair of cruck blades forming the hall truss. Almost all crucks have trenched side purlins, but here the clasped side purlins conform to the south-eastern tradition. Likewise cruck buildings commonly have ridge beams – but here there is no ridge, presumably because ridge beams are not part of the east Hampshire carpentry tradition of box-framed construction.

Boarhunt is on the very eastern edge of cruck distribution and this may partly account for the hybrid form of the roof. Within a few miles of Boarhunt is a house with a

Fig 3.19: Distribution of box-framed buildings
with trenched side purlin roofs in Hampshire

(Bob Edwards, Hampshire County Council)

57

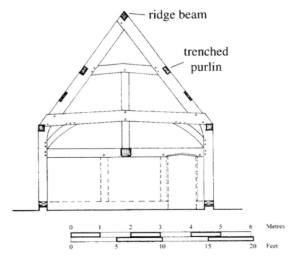

Fig 3.20: Lilac Cottage, Burgate, Hampshire
a house in the far west of the county where the
cruck tradition of ridge beams, trenched side
purlins and massive rafters affected the form
of roofs in box-framed buildings.

similar hybrid roof at Uncle Dick's Cottage, Hayling Island (Roberts 2003, 24). In both cases crucks were apparently chosen purely because they gave a graceful Gothic arch over the centre of the hall – a point that is discussed at more length below.

The side purlin became the standard roof type in Hampshire from the start of the 15th century and remained so until well into the 18th century (Fig 3.7). Of the various forms of side purlin, the butt or tenoned purlin roof was generally confined to larger and thus generally higher-status buildings. The earliest known example is in a cruck house, The Mount at Silchester (c.1405d, VA33, 93) and the earliest barn with a butt purlin roof is the Cross Barn, Odiham (1532d, VA 27, 98). Butt purlins were aligned along the length of the roof until the late 16th century, after which they were gradually super-seded by butt purlins staggered in alternate bays.

After 1400, the clasped purlin roof is by far the most commonly found roof in the centre and east of the county but in the west the cruck in-fluence emerges again with the trenched side purlin and ridge beam (Figs 3.19 & 3.20). Only a few trenched purlin roofs have been dated in Hampshire but the limited data so far accumu-lated suggests that they fall within the same date-range as that of the clasped purlin. Fi-nally, the threaded purlin has been found in a very few 15th and 16th century high-status houses.

Closed Trusses in Principal Rafter Roofs
At present, only two 14th century principal raf-ter roof trusses have been identified: at Church Farm, West Tytherley (1334/5d, VA38, 128) and the house from Boarhunt (1355-90d); the

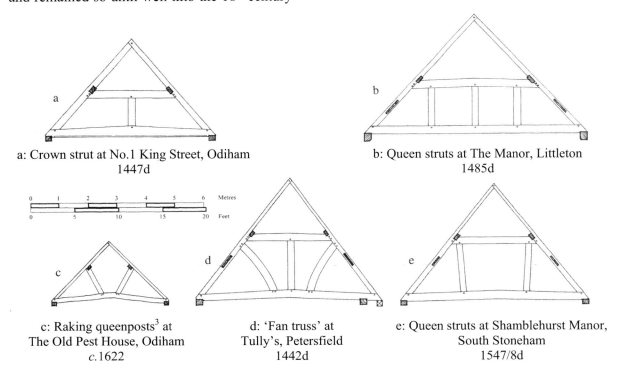

a: Crown strut at No.1 King Street, Odiham
1447d

b: Queen struts at The Manor, Littleton
1485d

c: Raking queenposts[3] at
The Old Pest House, Odiham
c.1622

d: 'Fan truss' at
Tully's, Petersfield
1442d

e: Queen struts at Shamblehurst Manor,
South Stoneham
1547/8d

Fig 3.21: Closed trusses in principal rafter roofs in Hampshire

58

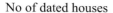

No of dated houses

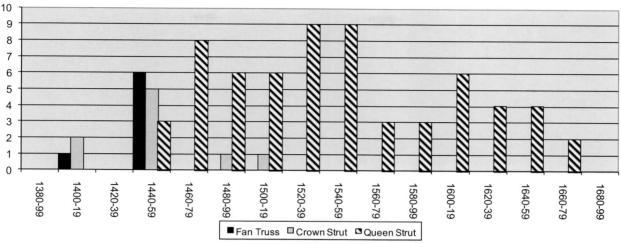

Fig 3.22: Chronology of some closed trusses in principal rafter roofs in Hampshire

former with short principals and the latter with diminished principals (Figs 3.17 & 3.18). The closed roof trusses in both examples are composed of no more than a simple collar and tie-beam with principal rafters and purlins. Without further examples, it is impossible to say whether this configuration is typical of the period. Between 1400 and 1600, however, it is possible to establish a more credible chronology of closed trusses in principal rafter roofs. There are three common forms in this period: namely, the crown strut (a single vertical timber between tie and collar beams and directly beneath the apex of the roof); the queen strut (at least two vertical timbers between tie and collar beams) and what might be called a 'fan truss'. In this form, a crown strut is flanked by two curved timbers that fan outward towards the junctions between the principal rafters and the collar beam (Figs 3.21 & 3.22).

The earliest dated crown strut roof in Hampshire is at Shepherd's Cottage, North Warnborough (1402d, VA31, 102) and, although this form is more common in the early 15th century, a late example has been found at Monk's Rest, Littleton (1500/1d, VA30, 107). The earliest dated example of what is here called a 'fan truss' is at Manisty Cottage, Odiham (1400d, VA27, 98). Thereafter, this form was common until the 1440s, the latest dated example in a box-framed building being at The Swan, Kingsclere (1448/9d, VA28, 175). The 1440s was a transitional period in which both 'fan' and queen strut trusses occurred in the same building, as at 6-8 West End, Sherborne St. John

(1444d, VA33, 93) and The Angel Inn, Andover where the roof was constructed between 1445 and 1453 (document). After 1450, the queen strut form dominated vernacular roof construction in Hampshire for over two hundred years. In a variant form the collar beam is dispensed with and raking (or slanting) queenposts from the tiebeam support and clasp the purlin to the principal rafter. (The term 'queenpost' is used here to denote a timber that rests on a tiebeam and supports a purlin as opposed to a queen strut, which supports a collar beam.[3]) This configuration is first found at Skyers Farm Barn, Wootton St. Lawrence (1580d, VA35, 105) and became common in the 17th century.

The apparent development in principal rafter roofs from the simple closed trusses found in two 14th century buildings to 15th century 'fan' trusses is paralleled by closed trusses in cruck buildings. Early closed trusses in cruck buildings lack vertical timbers between the collar and tiebeams and it is not until 1391d (VA24, 54) at Breach Farm Barn, Sherfield-on-Loddon that the 'fan truss' occurs in a cruck building. The latest closed cruck truss with the simpler form is at Pembroke Cottage, Hartley Wespall (1413d, VA27, 98) and thereafter the 'fan truss' was - with one exception - used in cruck buildings until the last dated crucks at Park View, Tichborne (1448-80d) (Fig 3.4), Rye Cottage, Mapledurwell (1487d, VA30, 107) and Hatch Cottage, Tadley (1496-1528d, VA41, 107). This approach to dating cruck buildings on typological evidence may be worth further exploration elsewhere.

59

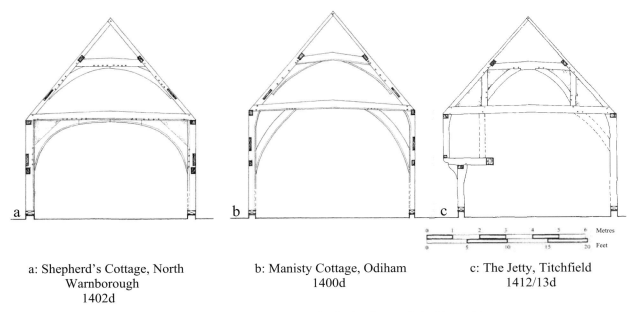

a: Shepherd's Cottage, North
Warnborough
1402d

b: Manisty Cottage, Odiham
1400d

c: The Jetty, Titchfield
1412/13d

Fig 3.23: Early open trusses in principal rafter roofs in Hampshire

Open Trusses in Principal Rafter Roofs

Turning to roof trusses over the centre of open halls, these were clearly intended to be seen and admired as statements of status, both because expense was lavished on their finish and decoration and because they replicated in wood the Gothic arch that was the hallmark of contemporary high-status buildings. Examples from the early 15th century are conservative and cautious in that the tiebeam is retained. As a result, arched braces beneath both collar and tiebeams produce two arches – one above another (Fig 3.23).

Later in the 15th century, the tiebeam is either effectively dispensed with by being reduced to a stub tie in the false hammer beam, as at Nos.

26-7 High Street, Lymington (1468-1503d) or dispensed with entirely; for example, by elongating the jowl of the principal post so that it can be joined to a substantial part of the principal rafter, as at The Crease, Micheldever (1463-83d) (Roberts 2003, 25), or by combining the jowl of the post and the arched brace in one timber, as at The Swan, Kingsclere (1448/9d, VA28, 175). An ambitious alternative was to create a Gothic arch with scissor braces, as at The Angel, Andover (1445-53) and, at an even greater extreme, the principal post is discarded altogether, as at The Manor, Littleton (1485d, VA26, 63). In all these examples, the hall truss presents an aesthetically pleasing single Gothic arch (Fig 3.24).

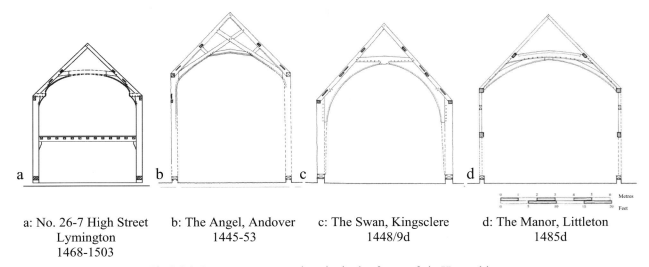

a: No. 26-7 High Street
Lymington
1468-1503

b: The Angel, Andover
1445-53

c: The Swan, Kingsclere
1448/9d

d: The Manor, Littleton
1485d

Fig 3.24: Later open trusses in principal rafter roofs in Hampshire

60

The Early Demise of the Crownpost Roof in Hampshire

An important and seminal study of early roofs in Surrey noted that the demise of the crownpost roof in that county coincided with the rise of the continuously floored house in which there was a chamber over the hall. Given this fact, it was reasonable to hypothesise that the two events were causally connected. It was suggested that the crownpost roof over an open hall is a more dramatic feature than the side purlin roof but that, when halls began to be floored over and attics created, the more aesthetically pleasing crownpost became less visible, redundant and even an obstruction (Harding 1993, 122).

The case for a causal link between the demise of the crownpost roof and the rise of the floor-ed-over hall cannot be sustained by an examination of the evidence from Hampshire, where the last flicker of the crownpost tradition precedes the first floored-over hall by several decades (Fig 3.7; Roberts 2003, 148 and 165). Nor in Hampshire does the crownpost seem to have been the preferred form either for beauty or status – at least on the evidence of the Gothic arch of the roof at the Brethren's Hall of St Cross Hospital. In the 1440s, the brethren's small lodging rooms at St Cross were given plain crownpost roofs similar to those at Kimpton Manor (Fig 3.15) but the great hall has a side purlin roof that was clearly meant to display the graceful Gothic arch (Fig 3.25). Building works had ceased at St. Cross by 1447 so that the hall roof cannot be later than the plain crownpost roof of the lodgings and probably – like it – dates to the 1440s; a date broadly con-

Fig 3.25: The Brethren's Hall at St. Cross Hospital, Winchester, Hampshire

(Milner 1839 & Warren 1899, 57)

firmed by recent dendrochronology (1437-1451d, VA41, 107). It is perhaps not surprising that the Gothic arch was preferred for the high-status hall for it was, after all, the preferred form for prestigious masonry buildings at the time.

Although the flooring over of halls did not cause the demise of the crownpost roof in Hampshire, it inevitably affected the scope for 'display' hall trusses. Now it was moulded ceiling joists that became the objects of display in halls, although occasionally a carpenter attempted a decorative truss in the chamber over the hall. This attempt was generally thwarted, however, by the introduction of attics or by hall chimneys. At Priory Farm, Monk Sherborne (1561d, VA36, 97) the carpenter's work was diminished by both! In the primary phase of construction, he placed decorative brackets beneath either end of the tiebeam in the centre of the chamber over the hall (Miles *et al.* 2005, 97). This was as much as he could do because it is evident that the attic was also a primary feature. In this primary phase, or very soon after, a large chimney was set in the hall so that a substantial part of one bay of the chamber over the hall was now occupied by brickwork. Thus, what seems to have been intended as an echo of the decorative hall truss of former times had lost its impact and meaning (Fig 3.26).

The widespread introduction in the late 16th century of attic floors and plaster ceilings in the first floor chambers of larger houses effectively removed the need for decorative roof trusses. Variations between roof trusses became the outcome of different approaches to effecting unencumbered access along the roof space. In smaller houses with single bay first floor rooms, rafters seem to have remained exposed well into the late 17th century and beyond. Single bay rooms, however, virtually preclude decorative open trusses and the queen strut truss, which had been established in the 15th century persisted, and remained the common form in closed trusses until the late 18th century.

Footnotes

1.   Unless otherwise stated, all dates given in the following discussion are referenced in Roberts 2003, 227-51. Since the publication of this book approximately 50 further dates of Hampshire buildings have been established by dendrochronology and published in Vernacular Architecture.

2   The term 'true cruck' is here used to denote a cruck associated with a purlin whose outer face is parallel to the rafters and is therefore set diagonally to the floor. This distinguishes true crucks from so-called 'base crucks' whose arcade plates are set parallel to the floor. Much has been written on whether this is a significant or genuine distinction but it may, at least, be said that base crucks, as defined here, tend to be associated with buildings of superior status and to have a different chronological and geographical distribution from true crucks (e.g. Alcock 1981, 16; Smith P 1988, 400-1).

3   The raked queenpost has no agreed name and is called a 'raked-purlin strut' in Chapters 6 & 7.

Acknowledgements: Nat Alcock, Chris Currie, Pam Solcombe and especially John Walker are warmly thanked for their advice during the preparation of this paper.

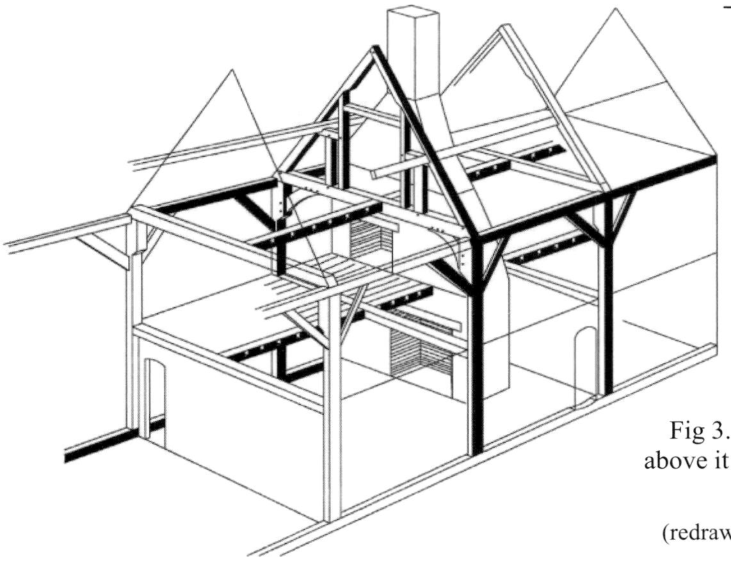

Fig 3.26: The chamber over the hall and the attic above it at Priory Farm, Monk Sherborne, Hampshire 1561d

(redrawn by John Walker from drawing by Bill Fergie).

4: MEDIEVAL ROOFS IN THE WEST MIDLANDS: THE POTENTIAL OF ARCHAEOLOGY AND TREE-RING DATING

By Bob Meeson

(Unless stated otherwise, all drawings are by the author)

Introduction

This article is based upon research undertaken for a talk at a day school in July 2008 to the Essex Historic Buildings Group, marking the fiftieth anniversary of the publication of J T Smith's paper on medieval roofs (Smith J T 1958). While he was by no means the only one to work on the subject, he was the first to systematically apply archaeological method to the classification of medieval roofs in England. J T Smith's work produced a new understanding of the subject at a time when relatively few roofs had been fully recorded and the attribution of construction dates relied primarily upon stylistic evidence, typological comparisons and documentary sources. During the half century that has passed since it was published, the main categories of roof discussed have changed little, but numerous archaeological excavations have thrown new light upon pre-Conquest buildings and the development of dendrochronology has enabled thousands of structural phases of later buildings to be accurately dated. Thanks to Dr Alcock, virtually all of the tree-ring dating results have been summarised in the pages of *Vernacular Architecture*, and available on-line at *http://ads.ahds.ac.uk/catalogue/library/vagbiblio*. The tree-ring dating lists are not without problems, but so many are now available that they can be used for more than the dating of individual building phases and they have become the first and main point of reference for anyone who wishes to know the dating parameters of a range of building types and carpentry techniques. Those lists were the springboard for this paper, the primary object being to explore how much more precision might now be applied to the emergence and duration of several of the main types of roofs constructed by carpenters working in the west midlands region. The outcome has been to show that new models are now possible because the dating profiles of a range of roof types can be systematically compared.[1]

For the present purpose the west midlands is deemed to include the historic counties of Gloucestershire, Herefordshire, Worcestershire, Shropshire, Staffordshire and Warwickshire, also taking in the West Midlands metropolitan area. If Wales is included, the geographical context of this region is not on the western fringe of our land mass but somewhere west of centre, and it might have been subject to influences from all sides. In the past it has been supposed that several of the types of roof discussed were products of the south and east of England, possibly under continental influence, giving the impression that the west midlands were less open than eastern counties to influence from the European mainland. This was to some extent the outcome of an early focus of research on the south-east resulting in some misleading distribution maps, but here an alternative thesis based on more contemporary data is proposed.

The paper begins with a summary of the growing correlation of evidence from archaeological excavations with that obtained from early dated standing buildings in order to identify a roof carpentry tradition that has been attributed to the European mainland, but which may already have existed throughout England long before the Norman Conquest. It continues with an assessment of the impact of tree-ring dating upon our understanding of the development of roofs in the west midlands region, and covers a span of approximately 600 years, beginning with a pre-conquest chapel in Gloucestershire and ending with a Staffordshire church that might have been designed by Sir Christopher Wren. The aim is to step outside the micro-analysis of jointing typologies and apex types in order to reflect upon very broad trends. The sequence in which several of the main forms of roof carpentry are discussed below was largely determined by the earliest tree-ring dates currently available for each type.

Before examining the rise and decline of the selected categories of roofs it is important to recognise that the available data varies through time (Fig 4.1). Of the 437 phases of buildings that have been tree-ring dated in the west mid-

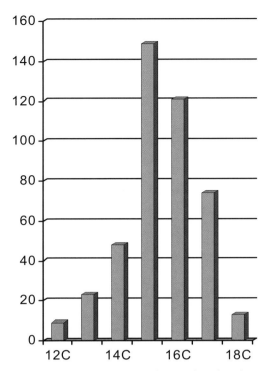

Fig 4.1: Distribution of tree-ring dated roofs in the west midlands by centuries

from documentary sources, and through parallels with inscribed dates, the relatively low number of tree-ring dated later buildings might be inhibiting progress towards a more precise understanding of trends in post-medieval roof carpentry.

Origins

Rare early vernacular roofs, some only in fragments, have generated much speculation about their origins and development, as for example with regard to cruck-framed buildings (Mercer 1996 & 1998; Alcock 1997), but reports from a growing number of archaeological excavations have enabled the range of earth-fast building techniques to be traced up to the 13th century and beyond. Because the nature of the material that can be recovered by excavators is inevitably different from that which can be derived by building recorders, the two groups formerly tended to interpret the evidence in different ways, with the result that there appeared to be a dichotomy between the evidence recovered from below the ground and that which was found in standing buildings. Although it is now generally accepted that during the later 12th and 13th centuries there was a major upheaval in the methods employed in the formation of foundations for buildings with timber walls, the implications of this knowledge for the interpretation of extant early roofs have yet to be fully explored. Only one aspect of wall construction will be summarised here, because it is relevant to the model that is proposed below for the development of some of the oldest roofs in the region. For lack of sufficient evidence from excavations within the west midlands, most of that cited below is from elsewhere in England, but it is crucial to avoid the trap of drawing premature conclusions from inadequate distribution maps (see below); the main exception is Catholme, Staffordshire, which at present provides the best excavated evidence of pre-Conquest buildings in the region.

lands only 48 were constructed in the 14th century, 23 in the 13th, and only eight were built before 1200; the attrition of old buildings is undeniable even if its causes and mechanisms remain open to debate (Currie 1988 & 1990a; Mercer 1990; Smith P 1990). Nevertheless, several very early buildings have been dated by various means, and they belong to an era during which many others were still being constructed with earth-fast foundations, some discussion of which is necessary as the basis of a model for early roofs. This model might be of particular significance in a west midland context where, in the absence of firm evidence for cruck-framed buildings as we know them before c.1262 (see below), there would otherwise be a lacuna of early roof types. The greatest number of tree-ring dates has been obtained from the 15th and 16th centuries – a fact largely explained by the number of buildings from this period that remain standing compared with those of the 12th to 14th centuries (Fig 4.1). Even though a yet larger proportion of the 17th and 18th century building stock remains available for study, far fewer of these have been tree-ring dated, so Fig 4.1 reflects a greater interest in the origins and development of the earliest building types. Although many more recent buildings are datable

Excavated pre-Conquest timber building foundations fall into two main categories – those with individual post holes and those with trench foundations for stave walls, which may or may not have been set upon base plates. Within the first category, across a wide geographical area including Bishopstone (Sussex), Chalton (Hampshire), Cowdery's Down (Hampshire), Mucking (Essex), Thirlings (Northumberland)

and West Stow (Suffolk), some foundations were comprised of post holes in pairs, one on each side of the building (James et al 1984). Testimony to the fact that such buildings were also constructed in the west midlands was provided by the major excavations at Catholme, where radiocarbon dates have suggested an occupation date range from the early 7th to the late 9th century (Losco-Bradley & Kinsley 2002, 42-98). One class of structures at that site has recently been interpreted as having employed a large number of tiebeams, each one spanning the gap between paired posts; in building AS29 the pairs of posts were approximately 1m (3 ft) apart (Fig 4.2a). A similar explanation was propounded for the possibly 10th century building P at Cheddar, Somerset (Rahtz 1979, Fig 36). The second category of earth-fast foundations, those which had trenches containing contiguous posts forming palisades, has been found at Cowdery's Down, Hampshire (Millett & James 1983), and at Goltho, Lincolnshire. In his detailed and well-argued discussion of the

9th century hall at the latter site, drawing on such parallels as the Hemse stave church in Sweden, the excavator postulated 'a roof of Romanesque form with a tie to the feet of every pair of rafters' (Beresford 1987, 38-53).

On most excavations in England relatively few extant timbers have survived for study, but although many of those that have been found in waterlogged or other anaerobic contexts belonged to such specialised structures as wells, watermills and waterfront revetments, there is now a growing corpus of *in situ* and re-used structural components from buildings which were supported by timbers standing on or in the ground. Two such groups are of particular relevance for this analysis: those with interrupted sill beams and those with ground plates. In York the former type has been found in 10th/11th century and earlier contexts, with earth-fast posts less than 1m (3ft) apart (Addyman & Hall 1991). Several examples of the latter type, ranging in date from 900 to 1400, were found

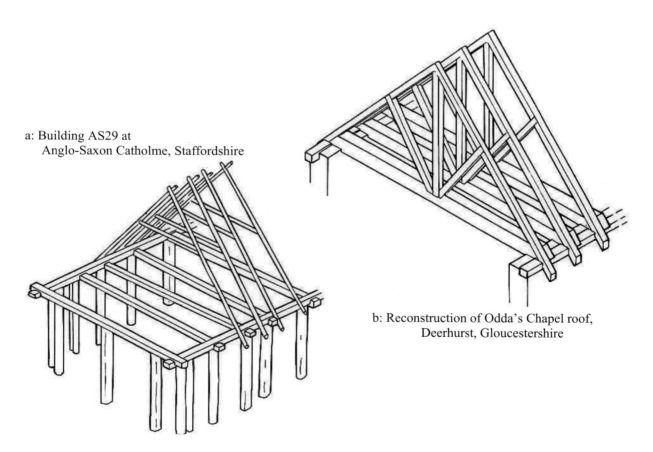

a: Building AS29 at
   Anglo-Saxon Catholme, Staffordshire

b: Reconstruction of Odda's Chapel roof,
   Deerhurst, Gloucestershire

Fig 4.2: Tiebeams and coupled rafters as envisaged for Building AS29 at Anglo-Saxon Catholme, Staffordshire and for the roof of Odda's Chapel, Deerhurst, Gloucestershire

(Based with consent on drawings by Philip Dixon 2002 and Christopher Currie 1983)

during the London Billingsgate Lorry Park excavations. Belonging to the second group, a number of re-used 11th century timber base plates (originally from non-waterfront contexts) were pierced by rows of mortices to house through tenons which must have supported wall posts at around 1m (3ft) intervals and, by inference, mortices could also have been employed in the associated wall plates (Milne 1992, 102-5 & 131-6). There is now also a Romano-British precedent for such broadly equal 1m (3ft) spacing of wall posts mortised into ground plates; discovered on the Southwark waterfront, London, this has been tree-ring dated to AD 152-53 (Brigham et al 1995).

A building at Weoley Castle, Birmingham, which probably had a life span from c.1200 to 1260, might have been a late example of this tradition; although it had earth-fast posts only at the corners, the ground plates supported wall studs at c.1m (3ft) intervals (Oswald 1962-3). Clearly there was a long evolution and wide variety of construction methods, but the regular spacing of paired posts and studs is a common characteristic. When Stuart Wrathmell embarked upon a reassessment of peasant buildings in the later middle ages his primary focus was on Wharram Percy, North Yorkshire, where he interpreted the excavated house-plans as cruck-framed buildings (Wrathmell 1989a, 5 -14), but less attention has been focussed on his conclusion that buildings east and south of the Vale of York were based not upon crucks but on pairs of upright posts (Wrathmell 1989b). For these later medieval vernacular buildings Wrathmell proposed a bayed roof system – one which had no need for a tiebeam at the foot of every rafter couple. Similarly, in the first published interpretation of the period 3 houses 18 and 19 at Goltho, Lincolnshire, the excavator was inclined to dismiss the notion that every pair of rafters might have been supported by a tiebeam, even though he was aware of polite Romanesque roofs of this kind (Beresford 1975, 41). The model that can be based on the above English examples, and on others not cited, is that in many early building systems consistent spacing of the wall posts might reflect the distance between the former roof trusses, and this is significant for three reasons. Firstly, a number of the earliest church roofs had tiebeam and coupled rafter trusses spaced at similar intervals to those that may have been employed on post-

wall buildings (see below), and they could have had the same indigenous origin, even if it fell within the broader European mainstream. Secondly, the trend towards a bayed roof system over secular vernacular buildings apparently reflects the same process over churches. Finally, if, as is likely, such post-wall buildings as those found at Catholme existed elsewhere in the pre-Conquest west midlands, they would belong to an older system of construction than full cruck and base cruck buildings.

Roofs with Tiebeams for Each Pair of Rafters

Odda's Chapel, Deerhurst, Gloucestershire, contained re-used timbers from a pre-Conquest roof until they were removed and burnt in 1965. Consistent with the above interpretation of evidence from excavations, the original church apparently had a single-framed roof with tiebeams for each pair of rafters; the ghost-lines of a king strut and two raked struts enabled the original structure to be interpreted as a type of roof for which there are numerous parallels on the continent (Currie 1983). Odda's Chapel was consecrated in 1056 so, had it survived, this would have retained the oldest extant roof so far identified in a west midland church (Fig 4.2b).

Closely-spaced tiebeams, each supporting coupled rafters, may well have been the norm in small stone parish churches before 1066, and there was probably a roof of this kind over the 12th century chancel at All Saints Church, Chebsey, Staffordshire. The primary roof was removed long ago, but when the wall was heightened the sockets which contained the original tiebeams were filled with recognisably later stones. The original tiebeams had passed right through the thickness of the wall, and no primary wall plates are now apparent, but the spacing between the sockets is about the same as that of the tiebeams at Odda's Chapel, and plausibly each one supported a uniform scantling rafter couple.[2] No doubt similar evidence could be found in more churches, but it seems that single-framed roofs over closely-spaced tiebeams continued to be built in west midland churches from at least the 1050s until the middle of the 12th century. There is no reason why the roofs over at least one class of wall-post structures should have been fundamentally different from contemporary stone buildings.

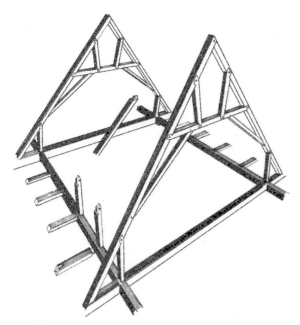

Fig 4.3: Nave roof at Roydon Church, Essex

(After Hewett 1982, 5)

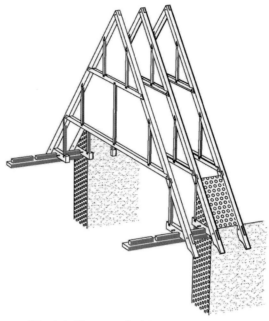

Fig 4.4: Nave roof of St Mary's Church,
Kempley, Gloucestershire
1128-32d

(© John Walker after Morley 1985 & Miles et al 1999)

Later Coupled Rafter Roofs

Some excavators have postulated bayed structures in pre-Conquest buildings, but in pre-Conquest west midland churches no roofs have yet been identified which dispensed with the need for a tiebeam under every pair of coupled rafters. On the near continent it has long been apparent that in post-Romanesque church roofs the number of tiebeams was gradually reduced to one under every fifth or sixth pair of rafters (Fletcher & Spokes 1964, 156), an observation that has been supported by such recent studies as that on church roofs in the Val d'Oise (Epaud & Bernard 2008). The nave roof at Roydon, Essex exemplifies this trend, having a tiebeam to every fifth truss (Fig 4.3) (Hewett 1982, 3-5), but a possible west midland example, at Madley, Herefordshire, attributed to about 1230 (Miles 1997; Currie 1990b), has yet to be analysed in detail, and the moulded and bar-stopped tiebeams might not be primary. Although such roofs can be deemed to be divided by the tiebeams into bays, each of the coupled rafter trusses imparted a broadly equal load from the roof to the walls.

As elsewhere, early west midland church roofs which did not depend upon tiebeams under every coupled rafter required various other means to resist transverse distortion. That over

the nave of St Mary's Church at Kempley, Gloucestershire, employing timbers felled in 1128-32d (VA39, 133), had sole plates and ashlar pieces to provide triangulation at the foot of each pair of rafters, and originally two tiers of collars were linked by vertical struts with bare-faced lap-dovetail joints. Here, unlike in many later English roofs, the struts were employed to suspend the mid-span of the lower collar from above (Fig 4.4) (Morley 1985; Walker 1999). In a similar manner, eight primary collars are linked by struts to the common rafters over the south bay of the hall at Temple Balsall, West Midlands (formerly Warwickshire), of 1176-1221d (VA24, 49) (Walker 1999, 39-41). The north transept roof of Holy Trinity Church at Wistanstow, Shropshire, tree-ring dated to 1200 -1221d (VA28, 161), was triangulated with sole plates and ashlar pieces near the feet of the rafters, and by soulaces in the angles between the rafters and the collars (Fig 4.5) (Miles 1997). At the Blackfriars Priory in Gloucester the roofs over the south range and the choir, dated respectively to 1230-69d (VA24, 47) and after 1238d (VA11, 34), both employ scissor braces halved across a collar (Fig 4.6) (Rackham et al 1978).

In the early roof at Kempley parish church (Fig 4.4), the common problem of racking

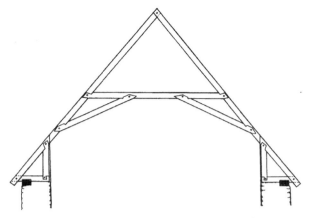

Fig 4.5: Holy Trinity Wistanstow, Shropshire
1200-1221d
(Reproduced with consent from D Miles 1997, 105)

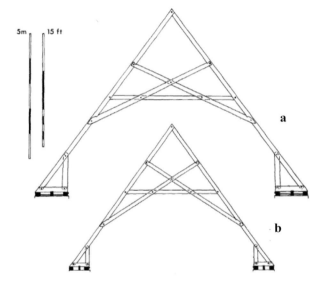

Fig 4.6: Roof trusses at the Blackfriars, Gloucester
a: over the choir, built after 1238d
b: over the south range 1230-69d
(After Rackham et al 1978, 108)

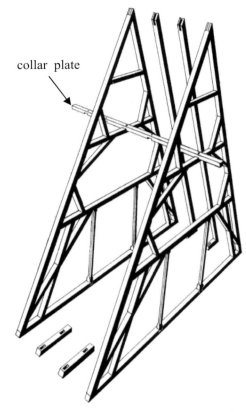

Fig 4.7: High roof of the nave of Lincoln Cathedral
1225-35d
(After Hewett 1985, 26)

(longitudinal distortion) may have been over-come by setting the feet of each truss into the top of the wall, but during the course of the thir-teenth century carpenters experimented with various other solutions to overcome this kind of instability. One such device was the collar plate – a timber running along the top of the collars. Such timbers have been described else-where as locking beams (Smith J T 2004, 310-11), and plausibly they were a precursor of col-lar purlins. At Madley doubt has been cast on the primacy of the collar plate, but it is typical of a number of medieval roofs elsewhere in Europe, including that over the nave at Lincoln, which has been attributed a felling date range of

1225-35d (VA12, 39) (Fig 4.7) (Hewett 1985, 26). Another early structural device that was intended to reduce racking was the rafter brace – a timber running obliquely across a number of common rafters (Fig 1.10) – as exemplified in the roof at Temple Balsall.

Passing braces and notched-lap joints were em-ployed in a group of church towers in Hereford-shire, that at Yarpole being the oldest, having been dated to 1195/6d (VA34, 100). Attributed to c.1300, the scissor braces in the chancel roof at Pontesbury, Shropshire, exemplify the persis-tence of such framing systems (Mercer 2003, 84-5). It has been suggested that this type of carpentry was similar to that which would have been used in the framed buildings in Norman motte and bailey castles, and if correct a strong Norman/French influence might be implied for some types of structures (Highams & Barker 1992, 244-5). While not denying this potential link, from the interpretation of excavated build-ing plans that can be traced back at least to the middle Saxon period, and from a number of early coupled rafter roofs with passing braces in England, it is again possible to construct a different model having indigenous roots within a wider European tradition.

Even if it was first employed in the west midlands in the Norman period, bayed coupled rafter roof construction continued in use in the region for more than 200 years (Fig 4.14). At least 20 west midland coupled rafter roofs have been dated to before 1300, but significantly at the time of writing only two full crucks and one raised cruck appear in the published tree-ring dating lists for this early period in the same region (see below). On the evidence of the surviving dated examples in the west midlands, the number of early wall-post and mass-walled buildings, the vast majority of which probably had coupled rafter roofs, far outweighs the number of early cruck-framed buildings.

Aisled Buildings

The small secular buildings and parish churches discussed so far could be covered by single-span roofs, but within the same mainstream building tradition, for those clients who required larger accommodation, either as expressions of status, for large-scale assemblies or for storage, aisled construction was necessary. The church, in its widest sense, was indirectly responsible for some of the most impressive early aisled buildings in the west midlands. One of the largest bishop's palaces was at Lichfield, where the hall was 30.5m long and 17m wide (100 × 56 ft), but that only remains as buried foundations (Tringham 1990, 63). Built around 1179d, the largest surviving medieval bishop's hall in the region is at Hereford (VA20, 46) (Blair 1987; Walker 1999, 33-4). It is shown in Fig 4.8 at the same scale alongside a section of the aisled hall at Temple Balsall, built for the Knights Templar with timber felled between 1176 and 1221d (VA24, 49), and which may plausibly have had both a tiebeam and a strainer beam in each truss (Alcock 1982; Walker 1999, 39-41). Many other substantial aisled buildings would have been constructed for manorial clients, as for example at Burmington Manor, Warwickshire, employing timber felled some time after 1159d (VA24, 49) and incorporating passing braces across collars (Walker 1999, 34-37). The manorial Handsacre Hall, Staffordshire, which collapsed in 1972, was broadly contemporary with these buildings; although it had been substantially rebuilt as a base cruck in or about 1300 (see below), elements of the spere truss and jointing recorded by Stanley Jones on a former arcade post leave little doubt that the first hall was aisled, and the felling date range for this is 1160-95d (VA21, 38). Now a

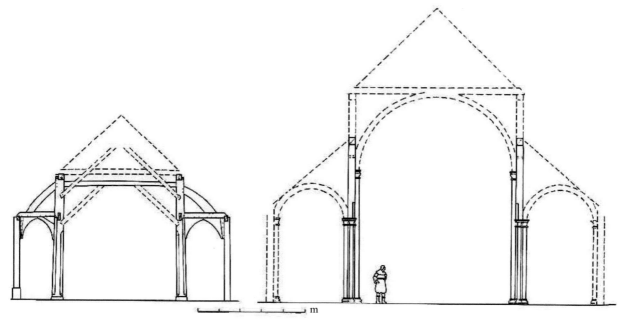

a: Temple Balsall, formerly Warwickshire, shown in its second phase; 1st phase dated to 1176-1221d

b: Bishop's Palace at Hereford, Herefordshire 1179d

Fig 4.8: Two early aisled halls

(a based with consent on a drawing by N W Alcock 1982; b based on various sources)

barn, the aisled hall of a canonical house constructed between 1253 and about 1288d in the Cathedral Close in Hereford (VA28, 143) exemplifies the continuing use of lap joints and scissor bracing during the 13th century (Morriss 2000, 178).

In common with the un-aisled buildings of the Norman and Angevin periods discussed above, the early upper roofs of west midland aisled buildings employed uniform scantling coupled rafters, variously stiffened with collars, soulaces, passing braces and scissor braces connected by lap joints, placing them in the mainstream carpentry tradition. The arcades of posts which separated the nave from the aisles supported arcade plates, which, unlike side purlins, were generally set square to the ground – a distinctive aspect that would be adopted in the great majority of base cruck buildings in the region.

Aisled buildings continued to be constructed in the west midlands for a wide range of clients and to serve a variety of functions throughout the 14th century. With a single-bay hall that was only 5.6m × 6.7m (18ft 6in × 22ft) (not including the crosspassage), Hill Top at Longdon, Staffordshire (Fig 4.15b), serves as a reminder that, as in Essex, the aisled form of construction was not reserved for the most affluent sections of society (Stenning 2003). Tree-ring dating failed at Hill Top, but from other coupled rafter roofs with lap-jointed collars of known dates in the region, and from the use of interrupted sill beams, it could have been built as early as the mid-14th century (Meeson 2001), notwithstanding that it has an edge-halved and bridled scarf joint, for which the earliest published date obtained elsewhere is 1370/1d in Coppwilliam, a single-aisled hall at Staplehurst, Kent (VA 22, 44, Pearson 1994, 155) (information from John Walker).

At Bredon, Worcestershire, a large barn was constructed on a fully aisled plan, with a strainer beam across the nave, employing timbers that were felled after 1344d (VA13, 49) (Fig 4.9b), and this was within a couple of years or so of the rearing of the full cruck-framed Leigh Court barn (see below and Fig 4.9a). By c.1411 when many manorial clients might have preferred a base cruck for their domestic halls, the large and prestigious Palmers' Guildhall in Ludlow, Shropshire, was given an eight-bay aisled plan (VA24, 57), and here, as in some other later aisled buildings, the carpenters employed side purlins in the roof (Moran 2003, 153-7). Not including spere trusses, the later examples of which were probably relict features

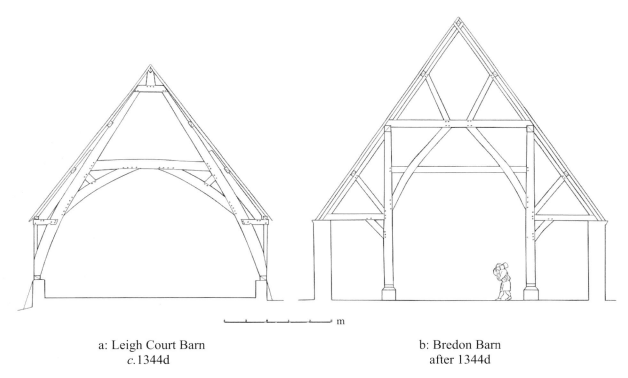

a: Leigh Court Barn
c.1344d

b: Bredon Barn
after 1344d

Fig 4.9: Contemporary cruck and aisled barns in Worcestershire

derived from aisled and base cruck construction, the latest date so far obtained from a secular fully aisled building in the west midlands is from a barn at Kings Pyon, Herefordshire, which was built of timber felled after 1490d (VA24, 47), but barns and parish churches continued to be constructed with aisles long after that.

Base Cruck Buildings

The discussion of mainly earth-fast post buildings at the Anglo-Saxon settlement of Catholme contains a short re-appraisal of such house-plans as one at Wijster in the Netherlands, which has been plausibly interpreted as a forerunner of base crucks (Dixon 2002). In the aisled byre of this longhouse, the earth-fast posts probably supported arcade plates, but at the domestic end of the building the living space was kept free of posts by moving the supporting timbers out to the line of the side walls; these were plausibly pairs of curved or inclined straight blades carrying tiebeams which in turn supported the arcade plates continuing through from the byre arcades (Dixon 1982, 277-8). However, the validity of extracting elements from later medieval vernacular buildings for the replication of structures from excavated evidence has been questioned (Wrathmell 1994, 189-90), and the hazards of such attempts are exemplified by the interpretation of foundations of a 6th-8th century building at Cowdery's Down as a base cruck (James et al 1984). This was subsequently re-interpreted as having had a roof of hefty coupled rafters (Alcock & Walsh 1993). Whether or not any such early medieval building foundations can be shown to have had a proto-base cruck frame, there is as yet no excavated evidence that any of them were directly comparable with their later surviving sophisticated fully carpentered counterparts.

The medieval base cruck truss was essentially a great timber arch which comprised two large curved blades rising to either one tiebeam or, as at Eastington Hall in Worcestershire, a pair of tiebeams, one directly above the other (Fig 4.10). It was J T Smith who coined the term 'base cruck' for carpentered frames which avoided the need for intrusive posts to carry the arcade plate – an especially useful design for the trusses which supported the roofs over the middle of open halls. He first discussed the type as a refinement of aisled buildings, but without the benefit of tree-ring dating he subsequently suggested that they might have been derived from full cruck carpentry, implying in turn that full or true cruck construction 'must be sought well before the middle of the 13th century' (Smith J T 1958, 140-1 & 1964, 129). The debate runs on, even though twenty years later the very wide distribution of base cruck buildings across most of England has been confirmed, placing many of them outside well-defined zones of full cruck construction (Alcock 1981, Fig 6). To explain this anomaly, it has been argued that a form of carpentry that might have been based originally on full cruck construction attained an independent identity before being adopted in the south-east about 1300 (Alcock 1997), and this would be all well and good if it were not for the fact that the earliest tree-ring dated full cruck is not as old as the earliest dated base cruck. At present the stance that base crucks developed from full crucks can only be supported by arguing that there were yet earlier full cruck precedents that have not survived.

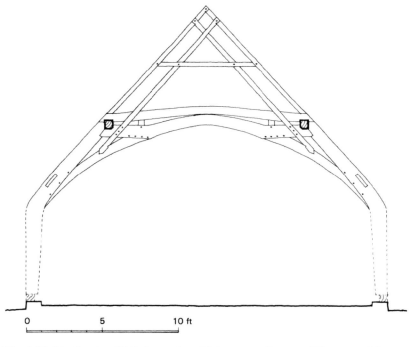

Fig 4.10: Eastington Hall, Longdon, Upton upon Severn, Worcestershire

(After Charles & Charles 1984, Fig 269)

71

Several well known examples of base cruck buildings show that this type of construction was employed elsewhere in Europe. The oldest base cruck building yet to be dated anywhere is part of St John's Hospital in Bruges, which was built of timber felled around 1229-38 (Alcock & Barley 1972, 143-4; Hill 2005, 4-5), and a yet larger raised base cruck, with an internal span of just over 16.7m (55 ft), was recorded at The Hall of the Knights in The Hague (Smith J T 1964, 148). It is a somewhat salutary experience for English recorders to compare the as-tonishing scale of the early Bruges base cruck with the slightly later English example of West Bromwich Manor, which has a span of a mere 8.2m (27ft). The most common form of base cruck truss has arcade plates carried on the ends of tiebeams which are supported by inclined blades, the angle between them being strength-ened by arch braces, as at West Bromwich Manor and Handsacre Hall (Fig 4.11a and b). This type of assembly was so strongly embed-ded in continental carpentry that it continued in use there at least until the 17th century.

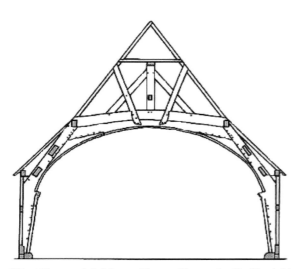

a: West Bromwich Manor House (formerly Staffordshire)
1270-88d

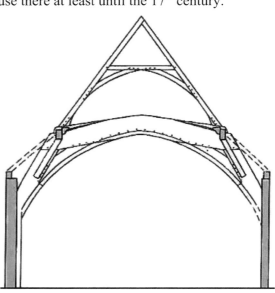

b: Handsacre Hall, Staffordshire
1291-1326d

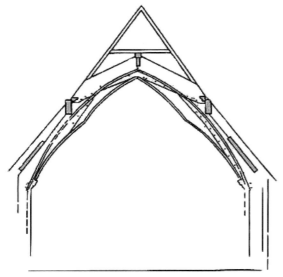

c: Mancetter Manor House, Warwickshire
early 14[th]C

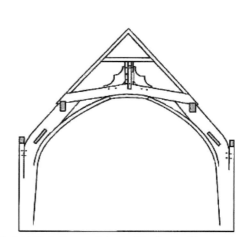

d: 15 High Street, Much Wenlock, Shropshire
1407-8d

Fig 4.11: Four west midland base crucks

(a based with consent on a drawing by S R Jones 1977
d based with consent on a drawing in M Moran 2003)

The earliest tree-ring date for any surviving English base cruck building was obtained from Siddington Barn, Gloucestershire, where both aisled and base cruck trusses were employed in a single construction phase in about 1245-7d (VA23, 44) (Figs 4.12a & 1.9) (Hewett 1980, 87-88). The base cruck halls at West Bromwich Manor House (Fig 4.11a), Wasperton Manor Farm, Warwickshire, and Eastington Hall, Longdon, Worcestershire (Fig 4.10), all have double tiebeams; although their functions differ this is redolent of the strainer beams that are paired with tiebeams in some aisled buildings (Fig 4.8a) (Crook 2002, 90-92). At Siddington and Eastington the carpenters employed arcade plates rather than side purlins, and in both buildings the upper roofs were of uniform scantling passing braces, scissor braces and lap joints, strongly suggesting that base crucks have the same roots as aisled halls and placing them firmly in the mainstream. The early base cruck truss at West Bromwich Manor House employed lap joints and scissor bracing; these are set on each side of the oldest crownpost and collar purlin yet recognised in the west midlands, and with a felling date range of 1270-88d it is one of the earliest such roofs in England (Fig 4.11a) (VA41, 101; Jones 1977). The combined use of base cruck and crownpost provides yet another early link with the mainstream in so far that the upper roofs of base cruck buildings followed the same development trend as those of the coupled rafter roofs discussed above. Exemplifying this trend, when the late 12th century aisled hall was rebuilt with a base cruck truss at Handsacre Hall (1291-1326d) (VA21, 38) the carpenters assembled an upper roof of coupled rafters and curved soulaces under the collars (Fig 4.11b), similar to those of 1291-1333d at Marwell Hall, Owslebury, Hampshire (VA25, 25) (Roberts 2003, 10-11); but in common with the early precedent at West Bromwich, the base cruck hall in the 14th century Mancetter Manor House, Warwickshire, was given a collar purlin roof (Fig 4.11c) (Alcock & Meeson 1999). At Siddington the carpenters introduced longitudinal stability to the upper roof of the barn with a pair of square-set side purlins, but others quickly adopted crownposts and collar purlins for this purpose.

At the time of writing, the latest tree-ring date for a base cruck building in the west midlands is 1407-8d for 15 High Street, Much Wenlock, Shropshire (VA24, 57), and that too has a crownpost and collar purlin roof (Fig 4.11d) (Moran 2003, 280-1). In the west midlands base cruck construction was first employed for high status clients, and it continued from the middle of the 13th century until at least the reign of Henry IV – a period of at least 150 years (Fig 4.13a).

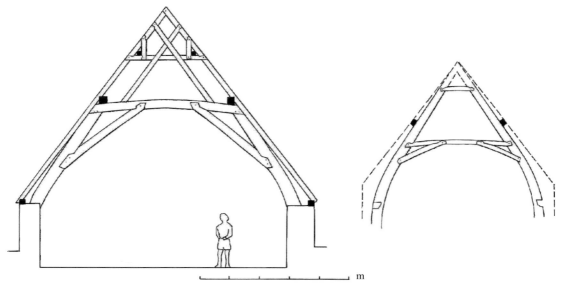

a: Early base cruck at
Siddington Barn, Gloucestershire
1245-7d

b: Early full cruck at Cruck Cottage,
Upton Magna, Shropshire as first interpreted
1269d

Fig 4.12: An early base cruck truss and an early full cruck

(a is from various sources. b is based on Alcock & Meeson 2009, 99)

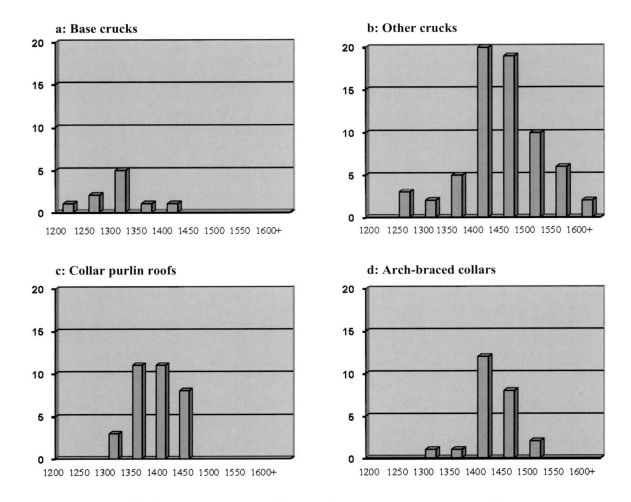

Fig 4.13: Tree-ring date ranges of four medieval roof types in the west midlands

As yet the samples are too small for firm conclusions to be drawn, but when the published tree-ring dates for west midland base cruck and full cruck buildings are divided chronologically into groups and plotted on bar-charts several related observations arise out of the patterns so derived (Fig 4.14). Firstly, the earliest standing examples of base crucks and full crucks were assembled during the period when the excavation of earth-fast wall foundations was being superseded by buildings with stone sills and continuous sill beams. Secondly, the oldest

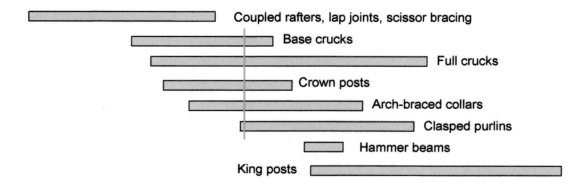

Fig 4.14: Tree-ring date ranges of some extant roof types in the west midlands

74

surviving dated base cruck is somewhat earlier than the oldest full cruck yet identified in the region. Thirdly, the growth and decline of the two types of construction are markedly different; west midland base crucks reached their apogee in the first half of the 14th century but their use declined during the first quarter of the 15th century, whereas full cruck construction was at its height during the 15th century and it continued until after 1600. In short, the currently available dating profiles allow the construction of a model in which base cruck construction began, increased and declined well in advance of the construction of full crucks (Fig 4.13a and b).

Across the country, most of the earliest standing base cruck trusses occur in conjunction with aisled frames, as at Siddington Barn, Gloucestershire (Fig 4.12a). What might be the oldest base cruck truss in Kent spans the open hall at the otherwise aisled Barnes Place, Hadlow; it is one of several in the county that have prompted the conclusion that their origins should be seen entirely outside the cruck tradition (Pearson 1994, 54-7). In the Pilgrim's Hall range at Winchester, Hampshire (1310/11d, VA32, 80) the smaller of two open halls is spanned by a base cruck truss set between two aisled trusses, and here as in other Hampshire base crucks it is considered to be a derivative of aisled hall construction (Roberts 2003, 9-13).

Full Cruck Buildings

Various attempts have been made to interpret excavated house-plans as full cruck buildings, both in England and on the continent. For example, an earth-fast post building discovered in 1935 at Westick in Germany, occupied from the 3rd to the 5th century (Smith J T 1964, 135-7), and a 5th century site at Odoorn in the Netherlands have both been interpreted as evidence of full cruck construction (Chapelot & Fossier 1985, 295-6). More recent excavations at Gomeldon, Wiltshire uncovered the foundations of a structure of 12th-13th century date which included two pairs of deep post holes that were inclined towards each other, prompting it to be identified as a cruck-framed building (Med Arch **8** (1964), 289), but as Philip Rahtz has argued, 'sloping posts can be interpreted in other ways, and true crucks may leave no evidence at foundation level' (Rahtz 1976, 88). A cruck blade in Cruck Cottage at Upton Magna,

Shropshire, may be either earth-fast, or simply standing on the medieval ground-surface (Moran 2003, 46-7), but neither this nor any other example within a standing building has yet been verified by systematic excavation in the west midlands. Likewise, potential examples of earth-fast cruck-blades on the Solway Plain, including one of 1564, have yet to be verified by excavation (Jennings 1997).

It has been argued that cruck construction might once have extended across all of England, but that it was superseded so early in the south-east as to leave no surviving examples, leading some archaeologists to interpret some post hole building foundations in that region as 'quasi crucks' (Green 1982), but not a single example has yet been substantiated and no re-used remnants have been reported from later buildings. Whilst on the one hand it would be churlish to argue that no one had hitherto thought to lean two lengths of timber together in order to support a ridge-pole, any such quasi-crucks may have been a far remove from the earliest surviving examples of well-carpentered cruck trusses, and to date the search for incontrovertible precursors has been fruitless. Debate on the emergence of full cruck construction may have been hampered to some extent by a reluctance to place it in the context of the great gulf that emerged in the 12th-13th centuries between wall-post buildings and more sophisticated carpentered framing. Improvements in the homes of the peasantry during the 13th century have been discussed in the context of generally rising living standards, which in turn might have enabled more people to employ carpenters to build their homes (Dyer 1989, 166). Such a trend might partially explain the shift away from earth-fast post buildings towards more durable construction systems, and this may have impacted upon the design and construction of cruck-framed buildings as much as any others.

A true cruck frame comprises a pair of timbers – or blades – which serve as the principals, often extending from a point well down the side walls to near the top of the roof. To emphasise a point already made, from the earliest known examples to the latest, all full cruck buildings employed side purlins, setting them typologically outside the coupled rafter roof tradition. Most side purlins were trenched into the outer edges of the cruck blades or supported on the backs of the blades or packing pieces (Fig 4.15d) or, less commonly, tenoned into the blades (Fig 4.15c). There are many variations of full crucks, especially in the design of the apex, though none have a purely west midlands distribution and some of the variant forms, such as end crucks, are not found in the region (cf. Fig 5.18) (Alcock 1981, 61-81). Although it is more than fifty years since the first reliable map showing the distribution of cruck-framed buildings was published, subsequent work, mainly by Dr Alcock, has served to reinforce some of

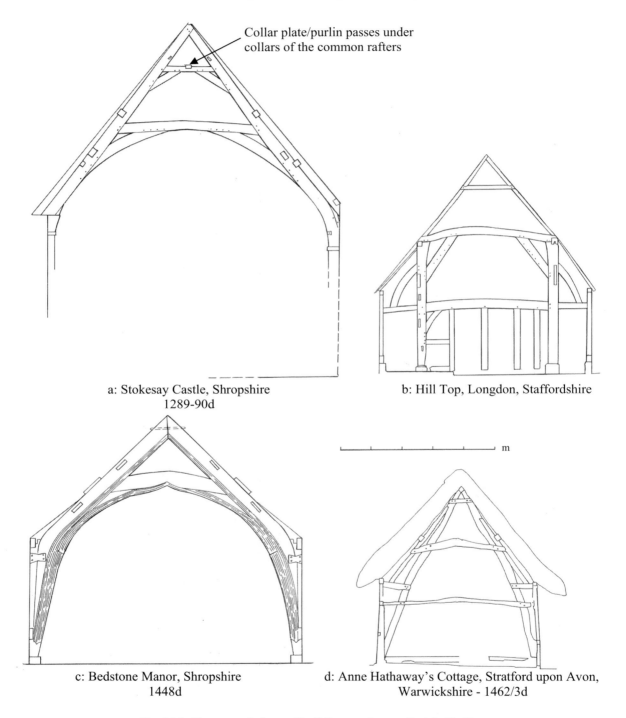

Collar plate/purlin passes under collars of the common rafters

a: Stokesay Castle, Shropshire
1289-90d

b: Hill Top, Longdon, Staffordshire

c: Bedstone Manor, Shropshire
1448d

d: Anne Hathaway's Cottage, Stratford upon Avon, Warwickshire - 1462/3d

Fig 4.15. Three cruck-framed buildings and a small aisled hall

(a from various sources
b Author
c Based with consent on a drawing by M Moran 2003, 54
d Based on a survey by the author for the Shakespeare Birthplace Trust)

the early conclusions; the value of distribution maps in the understanding of regional typologies, and local variants within them, has been more forcibly demonstrated for full cruck framing than for any other category of vernacular building (Smith J T 1958; Alcock 1981, 56-81). Full cruck framing has a demonstrably western bias, with not a single example in south-eastern England, and this is another factor which sets them apart from base cruck building construction, although even in the 13th century some buildings stepped across the dividing line between the two types. One such building is the hall at Stokesay Castle, built for the wealthy merchant Lawrence of Ludlow, and tree-ring dated to 1289/90d (VA28, 160) (Fig 4.15a). The hall roof is highly significant for various reasons, but two characteristics suggest that its carpenters were well aware of framing techniques not normally associated with cruck framing. Firstly the end trusses are of aisled form, and secondly the upper roof incorporated either a collar plate or collar purlin, both features more commonly found in base cruck halls. Nevertheless, at Stokesay the raised cruck blades extend all the way up to the apex of the roof, and they support double side purlins rather than arcade plates. It is possible that full cruck Stokesay was under construction at almost the same time as the base cruck hall at West Bromwich Manor, so already in the 13th century carpenters working for high status clients could adopt either technique.

Given access to the right timber, west midland carpenters could employ full cruck frames in the construction of very substantial buildings. The largest and most spectacular full cruck-framed building anywhere is the 10-bay barn at Leigh Court in Worcestershire (Fig 4.9a), which was built from timber felled c.1344d (VA37, 108); it is approximately 43m long and 10.7m wide (140 × 35ft), giving it an area of 460m² (4900 sq ft) (Charles 1997, 2-4). From the late 13th to the 15th century and for a wide range of clients, especially in rural areas of the west midlands, the full cruck became the preferred framing system, and it appeared in many guises (Fig 4.15a, c & d). Cruck-framing is not only the most numerous category of medieval buildings found in the region but also it continued to be used for a longer time-span than most of the other post-Conquest types discussed in this paper. Nevertheless, as the debate about

the origins of crucks continues (Hill 2005 & 2007; Alcock 2007), from an archaeological standpoint it must be admitted that the oldest remnants of a full cruck building so far recognised in the west midlands, at Cruck Cottage, Upton Magna in Shropshire, yielded a felling date of 1269d (Fig 4.12b) (VA26, 70) (Moran 2003, 45-47). Not including upper crucks (those with their feet resting on a ceiling beam), the latest full cruck frame so far tree-ring dated in Shropshire was constructed in 1576d (VA34, 115), but there are three later dated examples in north Staffordshire, including Old School House at Ford, built in or soon after 1600d (VA28,128). Although in due course the availability of more tree-ring dates might confirm the impression gained thus far, it would be rash to conclude from just three buildings that full cruck construction persisted longer in the north-east of the region than in the west, and in any case late 16th/17th century cruck buildings are found further north. However, so far as one can tell from the dates so far published, full cruck framing was employed in the west midlands for a period of not less than 340 years.

Crownposts and Collar Purlins
Alongside the strong cruck tradition many crownpost roofs were also built. The earliest tree-ring date for any crownpost in the region, and one of the earliest in England, was obtained from the open hall of West Bromwich Manor House of 1270-88d, and as noted above, this was also a base cruck (Fig 4.11a). It is comparable in some respects with York Farm at West Hagbourne, Oxfordshire (Fig 1.15), where the base cruck with crownpost open hall was constructed in 1284-5d or soon after (VA24, 55) (Currie 1992, 126-32), and it is worth emphasising that these crownpost roofs were built only a short time after 1262 – the earliest tree-ring date yet obtained from a full cruck building. Even the isolated and vernacular plank-walled Rushton Spencer Church, Staffordshire (c.1293-1318d, VA29, 107), had crownposts and a collar purlin, and so far these are the oldest identified in the region that stand on conventional tiebeams (Fig 4.16a) (Meeson 1983a). The crosswing roof at Mancetter Manor House, Warwickshire, dated on documentary evidence to c.1325 (Fig 4.16b) and the lodging range of 1391/2d at Mavesyn Ridware, Staffordshire (Fig 4.16e) (VA27, 79), have two of the finest west midland crownpost roofs, both of them

built on a large scale for high status clients. Crownpost roofs of various types also came to be employed on buildings of lower status, a number of urban examples of which have been dated. The Heritage Centre at Henley-in-Arden, Warwickshire, of *c*.1345d (VA33, 87), has 4-way up-swinging braces in the central open truss (Fig 4.16c) (Alcock & Meeson 1997), while a closed truss of the same date in 186-7 Horninglow Street, Burton upon Trent, Staffordshire (VA26, 49), is flanked by lap-jointed scissor braces (Fig 4.16d) (Meeson & Kirkham 1995), and at 169 Spon Street, Coventry, Warwickshire, there is an example of a closed truss of 1391-1404d (VA11, 34) which is only longitudinally braced to the collar purlin (Fig 4.16f) (Charles 1974). Crownpost roofs continued to be built in the west midlands until around 1430, the two most recent examples both being in Shropshire where, at the high

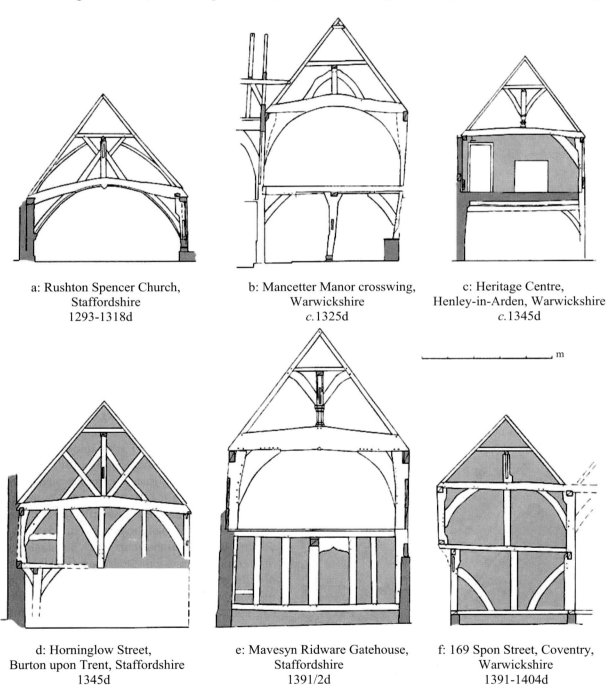

a: Rushton Spencer Church,
Staffordshire
1293-1318d

b: Mancetter Manor crosswing,
Warwickshire
*c.*1325d

c: Heritage Centre,
Henley-in-Arden, Warwickshire
*c.*1345d

d: Horninglow Street,
Burton upon Trent, Staffordshire
1345d

e: Mavesyn Ridware Gatehouse,
Staffordshire
1391/2d

f: 169 Spon Street, Coventry,
Warwickshire
1391-1404d

Fig 4.16: Some west midland crownpost roofs, all with coupled rafters with collars

(f based with consent on a drawing by S R Jones)

status Upton Cressett (1427-31d, VA25, 33) and at Cottage Farm, Easthope (1429-30d, VA25, 31), the crownpost and collar purlin roofs were over open halls. With a span of about 160 years between *c.*1273 and *c.*1430, crownposts and collar purlins can be found in some of the earliest surviving roofs of the west midlands (Fig 4.14).

The astonishing volume of work on the distribution of cruck-framed buildings has only served to reinforce the benefits of distribution maps, but their use can also entail pitfalls. During the early 1960s, when Fletcher and Spokes considered the origin and development of collar purlin roofs, apart from a couple of outliers at Leicester and Stokesay, the only recorded English examples were in the south and east; they concluded that the carpenters of that region followed France until *c.*1270 before developing their own form of crownpost roofs (Fletcher & Spokes 1984). However, as in the case of base crucks, more recent discoveries in the west midlands include some of the earliest crownpost and collar purlin roofs in England. Early examples include those in the hall at West Bromwich Manor (as above), and in the Buck's Head, Church Stretton, Shropshire, of 1287-1321d (VA26, 69) (Moran 2003, 117). None of these are substantially later than The Old Deanery in Salisbury, Wiltshire, attributed to the 1270s (back cover), and all of them were constructed during the same era as the earliest crownpost roof noted by Sarah Pearson in Kent, at Nurstead Court, which employed timber felled 1299-1334d (VA19, 48) (Pearson 1994, 53 &156). The earliest examples in Hampshire have been attributed to the 14th century (Roberts 2003, 30). With the aid of tree-ring dating it now appears that west midland carpenters began to construct crownposts and collar purlins for upper social level clients at much the same time as many of their counterparts elsewhere in England, if not earlier, suggesting that as soon as the benefits of longitudinal stability had been recognised the system was rapidly adopted.

The comparatively rapid widespread adoption of crownposts stands in marked contrast to the manner in which they were replaced by other roof types in some areas while they persisted in others. Whereas the tree-ring dating results at present imply that whilst the last crownposts in Shropshire were assembled around 1430 only

about 160 years after the technique was first used in the region, Kentish carpenters continued to build them until at least 1532, giving them a markedly longer duration (Pearson 1994, 156). One difference between the two counties is that in Shropshire crownpost roofs were employed in only a minority of buildings alongside the regionally dominant full crucks. Whereas some Kentish carpenters clung on to crownposts, their demise in the west midlands may have been due initially to the early adoption of such new types of roof framing as arch-braced collar trusses. These were part of a wider general category of roofs, the majority of which had side purlins which carried part of the roof load to the supporting transverse frames, rather than having it equally distributed along the tops of the side walls. F W B Charles proposed the term *post and truss* for this form of box-framed construction, arguing cogently that it was derived from the cruck-framed building tradition (Charles 1967, 44-5).

Arch-Braced Collar Trusses
Cruck-framed buildings continued to be constructed long after crownpost roofs ceased to be built and other forms of roofing were introduced, but the increasing use of arch-braced collar trusses supporting side purlins might have been one of the factors which led to the

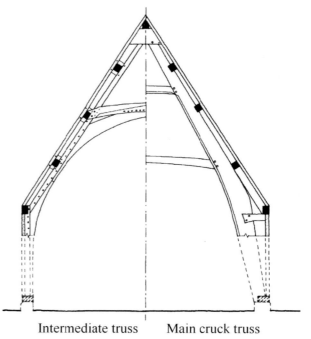

Intermediate truss   Main cruck truss

Fig 4.17: 81-82 Barton St, Tewkesbury, Gloucestershire sections of main & intermediate trusses in hall

(After Charles & Charles 1984, fig 69)

crownpost being abandoned by west midland carpenters sooner than those working elsewhere in England. F W B Charles cited instances of vernacular buildings like 81-82 Barton Street, Tewkesbury, Gloucestershire, where the main frame is a full cruck but the intermediate truss is of arch-braced collar form (Fig 4.17) (Charles & Charles 1984, 77). Charles's architectural practice was in Worcester, and he was more aware than others of the spectacular Guesten Hall roof in that city as he was instrumental in its re-erection at the Avoncroft Museum of Buildings, Worcestershire (Fig 4.18a). On documentary evidence, this arch-braced collar roof with side purlins was built about 1320 (Charles 1971). Apart from being one of the earliest roofs of its kind, it is also one of the largest, and if the cusped bracing is anything to go by, it was assembled by west midland carpenters.

Plausibly, arch-braced collar roofs with tenoned side purlins were spurred on in the west midlands by innovative large-scale display roofs like that over Worcester's Guesten Hall, but in 1340-58d carpenters working in Burton upon Trent assembled an arch-braced collar roof with a single central purlin that was surely derived from crownpost construction (Fig 4.25) (VA30, 95) (Meeson 2002a, 114-5 & 118). Those craftsmen were working for the Abbot of Burton, and they might have been brought in from elsewhere to construct this refined roof over his private first-floor chamber, but equally a variety of framing techniques was now available to local carpenters.

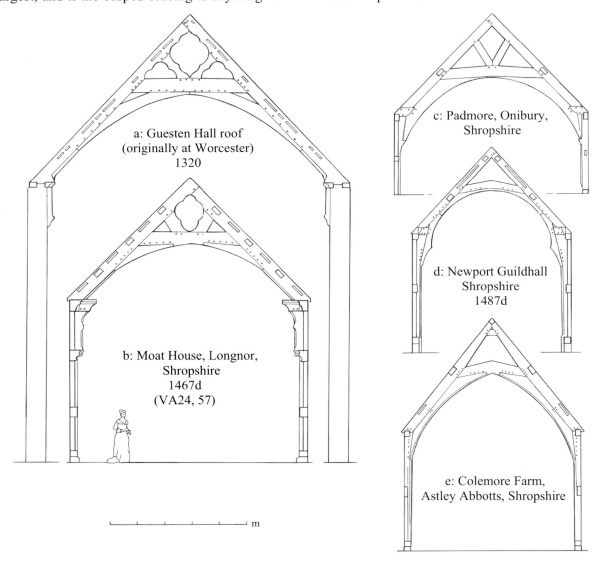

a: Guesten Hall roof (originally at Worcester) 1320

b: Moat House, Longnor, Shropshire 1467d (VA24, 57)

c: Padmore, Onibury, Shropshire

d: Newport Guildhall Shropshire 1487d

e: Colemore Farm, Astley Abbotts, Shropshire

Fig 4.18: Arch-braced collar roof trusses in the west midlands
(a is from various sources. b-e based with consent on drawings in M Moran 2003)

80

Notwithstanding the Abbot of Burton's roof, the majority of arch-braced collar trusses in the region had side purlins. All of the examples shown in Fig 4.18 are drawn at the same scale, and they range down from the Worcester Guesten Hall roof across almost the full gamut of functions and status. Some of the best roofs of this type are on stone walled buildings, but the majority are on buildings with timber-framed walls. In most of the latter, carpenters recognised the need to strengthen the angle between the wall posts and the principal rafters, so they designed the arch braces to extend down the walls to well below the eaves. In buildings like Newport Guildhall, built c.1487d (VA24, 57) (Fig 4.18d) and Padmore in Onibury (Fig 4.18c), both in Shropshire, the braces interrupted a stub tiebeam (Moran 2003, 470-76, Moran 1985). Elsewhere, as at Great Binnal, built 1460d or soon after (VA27, 102) (Fig 4.19), and at Colemore Farm (Fig 4.18e), both in Astley Abbotts, Shropshire, the base of the principal rafter was jointed directly into the wall plate. At the first of these houses, with elaborate cusped bracing above the collar, the arch braces appear to be soundly fixed with chase tenons whereas, in the much plainer second house, Colemore Farm, slip tenons were employed (Moran 2003, 379 & 380-1).

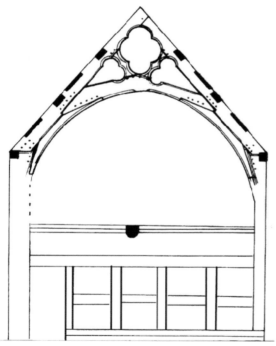

Fig 4.19: Truss at Great Binnal, Astley Abbotts, Shropshire
1460d

(With consent drawing by M Moran.(Moran 2003, 381))

On documentary evidence, the earliest arch-braced roof in the region was assembled in about 1320, and the latest published tree-ring date for a double arch-braced truss, at 1-4 Church Road, Eardisley, Herefordshire, is 1513d (VA37, 109), giving a probable life-span of almost 200 years for this type of open truss in the west midlands. Arch-braced collar roofs persisted until a later date than did crownposts, but neither form of roof carpentry could survive the demise of the open hall (Figs 4.13d and 4.14).

Roof Trusses with Principal Rafters, Tiebeams and Collars

In 1960 J T Smith remarked upon the lack of detailed knowledge of principal rafter tiebeam trusses. During the intervening years there has been no systematic attempt to enhance understanding of the type, and even now the earliest principal rafter, tiebeam and collar roofs in the west midlands cannot all be reliably singled out from the tree-ring dating lists. One problem in this regard is the use of the word *collar* to refer to the small scantling timber which connects coupled rafters in the early roofs of one tradition and also to the more substantial timbers which link cruck blades and principal rafters in another (compare Figs 4.16 and 4.18). It might be because such roof structures were very common by the 17th century that only a small proportion of them have been tree-ring dated. In the quest for early carpentry the type has been insufficiently appreciated, and consequentially it has proved more straightforward to determine the duration of relatively less common medieval crownpost roof construction than to reappraise the development of the most common post-medieval roof types in the region.

In the tree-ring dating lists the earliest entry for the west midlands which refers to a conventional principal rafter, tiebeam, collar and queen strut roof is for Manor Farm in Tredington, Gloucestershire, of 1366-95d (VA34, 99). This would seem rather late when compared with The Vicarage at Martley, Worcestershire, formerly attributed on general grounds to c.1300 (Charles 1967, 54-5), but for the fact that the very deep arch braces under the tiebeam at Martley are so similar to those in the tree-ring dated collar purlin Mavesyn Ridware Gatehouse of 1391-2d (Fig 4.16e). This only serves to demonstrate how difficult it is to attribute dates on grounds of style and how much need there is for more firm tree-ring dates for a type of building that was at one time thought to be better understood than most. Despite the reservations, only dendrochronology could rule out an early to mid 14th century date for the Martley Vicarage, and in the meantime the first use of this type of roof in the region can only be tied down to a time-span of more than half a century. Making extensive use of second-hand timber, the roofs at 6 Market Street, Tamworth, Staffordshire, including trusses comprising principal rafters, tiebeams, collars and queen struts, might have been assembled as late as c.1695d (VA25, 38) (Meeson & Kirkham 1993, Fig 1).

Various numbers, types and arrangements of struts are found between tiebeams and collars. For example, the tiebeam and collar roof of The King's Head, Mardol, Shrewsbury, of c.1404d (VA26, 69), had a crown strut flanked by raking struts rising to clasp the side purlins[3] (Moran 2003, 227-30), and in the Ludlow Palmers' Guildhall roof of 1411d the crown

struts are flanked by cusped braces (VA24, 57). By far the most common form, especially during the 16th and 17th centuries, had a pair of queen struts between the tiebeam and the collar, as at 88 Main Street, Alrewas, Staffordshire (Fig 4.20c), which has been attributed on general grounds to the 17th century. An internal truss of 1450-75d (VA 33, 115) at 8 Vicars' Close, Lichfield, Staffordshire, exemplifies a closely related form in which the tiebeam and the collar are connected by raking struts (Fig 4.20a) (Arnold, Laxton & Litton 2002, 1-3 & 8). This broad group of trusses includes those with multiple struts but also encompasses several examples which have none, and at Baddesley Clinton, Warwickshire, these two variants can be compared in the adjacent roofs over the east range (Fig 4.20b and d) (Alcock & Meeson 2007, Figs 16 & 17).

Side Purlins
One characteristic common to most of the west midland box-framed roofs described above is the side purlin, and when sufficient examples of the various forms have been recorded and

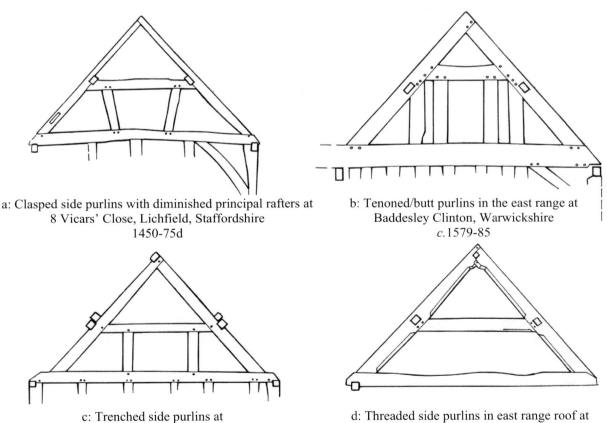

a: Clasped side purlins with diminished principal rafters at 8 Vicars' Close, Lichfield, Staffordshire 1450-75d

b: Tenoned/butt purlins in the east range at Baddesley Clinton, Warwickshire c.1579-85

c: Trenched side purlins at 88 Main Street, Alrewas, Staffordshire 17th century

d: Threaded side purlins in east range roof at Baddesley Clinton, Warwickshire c.1703d

Fig 4.20: Four principal rafter, tiebeam and collar trusses with four types of side purlins

closely dated they may one day contribute to a better understanding of the development of conventional principal rafter, tiebeam and collar trusses. J T Smith deduced from the distribution of principal rafter roofs as it was understood in 1960 that they may have developed from full cruck construction and, as noted above, Charles agreed (Charles 1967, 43). The earliest and the latest published tree-ring dated full cruck buildings employed trenched side purlins, indicating that they continued in use alongside their box-framed counterparts for a considerable time.

In most west midland box-framed buildings the common rafters are supported by side purlins which span the gaps between principal rafter, tiebeam and collar roof trusses. There are relatively few types of junction between side purlins and the supporting principal rafters, yet despite the attempts in the CBA Glossary (Alcock et al 1996) to promote a common vocabulary some disparity of terminology remains. An example of this is the confusion in some of the literature between tenoned purlins and threaded purlins, especially as it is sometimes difficult to discriminate between the two forms from a distance in a tightly-jointed roof (Fig 4.21). Given the absence of clear and consistent usage of a common vocabulary and problems of misidentification, caution is re-

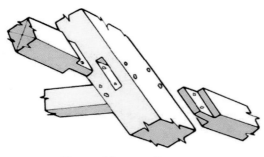

a: Tenoned/butt purlin

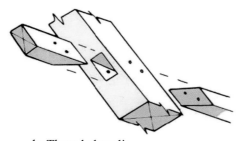

b: Threaded purlin

Fig 4.21: The difference between a tenoned or butt purlin and a threaded purlin

quired when using the tree-ring dating summaries for any analysis of the dating and distribution of purlin types, particularly as so few of them contain relevant information.

In the west midlands the majority of side purlins sit in trenches cut across the backs of principals, probably mainly in simple or rural buildings like that at 88 Main Street, Alrewas, which also retains a ridge purlin (Fig 4.20c). The predominance of trenched side purlins is particularly noticeable in 17th century lower-status box-framed structures, but because they were employed throughout the period of study they are less useful than other types for tracing the development of west midland roof carpentry. Conversely, clasped purlins and tenoned purlins appear to have been employed for shorter time-spans.

Rather than being laid in trenches across the backs of the principal rafters, clasped purlins were contained in the angle between the collar and the principal rafter. A common but not invariable characteristic was a reduction in the scantling of the principal rafters above the level of the purlins, which can be seen in the roof of a 'renter' at 122 Spon Street, Coventry (Meeson 2002b), built around 1455d (VA30, 104), and at 8 Vicar's Close, Lichfield, Staffordshire (Fig 4.20a). Elsewhere, especially in roofs that were not open to view from the room below, the collar was sometimes dispensed with and the purlin was clasped over the head of a raking strut[3] (as in Fig 3.21c). An example of this kind at Baddesley Clinton, Warwickshire, was built between 1526 and 1536 (Alcock & Meeson 2007, 311-13). The apogee of clasped purlin roof construction in the west midlands was probably in the 15th century, but until the advent of tree ring dating it was not possible to determine when the type was first used or how long it persisted, and uncertainty has grown as specialists working in other areas have found both earlier and later examples. Tree-ring dating has now served to extend the known date-range of this type of construction in the region to more than 200 years; the earliest example found to date is at Tredington Manor Farm, Gloucestershire, of 1366-95d (VA34, 99), and the latest known instance of its use is in the Polesworth Abbey Gatehouse annexe, Warwickshire, with a felling date of 1582d (VA38, 113) (Alcock, Meeson & Meeson 2007, 29-30).

Tenoned side purlins (sometimes described as butt purlins) were employed in conjunction with the arch-braced collar trusses over Worcester's Guesten Hall roof of c.1320 (Fig 4.18a) (Charles 1971). They were used in the 1430s tiebeam and double collar roof of Thomas Ferrers' open hall at Tamworth Castle, Staffordshire (VA18, 53) (Meeson 1983b), and in the arch-braced collar roof of the abbey infirmary at Burton upon Trent, Staffordshire, in 1445-1470d (VA30, 95). A tenoned purlin roof remains in situ over the east range at Baddesley Clinton, dated to 1579-85 (Fig 4.20b), but the later roof of c.1703 over the same range apparently employed threaded side purlins (Fig 4.20d) (VA33, 86) (Alcock & Meeson 2007, 329-30). Particular caution is required in roofs that might have been altered. The jettied gatehouse of 1591/2d (VA20, 41) at the front of West Bromwich Manor House now has trenched purlins, but although they were always trenched across the internal principals, in the original building they were threaded through the gable principals (Jones 1977, 31).

Other Roof Types

So far this review has briefly considered some of the main types of roof structures employed in the west midlands on both secular buildings and churches from before the Norman Conquest until the 17th century, but other forms of construction are briefly considered below as they raise questions regarding dissemination, function and status.

Hammer beam roofs were constructed elsewhere in England from the early 14th century, the Pilgrim's Hall, Winchester, Hampshire having been tree-ring dated to 1310-11d (VA32, 80), but in the west midlands dated roofs of this kind are somewhat later. It has been suggested that the

roof that once spanned the hall at Kenilworth Castle, Warwickshire, could have employed hammer beams in 1389-93, and it might have been assembled by carpenters linked with royal service (Courtenay 1984). When it was first rediscovered, the hammer beam hall encapsulated within the later Booth Inn, Hereford, was attributed by F E Howard to 1380-1400 (Watkins 1918-20), but the tree-ring date-range is now known to be 1454-92d (VA28, 144) – more than 60 years later than royal Kenilworth. Types of construction whose first patrons were at the highest level of society may have been taken up more slowly and on a smaller scale by others with lesser means but who were nevertheless encouraged to follow a trend. The latest tree-ring dated example of a hammer beam roof in the region, at The Commandery in Worcester, is of 1465-70d (VA29, 105), but it is plain to see that this type of roof persisted into the 17th century. None of the fifteen hammer beam roofs in Shropshire churches have been tree-ring dated, but that at Donington has been attributed to about 1635 (Fig 4.22) (Mercer 2003, 304).

Although kingpost roofs are generally associated with the north of England they are also found in southern England and in the west midlands, where they range across a span of more

Fig 4.22: Simplified section of a double hammer beam roof based on that over the nave of Donington Church, Shropshire - attributed to 1635

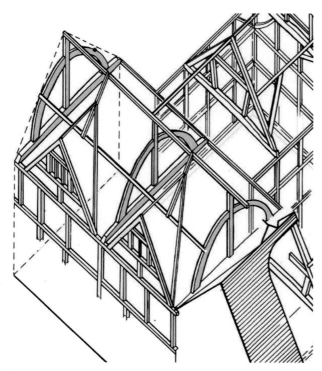

a: 44-45 Church Street, Tamworth, Staffordshire
16th century?

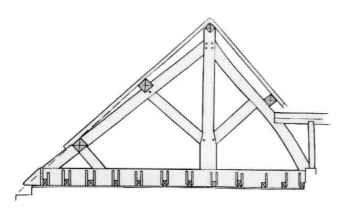

b: Baddesley Clinton, Warwickshire
*c.*1790

Fig 4.23: Kingpost roofs

than 300 years. In an undated roof in Tamworth (now demolished) the kingposts were flanked by curved braces which doubled as principal rafters and carried trenched side purlins (Fig 4.23a) (Meeson 1971). On general grounds this roof was originally attributed to the 16th century, but the date range of 1453-76d was obtained for a kingpost roof in Minworth Greaves Farm Barn, Warwickshire (VA32, 90), and a similar roof over a barn at Carlton Court, Steyning, West Sussex was erected with timber that had been felled in 1404/5d (VA26, 61)

(Aldsworth 2007). In Hampshire kingpost trusses have been found in some of the earliest surviving houses, including 1292-93d at 42 Chesil Street, Winchester (VA27, 99) and 1279-1311d at 15 High Street, Fareham, (Fig 3.12b) (VA29, 117) (Roberts 2003, 27-29). A kingpost roof at Baddesley Clinton was constructed in or about 1790d, and at the time of writing this is the latest tree-ring dated example in the west midlands (Fig 4.23b) (VA33, 86).

In all of the examples cited above the tiebeams were conceived by their carpenters as the means by which posts in compression offered support to a ridge plate, but from the 17th century 'trussed rafter' roofs became increasingly common (Yeomans 1999, 189-193), and this type persisted throughout the 19th century. In many such trusses kingposts and king struts were in tension, providing support to the centre of the tiebeam. Often the mortice and tenon joint was supplemented by a metal strap placed under the tiebeam soffit and folded up each face of the kingpost or king strut. Although this general category of trusses became commonplace in the roofs of agricultural buildings (Peters 1969, 240), it probably owes its origin to polite architecture. In 1676-7, while vernacular timber-framed houses were still being built nearby, the roofs over St Mary's Church at Ingestre, Staffordshire, finally marked the break from what had hitherto been a gradual development of medieval carpentry. Almost certainly emanating from Sir Christopher Wren's practice – if not from Wren himself – the shallow-pitched roof over the nave retains primary kingposts in trussed rafter trusses (Fig 4.24). More experimentally, the arched ties across the chancel were formed out of two curved timbers fastened together by slip through tenons with face pegs and metal forelock bolts, and a metal tie-rod was employed at the outset in the east gable; the post-medieval engineered roof had arrived in the west midlands (Meeson 2009).

General Discussion and Conclusions
However well-argued, the replication of structures from excavated house-plans has been fraught with difficulties, and it will remain so, because the constructs that can be applied to the evidence are so subject to the objectives of the interpreter. Equally, for historians arguing one case or another, different meanings can be argued from similar terms in the documentary

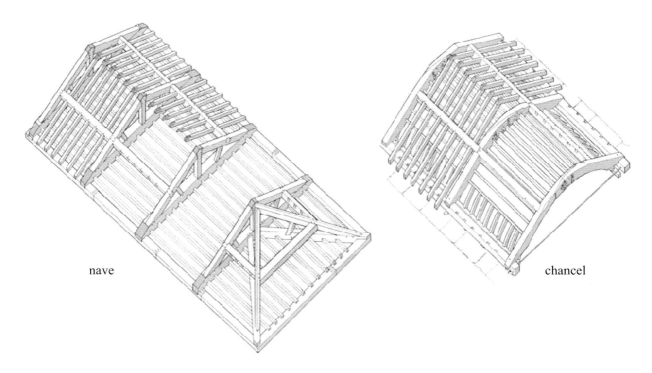

nave

chancel

Fig 4.24: The nave and chancel roofs of Ingestre Church, Staffordshire

sources; that, after all, was the crux of the recent published debate on the origins of crucks (Hill 2005 & 2007; Alcock 2007). As Eric Mercer once remarked, 'Theories would be fine if it were not for the evidence...' (*pers. com.*); now there is so much new evidence that it is sometimes difficult to see the wood for the trees, and yet in many regards there is still not enough. A consensus has emerged amongst archaeologists that a revolution in building construction methods occurred during the 12th-13th centuries. For one form of roof construction that might have preceded that revolution there is now a potential overlap of evidence recovered by trowel with that which remains *in situ* above the eaves; closely-spaced tiebeams and coupled rafters could have been employed both on pre-Conquest wall-post and stone walled buildings. It is a model that has yet to be properly tested, but one which has the advantage in a west midland context of offering a form of construction that might have preceded the properly carpentered cruck frame or stood alongside its precursors.

The problems caused by fragmentary and differential survival apply as much to coupled rafter roof types as to crucks and base crucks, but the scarcity of early church roofs in the west midlands is likely to be due more to the predi-

lection for reconstruction than to their former absence. Roof replacement has been so thorough that in their magisterial survey of Anglo-Saxon architecture the Taylors were reduced to analysing roof pitches from gables and from crease lines on towers (Taylor 1978, 1060), but despite the dearth of extant roof carpentry some deductions are possible. Following excavations and detailed fabric analysis it was concluded that the phase 2 nave (7th or 8th century) of St Mary's Church at Deerhurst, Gloucestershire, would have had a roof with a pitch of *c.*50° (Rahtz & Watts 1997, 156-9 & 190-1), so it might have been similar to a small number of 11th and 12th century church roofs in the area. Coupled rafter roofs like that of about 1056 over Odda's Chapel, Deerhurst, Gloucestershire, (Fig 4.2b) and collar plates like that at Madley, Herefordshire, (of about 1230, or plausibly not long afterwards if it was secondary) have provided fragments of evidence. Over time the number of tiebeams was reduced and crown-posts were introduced to provide support at intervals to collar purlins, thereby further enhancing longitudinal stability (Currie 1990b, 18-22). If it is accepted that early in this process most if not all Anglo-Saxon churches had coupled rafter roofs there may have been no great time-lag between developments on the continent and those in England.

Attempts in 1964 by Fletcher and Spokes to analyse and explain collar purlin and crownpost roofs were hampered by a lack of data from beyond south-east England and the consequential inadequacy of the distribution maps that could be compiled (Fletcher & Spokes 1964), but the gaps in the distribution and dating of early buildings are being filled, and the comparison of English with European tree-ring dates is beginning to further inform research (Alcock 2008). We now know that some of the earliest collar purlin roofs in England can be found in the west midlands. Many new discoveries, and the advent of dendrochronology, have conspired against early theories of diffusion; a more complex process might now be entertained involving the simultaneous exchange of ideas between workshops on both sides of the English Channel, and a social explanation may lie at the heart of this model. Even in 1100 the English Channel was not a barrier, but a means of communication, and communication in another sense lay at the heart of social and cultural divisions. Latin united the upper clergy across Europe, and the languages of the court were Latin and Norman French, while the peasantry spoke Old English, Cornish, Welsh, and a wide range of dialects (Brooke 1969, 22-42). The Anglo-Norman aristocracy and the clergy, most of whom had stronger affinities with the European mainland than with the English peasantry, formed a client base across all of England for masons and carpenters alike; the difference between the roofs of their baronial and manorial halls, or of their churches, and those on the Continent, was probably less than was formerly imagined. Diffusion may have been influenced as much by social as by national boundaries.

Circumstantial evidence that the closely-spaced tiebeam roof was relatively common on a wide functional and social range of buildings might belie the full diversity of roof structures that have not survived. One of the biggest outstanding questions about the framed buildings that emerged during the 12th-13th centuries rebuilding is whether they evolved from precursors or were innovated during this period. The level of precision that can be obtained by dendrochronology has raised issues of this kind concerning the origins and development of cruck-framed and base cruck buildings. Full crucks have yet to yield examples that are as old as the earliest dated base crucks, potentially reversing old assumptions and nullifying former lines of enquiry, but the dates of the earliest recognised examples of each form of construction are so close as to demand caution. After all, in 1995 the cruck blade of c.1269d at Cruck Cottage, Upton Magna, Shropshire (Fig 4.12b), was the oldest then known, but already by 2001 it had been knocked off its perch by The Royal George, Cottingham, Northamptonshire, cruck of 1262d (Hill & Miles 2001), and neither of these dates is much later than that of the earliest English base cruck of 1245-7d at Siddington, Gloucestershire (Fig 4.12a). For these reasons the currently perceived sequence may be based upon no more than accidental survival, but the same argument would apply if a yet older example of one sort or the other were to be identified. The over-riding significance of these dates is not so much the difference between them as their closeness. The fact that the earliest known examples of the two types of building are nearly contemporary raises questions about theories that one form of construction evolved out of the other. Although the earliest survivors might not have been the first of their kind, the rates of development and decline that seem to be implied in Fig 4.14 suggest that base crucks gained currency and then declined well in advance of full crucks. It has been suggested that at a high social level base cruck construction could have been adopted relatively quickly whereas full crucks, generally built for clients of a lower social order, might have been slower to spread over a wide area (Alcock 2006). Even if cruck precursors of what may be loosely described as the product of the first 'great rebuilding' of the 12th-13th centuries can be suggested from excavated building plans, they may have been different in their quality of construction and methods of assembly. The temptation to use only the tree-ring dates as a means of reversing the old hypothesis and concluding that full crucks were derived from base crucks should be resisted – at least at present – as the two types have so little in common. Whatever the sequence was, there is more that divides the two types than unites them; in particular, base cruck structures have clear affinities not just with aisled halls but also with the widespread uniform scantling coupled rafter upper roof forms whereas full crucks do not, having employed an entirely different side purlin system from the outset.

It is becoming untenable to argue that the two types have a common origin simply because they both employed curved blades. In any case, as Edward Roberts has observed, some timbers that have been described as base cruck blades can be regarded as inclined versions of arcade posts (Roberts 2003, 10). One such example, The Old Deanery in Salisbury, Wiltshire (back cover), has been dated on documentary evidence to some time before 1274 (Drinkwater 1964). It is one of a number of so-called base crucks in which the arcade plates pass under the ends of the tiebeams instead of above them. The variety of designs that have now been identified make it more difficult to explain the development of medieval carpentry only in terms of linear diffusion within given traditions, and perhaps individual carpenters should be given greater credit for their ingenuity in solving particular problems in given buildings. What might have been an independent decision to adopt solutions from two different building technologies can be found in Stokesay Castle. It is highly plausible that the original hall at nearby Ludlow Castle and several local churches all had coupled rafter roofs so when, around 1289-90d, the carpenters of the cruck-framed and trenched side-purlin roof of the hall at Stokesay Castle also employed a collar purlin they were borrowing from a methodology that had already been used in the area (Fig 4.15a). The means and rates of transmission and hybridisation varied through time and from place to place, but in the 13th century the boundaries between coupled rafter and side-purlin roofs were already blurred.

The difficulties in tracing the early use and subsequent development of various roofing members can be further illustrated with reference to side purlins. As summarised above, the conventional wisdom is that west midland side-purlin roofs were derived from cruck-frame carpentry, but other influences may also have been at work, especially in larger buildings. In the roof with paired coupled rafters over the cathedral nave at Chichester (Fig 6.7), attributed by Hewett to the late 13th century and subsequently dated to 1272-1307d (VA23, 54), the clasped side purlins substantially precede

any that have been found in secular west midland roofs (Hewett 1985, 14-15). The aisled Great Coxwell Barn, Oxfordshire (1300-1310d, VA11, 33), with intermediate trusses employing curved blades redolent of base crucks, has purlins that pass along the sides of the roof between paired common rafters, although in this context they might have been conceived as a means of restricting racking. Built after 1344d (VA13, 49), Bredon barn made similar use of such timbers (Fig 4.9b) (Charles 1997, 17-28). Even as the crownpost West Bromwich Manor House was being built with collar purlins (Fig 4.11a), master carpenters elsewhere were also making increasing use of side purlins. In Chichester, and in both of the barns, the placing of the side purlins between paired rafters is markedly different from the trenched purlins employed in full cruck buildings but, plausibly, clasped purlins could have been derived from either form of construction, again illustrating how complex the mechanics of change might have been in medieval carpentry.

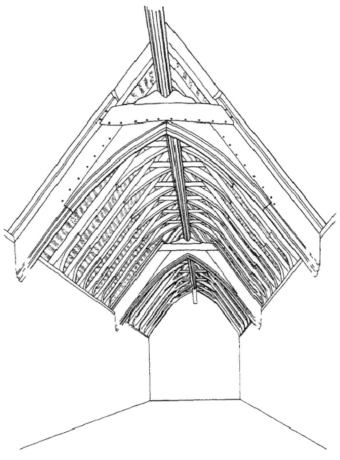

Fig 4.25: Solar wing of Abbot's House, Burton Abbey, Burton upon Trent, Staffordshire

The third quarter of the 14th century was the high point of medieval carpentry in the west midlands, as around 1380 a carpenter might have been commissioned to assemble an open hall with a base cruck, a full cruck, a crownpost and collar purlin, or an arch-braced collar truss. West midland carpenters could call upon a wide and sometimes bewildering array of roofing techniques, not all of which were ultimately successful (Fig 4.14). The innovative arch-braced collar roof of *c.*1320 over Worcester's Guesten Hall employed tenoned side purlins (Fig 4.18a), but twenty or thirty years later in the smaller arch-braced collar roof over the Abbot's solar at Burton upon Trent a collar purlin was used (Fig 4.25). The fact that one arch-braced collar roof had tenoned side purlins whilst another was given a collar purlin serves to emphasise the breadth of repertoire that west midland carpenters could call upon. In the solar roof of 1405-35d at Rigg's Hall, Shrewsbury, Shropshire (VA32, 81), the collar purlin was supported by a crownpost at one bay division, but was threaded through a mortice in an arch-braced collar at the next (Fig 4.26), whereas both 'threaded and trenched purlins' are claimed for an adjoining broadly contemporary roof (Moran 2003, 221). At Upton Cressett, Shrop-

shire, a crownpost and collar purlin roof was assembled for the manorial hall of 1427-31d (VA25, 33), but in the contemporary crosswing arch-braced collars and clasped side purlins were employed. The roof of 1445-70d over the infirmary at Burton upon Trent Abbey (VA30, 96) has a long arch brace passing the stub tie-beam, but the trusses are failing because the carpenters, like those at Astley Abbotts (Fig 4.18e), used only slip tenons instead of chase tenons to connect the arch braces to the principals. Alongside all of this variety and innovation full cruck construction continued unabated.

The emergence of arch-braced collars in the 14th century, most often as the means of supporting the roof over an open hall or a church, and the manner of its adoption in several regions in both vernacular and polite buildings, remain difficult to explain. Was it the outcome of an ingenious new solution for a grand roof over a polite stone walled building such as that at Worcester's Guesten Hall (Fig 4.18a), later emulated in smaller stone and timber buildings? Or was the arch-braced collar truss the ultimate development of a much older bladed or base cruck roof like that over The Old Deanery in Salisbury, Wiltshire (back cover)? The roof over the stone walled Prior's Hall at Much Wenlock, Shropshire, might fall into this category; it was built in or soon after 1425d (VA25, 32), but even at this late date the carpenter elected to combine the splendid arch-braced collar roof with both side purlins and a collar purlin (Moran 2003, 20-21 & 346-7). A less hybridised example can be found over the church nave at Bettws-y-Crwyn, Shropshire, with three tiers of cusped bracing. In marked contrast with such spectacular display roofs, many arch-braced collar roofs are found singly, spanning the middle of open halls in timber-framed buildings (Alcock & Woodfield 1996). Whether or not the arch-braced collars in vernacular timber-framed buildings were influenced primarily by the grand display roofs, there was clearly some element of independent innovation by local carpenters, but all of them faced the common problem of how to secure the junction between the principal rafter and the top of the wall. The solutions included stub tiebeams, deep passing braces, jointed crucks, extended jowls and sling braces, to name but a few; so many varieties have been recorded that it has become difficult to categorise them. As

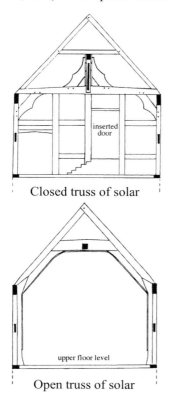

Closed truss of solar

Open truss of solar

Fig 4.26: Rigg's Hall, Shrewsbury, Shropshire
(With consent drawing by M Moran (Moran 2003,221))

no single method of solving this structural problem was adopted from the outset, it is plausible that when commissioned to build arch-braced collar trusses carpenters could call upon a wide range of solutions to suit the available materials and their personal predilections.

To summarise, at the outset this paper was intended to discuss how recent archaeology, building analysis and tree-ring dating had reinforced knowledge of roof construction in the west midlands, but the attempt has generated new avenues of enquiry. Single-framed roofs with tiebeams for each pair of rafters (as above) had already been published elsewhere, but it is both instructive and surprising to recognise how much older the type might be than the earliest surviving examples of any other form of construction in the region (Fig 4.14). With the benefit of a chronological overlap between evidence from standing buildings and archaeological excavations it has been possible to suggest a substantially pre-Conquest origin of this type of roof in the region. Attempts to identify early proto-cruck buildings from excavations have been controversial, and the earliest dated base cruck and full cruck buildings are substantially later than the oldest tiebeam roofs. The numbers of dated buildings are small, but on present evidence the development and decline of base cruck construction proceeded in advance of full cruck construction. Base crucks, many of which occur outside the full cruck zone, appear to have been a product of aisled hall construction. There are more differences than similarities between base crucks and full crucks. The fact that the earliest crownpost yet found in the region might have been assembled within a decade or so of the oldest full cruck building in Shropshire adds weight to the evidence of a widespread evolving coupled rafter roof tradition. Is the Upton Magna cruck a remnant of a much older tradition that has yet to be convincingly demonstrated in an archaeological excavation, or was it amongst the first of a new generation of well-carpentered buildings that were produced in a 12th-13th century 'great rebuilding'? If full cruck construction grew out of the same period of rebuilding as crownposts why did it come to dominate rural Shropshire in the medieval period in a way that crownposts did not? Coupled rafter trusses, aisled halls, base crucks and crownposts all belonged to a changing tableau of roofs in a sequence of main-stream developments primarily for higher status clients, and full cruck buildings, albeit that they display their own sequence of changes, were constructed mainly to meet the needs of an orthodox majority. But even in the mid-13th century there were exceptions, as demonstrated by the aisled Lime Tree House, Harwell, Oxfordshire, originally identified as the former manor house, but now recognised as part of a 21-acre peasant yardland (Currie 1992, 152-59), and by the 14th century similar styles and techniques of carpentry were commonly found within a wide social range of buildings. The current orthodoxy that box-framed side-purlin carpentry grew out of west midland cruck-framed construction will only be fully tested when more such buildings have been closely dated across England. Generally, the results of this specifically regional analysis suggest that the potential now exists to compare developments in the west midlands in some detail with those elsewhere by means of a wider study involving the detailed comparison of closely datable buildings.

Footnotes

[1] Tree-ring dating lists have been published annually from *Vernacular Architecture* **11** (1980). Compiled by N W Alcock, indexes of dates published up to 1998 can be found in *Vernacular Architecture* volumes **18** (1987); **24** (1993); **29** (1998).

[2] Unpublished survey by a Keele University Continuing Studies class under the supervision of the author.

[3] Referred to as 'raked-purlin struts' in Chapters 6 & 7.

Acknowledgements

John Walker is thanked for the invitation that provided the impetus for this paper to be written, and for help throughout. N W Alcock, N Hill and C Tyers are acknowledged for their comments on an early draft. P Dixon, S R Jones and D Miles are thanked for discussing their work as cited, as is C Currie who also copied various papers to me. Most of the drawings of buildings in Shropshire are based, with thanks, on work by M Moran and H Hand. Jean Meeson has shared much of the pain involved in numerous redrafts of the text.

5   ROOF CARPENTRY IN DEVON FROM 1250-1700

By John R. L. Thorp, Keystone Historic Buildings Consultants
(Unless stated otherwise, all drawings are by the author)

This paper attempts to outline the development of the historic roof carpentry in a county with two distinct traditions, which can be conveniently labelled the vernacular and the polite. These ran parallel to each other from the earliest roofs into the 18th century, but the most interesting period was that before c.1550 in terms of development and hybridisation. This coincides with the development of Gothic architecture in Europe, providing an interesting insight into the phenomenon from a local context as expressed in carpentry. However, most of the serious work in Devon in the past 50 years or so has focussed on vernacular building and therefore the polite tradition, particularly in church roofs, is very much under-represented in the following account.

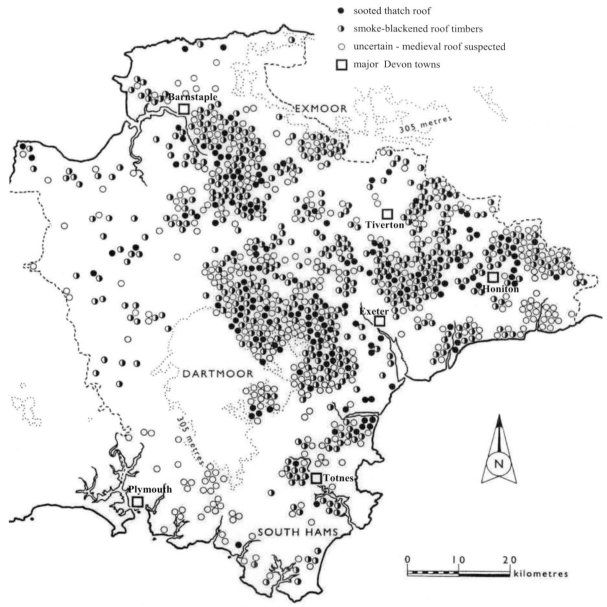

Fig 5.1: Smoke blackened thatch in Devon.
This map effectively shows the survival of medieval roof carpentry in the county

(Cox & Thorp 2001, 40)

Introduction and Survival

The first thing to understand is the nature of the survival of historic houses and their roofs in this part of the world. Rural Devon is an area of early enclosure and most steadings have medieval origins. Moreover the county was increasingly prosperous throughout the whole period under discussion on the back of the export trade of woollen cloth. Fig 5.1 is taken from *Devon Thatch* (Cox and Thorp 2001, 40) and shows the survival and distribution of sooted thatch in Devon. It effectively illustrates the widespread survival of rural medieval roofs. A good few date from *c*.1250-1450, but the majority date from the period between *c*.1450-1550. Most of these medieval houses were improved in the 16th and 17th centuries. Many other farmhouses were extensively, if not completely, rebuilt in the immediate post-medieval period, particularly in the 17th century. A few were clearly new foundations.

The survival of a large number of medieval roofs in the countryside is in stark contrast with the early towns of Devon. Here the growing profits from an expanding overseas trade created pressure on the land in the main trading streets, which led to their wholesale redevelopment in the 16th and 17th centuries. With the exception of a handful of medieval houses in Exeter's Cathedral Close there is hardly any medieval domestic carpentry left in the early towns.

A third factor which contributed to the survival of old houses in Devon is the relative decline of the county's economy after the mid 18th century, when technological innovation took the wool trade to the industrialised factories of the north of England. This affected both town and countryside and meant that there was less 18th and 19th century rebuilding than in many other parts of England.

The Devon rural building tradition is exclusively of mass wall construction (Fig 5.2). The geology is varied, providing regional variations of rubble masonry and provides some stones which can be worked for dressings or even ashlar for the finest buildings, notably the limestone from Beer, the granite from Dartmoor, or the mid Devon volcanic traps. Earth or cob walling was also extensively used for all types of domestic houses, particularly in east and mid Devon. Commonly the cob was raised on low stone rubble footings but a number of historic cob buildings, some of quite high status, have no footings at all.

Even when timber framing became fashionable among the merchants of the larger towns from the early 15th century onwards, their houses were built French-style of mixed construction with timber fronts and stone side walls.

Early Polite Roofs in the Romanesque Tradition

There is evidence of two aisled halls in Devon. One, from an unnamed manor in Stoke Fleming, is known from historic accounts as a ruin. Now all that remain are a couple of stone scalloped capitals suggesting a 12th century date. The other is the Bishop's Palace in Exeter. Although massively rebuilt after the Civil War the shell of a three-bay aisled hall remains of the palace built for Bishop Brewer (1225-45). This incorporated one and re-used fragments of other original oak aisle posts, square in section with

a: Cob built house, Hayne, Zeal Monachorum, Devon   b: Stone built South Wood, Cotleigh, Devon

Fig 5.2: Mass wall construction

Fig 5.3: Fragment of aisle post in
Bishop's Palace, Exeter, Devon
1225-45

attached shafts, moulded bases, and stiff-leaf carving to the capitals (Fig 5.3) (Blaylock 1987 & Wood 1965, 39). However there is no evidence of the actual roof carpentry of either house.

A grainy mid 20th century photograph (preserved in the West Country Studies Library) is all that remains of the roof over the domestic chapel at Fardel in Cornwood parish. As far as one can see it is a collared common rafter roof with passing braces and ashlar pieces (Fig 5.4). John Allan of Exeter Archaeology, who brought this photograph to my attention, is of the opinion that the chapel is 13th century rather than 12th century. At Elmside, East Leigh, Coldridge there is a range with collared common rafter trusses with ashlar posts and mortices for soulaces dendro-dated to shortly after 1302+d (VA23, 44)[1]. The boarded roof cover indicates slates or shingles on the roof which means a high status building. In 1968 Nat Alcock published a similar collared common rafter roof, this one without soulaces, and surviving over the oldest part of a multi-phase medieval house at Fishleigh Barton, Tawstock (Fig 5.5) (Alcock 1968, 14-16).

These early collared common rafter roofs are quite rare in Devon houses. They represent a survival from a polite tradition deriving from a northern European mainstream. They are characterised by the employment of timbers of similar, relatively light-weight scantling, the use of wall plates and the absence of a bay system, purlins and ridges.

Fig 5.4: Domestic chapel at Fardel, Cornwood, Devon

(Reproduced with permission of Dartmoor Trust)

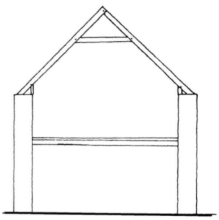

Fig 5.5: Oldest part of
Fishleigh Barton, Tawstock, Devon

(© Nat Alcock 1968, Fig 1)

The Bay System in Vernacular Roofs

The early 14th century roof at Townsend in Stockland (east Devon) – a farmhouse of no particularly high status, appears to reuse timbers from a mid 13th century roof (Fig 5.6), which have been dated by dendrochronology to c.1258-63d (VA34, 98). The timbers include halvings for notched lap-jointed collars, and similarly-jointed soulaces, which were in common use in traditional common rafter roofs of the late 12th and 13th centuries. However these are significant since they are large enough to indicate that they derive from a trussed roof system. A roof divided into bays by trusses

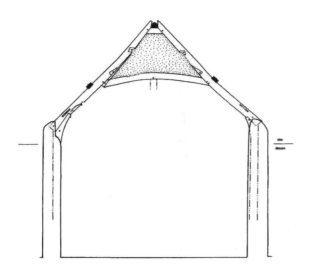

Fig 5.6: Reused timber dated to 1258-63d
in Townsend, Stockland, Devon

built of large timbers connected laterally by longitudinal timbers represents a serious improvement on the old common rafter truss tradition. It signals the arrival, both of stronger roofs which stand a better chance of lasting, and marks the introduction of a period of experimentation which, in polite terms, characterises the period of Decorated Gothic architecture.

The oldest dated original vernacular roof in Devon so far is the three bay roof over the hall and cross passage of the Old Rectory in Bridford, comprising two trusses and attendant timbers, dated by dendrochronology to 1279d[2] (Fig 5.7). Based on the name, and with the manor house the other end of the village, this was a middling-status building using face-pegged, jointed crucks of massive (whole-tree) scantling. The posts have expanded heads, curving inwards, to accommodate the principals at the elbow (that is to say at eaves level) with a simple, pegged scarf joint. Here this is also locked by unique mirror-dovetail (bowtie-shaped) blocks set into the sides of the joints (Fig 5.8). The trusses have cranked collars mortice and tenoned into the principals, yokes and a square-set ridge (Fig 5.9). Incidentally the ridge has canted upper corners so as not to interrupt the common rafter couples. The trusses carry a single set of back purlins (the simplest form of side purlin where it is carried on the back of the principal rafter). The point here is that this dated jointed cruck truss roof apparently illustrates a mature tradition as early as 1279.

Fig 5.7: Old Rectory, Bridford, Devon
1279d

Fig 5.8: Mirror-dovetail at
Old Rectory, Bridford, Devon
1279d

Fig 5.9: Roof with yoke and square-set ridge at
Old Rectory, Bridford, Devon
1279d

Fig 5.10: Barn, Shamlands, Abbotsham, Devon

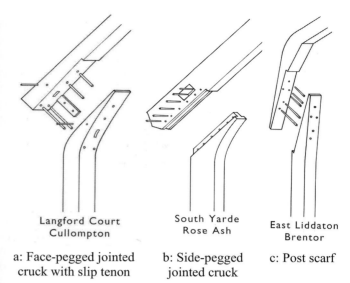

Langford Court
Cullompton

South Yarde
Rose Ash

East Liddaton
Brentor

a: Face-pegged jointed
cruck with slip tenon

b: Side-pegged
jointed cruck

c: Post scarf

Fig 5.11: Scarfed crucks

The vernacular tradition of domestic roof carpentry in Devon is the cruck truss system, using timbers from specially chosen trees to curve in from the walls looking almost like a series of Gothic arches (Fig 5.10). There is a great difference between the curving principals of the crucks and the polite system of the common rafter trusses. The latter are built on top of the finished walls. Cruck trusses are raised at an early stage of the construction of the building. An increasing number of medieval examples are being recorded with posts descending to the ground. These were raised before any walling was erected. However it was more usual to build them on stone rubble footings, and then the upper walls were built around the cruck posts. Sensibly, many were built onto horizontal spreader plates but many were not. Depending on the available timbers they could rise from ground level, or from about 1m (3ft) above (particularly common in cob-walled buildings) or even higher. In these roofs the common rafters hang from the ridge. There is clear evidence that, in most Devon cruck truss roofs, the common rafters are in position before the walls have been built up to their full height. The early cruck blades are often made up of two timbers scarfed together. When connected at the elbow (eaves level) they are called jointed crucks (Fig 5.11a & b), but there are many early examples of such joints in the posts or principals (Fig 5.11c).

Old Cheriton Rectory, Cheriton Bishop, is a middling-status house roof which has been dated by dendrochronology to 1299-1300d (VA28, 140) (Fig 5.12). Here the main trusses are true crucks, but not quite in every case. The principals of Truss 4, for instance, needed extra pieces, scarfed on, to get them to the saddle

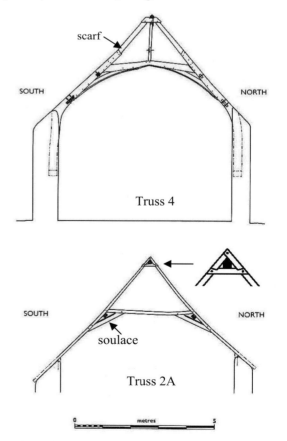

Fig 5.12: Old Cheriton Rectory, Cheriton Bishop, Devon
1299-1300d

95

Fig 5.13: A king stud acting as a false kingpost[3]
Old Cheriton Rectory, Cheriton Bishop, Devon
1299-1300d

apex and square-set ridge (a variation on the yoke form of apex at The Old Rectory in Bridford (Fig 5.9)). However this roof is more sophisticated. For instance, the trusses are arch-braced. It is not full arch bracing since the curve of the crucks is used to continue the lower section of the arcs into the walls. These curve into an apex formed out of the underside of the collar demonstrating a development of the straight soulace. Also they have butted side purlins and windbraces. In the national context this is an early use of butt purlins. This roof also incorporates a false kingpost arrangement designed for arch braces from it to provide support for the ridge (Fig 5.12 & 5.13)[3]. Furthermore the roof includes intermediate trusses which seem to derive more from the common rafter tradition rather than the local vernacular (Fig 5.12, truss 2A). It is made up of common rafter sized timbers and appears to include ashlar posts. Soulaces clasp the purlins under the collar and a yoke (engaging the rafters with dovetail-shaped lap joints) clasps the ridge under the apex of the rafters.

The Church Wagon Roof Tradition
The Church of St Mary, Luppitt has a collared common rafter truss system with curving arch braces (Fig 5.14). With an impressively engi-

Fig 5.14: St Mary, Luppitt, Devon

neered transeptal crossing, the four roofs sit very happily in the late 13th – early 14th century fabric. It seems very likely that these are the original roofs, and, if so, (taken together) one of the earliest church roofs in Devon. As such it represents the beginning of a form which developed in a different direction from the domestic vernacular tradition. From this time onwards the churches of Devon maintain and develop the old polite tradition, evolving the style to produce the distinctive wagon roof form found exclusively in churches and chapels. There are no cruck trusses in Devon churches and no wagon roofs, with one arguable exception, in medieval houses. The dating and typology of the wagon roof must await much more research. Very few have been recorded due to the problems of accessibility[4].

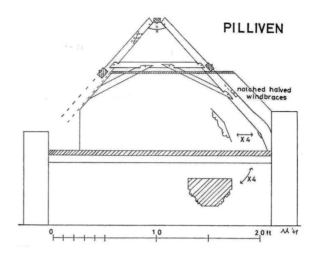

Fig 5.15: Pilliven, Witheridge, Devon

(© Nat Alcock 1972)

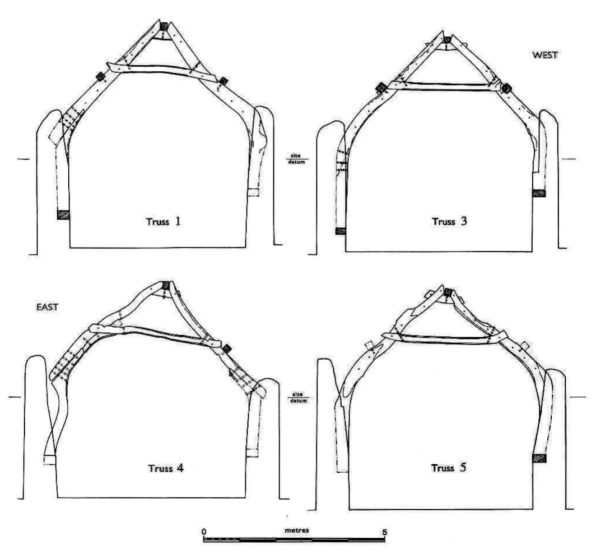

Fig 5.16: Chimsworthy, Bratton Clovelly, Devon
1305-6d

The Development of Early Vernacular Roofs
Nat Alcock recorded Pilliven in Witheridge in the 1960s (Fig 5.15) (Alcock 1972, 36-40). It is the most urbane of this group of early roofs and the closest in detail to the reused principals at Townsend in Stockland described above (Fig 5.6). It must date from the 13th century, but it has not been subjected to dendrochronological analysis. The surviving truss comes from a truly vernacular roof, but one which includes significant elements referenced from the old northern European common rafter roof tradition. Typical of the early Devonian roofs of the period it is a whole-tree cruck truss with a yoked apex-arrangement for a square-set ridge and carries a single set of trenched side purlins. One of the principals includes a scarf joint above collar level. However, archaic elements include a collar which engages the principals with notched and halved lap joints, and has similarly-connected prototype straight arch braces (soulace-like) and windbraces. Also, uniquely amongst these early roofs, a horizontal moulding stands proud from the blade at elbow level. Alcock is probably correct in speculating that it may represent, or correspond to, a moulded corbel.

The roof at Chimsworthy in Bratton Clovelly is dated by dendrochronology to 1305-6d (VA28, 139). It is made up of a series of massive truss and face-pegged jointed cruck blades, built from massive tree trunks (Fig 5.16). It must have been rather difficult to raise with the feet at different levels, and the timbers are so irregular that a clasped purlin was contrived in Truss 4 (east side). It has a square-set ridge carried on a yoke so that the principals extend to clasp the sides of the ridge. It has lap-jointed collars

Fig 5.17: Higher Horselake, Chagford, Devon

(maybe echoing polite forms), back purlins and the scarf joints are not necessarily on the elbow. Such irregular whole-tree trusses which are jointed in different positions probably indicate that the oaks were felled from the wild wood rather than managed woodland. The drawings do little credit to the impressive appearance of this roof when seen on site. Higher Horselake in Chagford is very similar but here the collars are mortice and tenoned into the principals (Fig 5.17). Another analogous example from Higher Tor in Widecombe in the Moor is made up of true crucks and has no collars at all.

Just a couple of hundred metres from the collared common rafter roof at Elmside in East Leigh (described above p93) stands Leigh Barton in Coldridge with a remarkable early roof of which three bays of the original four remain intact (Fig 5.18). Although it is built of whole-tree crucks, which rise from ground level, the oak timbers used were fast-grown and failed to date after dendrochronological sampling and analysis. The trusses variously employ saddles or yokes at the apex, supporting the square-set ridge, and face-pegged scarf joints (augmented by blocks) in the posts or principals. None of the joints is at the elbow. The collars are cranked with chamfered soffits with simple circular bosses. At the upper east end there is an arch-braced hip cruck. There are gabled end walls to some farmhouses but the most common end wall was a half-hip, particularly in cob areas. The walls rise high enough to carry the purlins but the ridge is supported by a hip cruck in the centre of the end wall.

Base Crucks
At the same time as the whole-tree cruck roofs were being raised over the superior farmhouses, the larger gentry houses were being built with base cruck roofs. There is one in the Gatehouse of Dartington Hall, Totnes (Fig 5.19), another in one of the canons' houses in Exeter's Cathedral Close, and archaeological evidence for others at Okehampton Castle and Buckfast Abbey. The base cruck is a two-tier roof which used large timbers curving out from the walls to support the arcade plate and tiebeam of the upper roof, and thus dispensing with aisle posts. Whilst there are obvious analogies with the local cruck tradition – not least the curving blades and the bayed truss system – these base crucks incorporate a level of technical sophistication

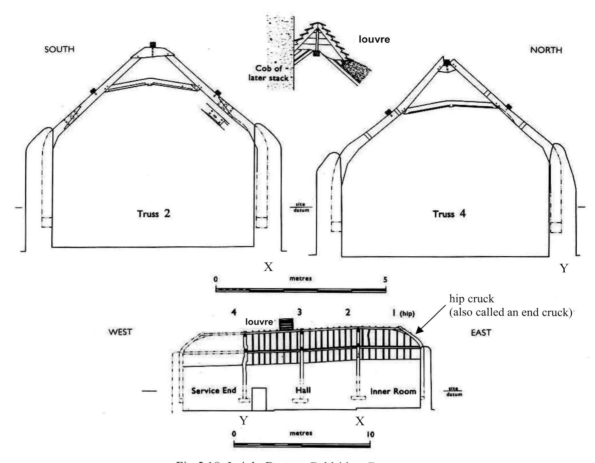

SOUTH

NORTH

louvre

Cob of later stack

Truss 2

Truss 4

site datum

X

Y

0   metres   5

hip cruck
(also called an end cruck)

4   3   2   1 (hip)

louvre

WEST

EAST

Service End   Hall   Inner Room

site datum

Y   X

0   metres   10

Fig 5.18: Leigh Barton, Coldridge, Devon

Fig 5.19: Gatehouse of Dartington Hall, Totnes, Devon

(photograph by John Walker)

Fig 5.20: Base cruck truss over hall of Moorstone Barton, Halberton, Devon
1304-29d

not found in other domestic medieval roof carpentry in Devon. The craftsmen making these roofs were under the direction of a master carpenter who was in contact with others working for the richer patrons throughout southern England and northern Europe. They are impressive polite roofs, representing, at household level, the experimental progress and elegant execution of the engineering revolution that is called, in art historians' terms, the Decorated Gothic style.

The earliest known is the one at Bridford Barton, dendro-dated 1298d[2]. The main block is a large-scale three-bay range with an aisle-type spere truss at the service end of the hall, and a base cruck over the hall. The hall truss is arch-braced in a very similar manner to the main trusses at the Old Rectory in Cheriton Bishop (Fig 5.12). It is however a base cruck with a top-tier roof of collared common rafters resting on the arcade plate. With no longitudinal strengthening the roof began to fail due to severe racking at this level, that is to say that these common rafter trusses started to move and lean over. This was arrested by works within the medieval period although it seems that a whole bay was lost. In hindsight racking of a

Fig 5.21: Truss at end of open hall of
Moorstone Barton, Halberton, Devon
1304-29d

common rafter roof is an obvious danger. The solution to this problem is demonstrated at places like Moorstone Barton in Halberton, where an admittedly better timbered roof incorporated a support to the upper roof by means of a crownpost arrangement (Figs 5.20 & 5.21). This roof, dendro-dated 1304-29d[2], survives so completely that only a couple of common rafters are missing. The other feature of the two base cruck trusses at Moorstone Barton is that

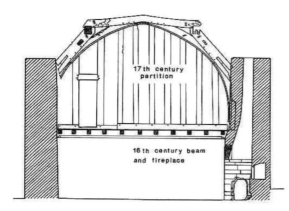

a: Base cruck truss in open hall

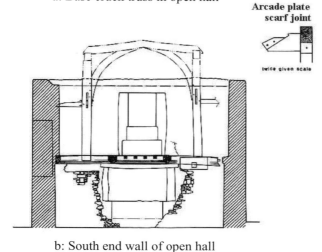

b: South end wall of open hall

0   1   5 metres

Fig 5.22: Uplowman Court, Uplowman, Devon
*c.*1310

they are fully arch-braced, creating a continuous (slightly arch-headed) curve from wall to wall. Here the lower springing of the arch bracing rises from carved corbels, but all this is carved out of the solid of the base cruck blade. Moreover a small block descends from the centre of the tiebeam, which here is carved as an ornamental boss. In this way the actual arch braces are locked tight top and bottom.

Remnants of base cruck roofs also remain at Uplowman Court (dated from the chapel stained glass to *c.*1310), without a crownpost system but with full arch bracing (Fig 5.22), and Woodbarton, Kentisbeare (dated by documentary research to *c.*1336) with a crownpost system and full arch bracing (also with evidence of unusually rich decoration) (Fig 5.23). It is interesting to note that a crownpost arrangement was included in Master Thomas Witney's early 14th century roof design for Exeter Cathedral which also included a bay system (Hewett 1980, 149-152). Here the collar purlin is tenoned into the crownposts, indicating that the roof was reared in bays. Once the first bay had been erected, the next bay, consisting here of three common rafter couples plus the crownpost truss, was erected and then stabilised by tenoning and pegging the short collar purlin

Fig 5.23: Base cruck truss over hall at Woodbarton, Kentisbeare, Devon
*c.*1336

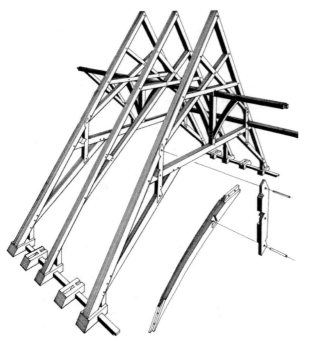

Fig 5.24: Roof of the nave of Exeter Cathedral
early 14th C
(After Hewett 1985, 46)

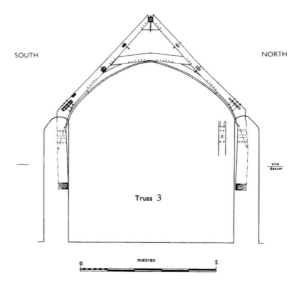

Fig 5.25: Rudge, Morchard Bishop, Devon
1316d

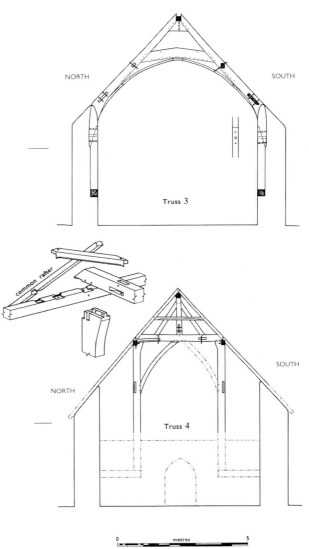

Fig 5.26: Bury Barton, Lapford, Devon
1328-39d

into the two crownposts (Fig 5.24). This also occurred in the base cruck roof over the gatehouse at Dartington Hall (Fig 5.19).

The Mid-Devon Three

There are three large and impressive vernacular roofs in mid Devon dating from the second and third decades of the 14th century, coinciding with the dates for the developed base cruck roofs. Rudge in Morchard Bishop, Bury Barton in Lapford and Thorne in Clannaborough are so similar in detail to each other that they are assumed to come out of the same carpenter's workshop. They have massive whole-tree cruck trusses with regular post scarfs, each fixed by four large face pegs (some wedged) neatly arranged above and below a rectangular block. They have massive yokes to carry square-set ridges and butt purlins. The collars are morticed, tenoned and pegged to the principals. They have full arch braces creating continuous curves from wall to wall (just like the base crucks). In what was becoming the common form of construction the lower springing of the arch bracing was cut out of the solid of the post. They also have curving windbraces. Rudge in Morchard Bishop, dendro-dated 1316d (VA28, 140), survives virtually intact five bays long (Figs 5.25 & 5.27). Thorne in Clannaborough, dendro-dated 1319-20d (VA28, 140), is four

102

Fig 5.27: Truss 3 of Rudge, Morchard Bishop, Devon
1316d

(photograph by John Walker)

Fig 5.28: Truss 3 of Bury Barton, Lapford, Devon
1328-39d

(photograph by John Walker)

bays long with a regular series of scarf joints in the principals above collar level as well as the signature post-scarfs. Bury Barton in Lapford, dendro-dated 1328-39d (VA28, 139), is a larger complex and was probably built as a gentry house (Alcock 1966) with a four-bay hall range, a three-bay service block and ancillary two-bay block (Figs 5.26 & 5.28). Rudge appears to have polite pretensions having collared common rafters, whilst Thorne is satisfied with its impressive arch-braced roof. However Bury Barton attempts to incorporate other elements from contemporary polite architecture. For instance the main purlin is set square to look like an arcade plate and the common rafters are collared. Moreover the end trusses, which are set into the rubble masonry of end walls of the two main ranges, are of aisle-type construction with all the technical sophistication of those in the contemporary base cruck roofs. Also there is one surviving kingpost directly supporting the ridge above the east end truss of the hall range (and evidence that other end trusses were simi-

lar). These are the only true kingposts known in Devon before the 18th century.

Late 14th and 15th Century Vernacular Roofs
Cleavanger in Nymet Rowland is dendro-dated to 1396-1400d (VA36, 84). By the end of the 14th century the timbers are no longer whole trees and the jointing of the crucks has settled onto the elbow – the eaves level (Fig 5.29). This might indicate the development of managed woodland and an increasing confidence in carpenters to understand the capabilities of the oak timbers they were using. The apex has also evolved. The yoke has shrunk to a triangular shape and the ridge is set diagonally, which makes it easier to accommodate the common rafter couples.

Two types of joint are used in the elbows in Cleavanger. The traditional face-pegged form is employed in the service end, and is augmented by a full slip tenon, that is to say the block is now pegged both sides of the joint

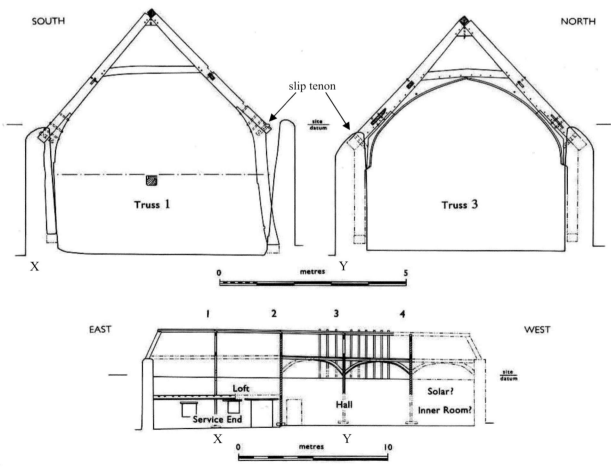

Fig 5.29: Cleavanger, Nymet Rowland, Devon
1396-1400d

104

(truss 1 Fig 5.29). With the reduction in the thickness of the main timbers the slip tenon has moved below a vertical series of the face pegs.

The other trusses employ an improved form of jointed cruck. The open truss over the hall and

Fig 5.30: Hall centre truss, South Wood, Cotleigh, Devon

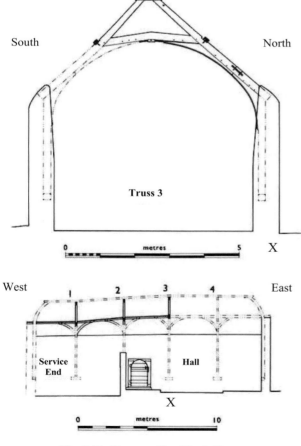

Fig 5.31: Prowse, Sandford, Devon

those in closed trusses at each end are side-pegged jointed crucks in which the curving head of the cruck post is fashioned to provide a tenon on its long upper edge. The principal rafter is provided with a corresponding long mortice in its underside and the joint is secured by a series of pegs and, like the service end truss, this is also augmented by a slip tenon at the base. Yeo Barton, Mariansleigh, in north Devon, dendro-dated to late 1396-99d (VA36, 84), has the same apex form and side-pegged jointed cruck assembly.

There are a group of roofs in east Devon which have the same type of triangular yoke with consistently face-pegged jointed crucks (all augmented with slip tenons) (Fig 5.11a). These are Membury Court, Poltimore in Farway, the arch-braced truss at Townsend in Stockland and at South Wood in Cotleigh (Fig 5.30). Most, unfortunately, have been rejected for dendro-dating because the timbers either have insufficient tree rings to date or have failed to date. Over the hall their roofs are fully arch braced which requires the large 40mm-diameter (1½in) face pegs to be very long to accommodate the thickness of the springing of the arch bracing. Where exposed, there is always a slip tenon at the base. This does not happen in mid Devon. All the full arch-braced roofs here have side-pegged jointed crucks (Fig 5.11b), including Prowse (Fig 5.31) and Bremridge, both in Sandford parish. Until dendrochronology sorts out this difference, we are left with the question of whether the east Devon roof took on the diagonal ridge form before the mid Devon roofs or whether the mid Devon roofs invented the side-pegged jointed cruck to avoid the long face pegs? The side-pegged jointed cruck type certainly makes full arch bracing easier.

By the mid 15th century the side-pegged jointed cruck was established as the standard form of vernacular roof construction in east and mid Devon and continued in widespread use through to the late 17th century. By this time the yoke had gone and the principal rafters were generally mortice and tenoned together at the apex, often notched (as in Fig 5.47). Commonly V-notches were provided to carry the ridge. The joint had settled at the elbow and the main timbers were usually fashioned from half-tree timbers, which clearly made it easier to mirror the main timbers.

Fig 5.32: Hall roof of Cullacott, Werrington, Cornwall
1472d

Raised Crucks

There are no known examples of the raised cruck before the second half of the 15th century, but very few of these roofs have been considered suitable for dendrochronological analysis. Moreover none of the remaining examples include the scantling or type of apex arrangement to ally them to earlier types. It is a variant cruck-form found commonly in the late medieval roofs of west and north Devon. With some notable examples, like Chimsworthy in Bratton Clovelly, these areas have not featured in the previous development of early roofs. They are defined as having principal rafters which curve cruck-like into the wall with short posts. Thus they were raised once the house walls were built at least three-quarters high and maybe higher. The areas where these are found tend to be those where stone rubble is the common walling material, but the cob-walled Cullacott, Werrington in the Tamar Valley is dendro-dated to 1472d (VA26, 60), and is a well-recorded example of the form (Fig 5.32). It lies just a couple of kilometres north of Launceston and is now in Cornwall, but was in Devon up until 1971 and, therefore, can be included here. In most cases such trusses sit on spreader plates, as for instance at Umberleigh House in Alherington, Cross in Bishop's Nympton and Hill Farm in Landkey. At Cullacott they are simply set into the upper level of the cob walls. The raised crucks vary to a point where the feet are so short they may be described as having principals with short curving feet.

Decoration

At vernacular level decoration is rare in the late medieval period. Arch braces and windbraces

Fig 5.33: Chamfered purlins,
Lower Chilverton, Coldridge, Devon
1488-1518d

Fig 5.34: South Yarde, Rose Ash, Devon
1447-8d

Fig 5.35: Old Rectory, Lustleigh, Devon

might well be chamfered. Less commonly the purlins too are chamfered and occasionally, as at Lower Chilverton in Coldridge (dendro dated 1488-1518d, VA28, 140) they are stopped (Fig 5.33). Bosses are extremely rare. Arch and windbraces were evidently sufficient to indicate status. An exception is South Yarde in Rose Ash (dendro-dated 1447-8d, VA24, 47), which was built as the house of Richard Yard and it seems he built the classic vernacular house of a social climber (Fig 5.34). It employed a full three tiers of windbraces to double-chamfered and stopped purlins with a false double ridge. Moreover the upper hall truss has the uncompleted remains of a carved blind arcade of trefoil-headed panels.

Cusping is rarely found in the vernacular repertoire but there are a couple of exceptions to prove the rule. The cusped windbraces at Tytherleigh Cott (now New Inn House) in Chardstock might be explained by the fact that it is situated on the Dorset border, but the Old Rectory in Lustleigh is on the eastern fringes of Dartmoor (Fig 5.35). However, the closest parallel to this form of the roof is Fiddleford Manor in Dorset, believed to date from c.1370.

Vernacular Influence on Grand Roofs

Decoration was certainly not lacking from the late medieval hall roofs of the elite strata of Devon society. Six grand and highly ornamental roofs make up the nationally-important 'Exeter Group' from the 15th century and early 16th century[5]. Characteristically they copy, develop and embellish re-created archaic forms. All feature strongly expressed and richly moulded arch bracing, square-set upper purlins in the form of arcade plates, decorative intermediate trusses, distinctive straight windbraces and coved arch bracing of the upper roof, which traps a crown purlin – very much in the fashion of a church wagon roof. They are thoroughly theatrical in concept (Fig 5.36). For example the roof of the Archdeacon of Exeter's House, dated to 1414-40d (VA33, 104), appears as a two-tier, short principal roof, but it shows none of the technical sophistication of the earlier base crucks described above (Figs 5.36a & 5.37). Nothing more complicated than a mortice-and-tenon or slip tenon joint is employed in the roof construction. Moreover the arcade plate is false consisting of suitably large, square-set lengths of moulded timber mortice and tenoned each end into the ties of the trusses.

The other five roofs are essentially arch-braced A-frames with side purlins and use similar decorative details. These are the Law Library (Fig 5.36b) and the Deanery (both in Exeter's Cathedral Close), Exeter Guildhall (Fig 5.38), Bowhill on the outskirts of Exeter and the gentry outlier at Cadhay in Ottery St Mary (Fig 5.36c)[6]. The roof at the Law Library has a hammer beam form and is said to be (and does look like) a copy of that at Westminster Hall (Figs 5.36b & 5.39). As such, it is pure architectural theatre. It is a very good-looking roof, but the hammer beam assemblies have little or no structural function. Cadhay originally had a similar hammer beam form but these were removed and the roof remains perfectly sound, supported on its arch braces (Fig 5.36c).

In most of the grand roofs of the Exeter group the principals sit on sole plates which are engaged to the arch braces, which take much of the weight of the roof. At Bowhill the basic truss form is the jointed cruck with the lower arch braces carved out of the solid of the inclined heads in the established vernacular fashion (Blaylock 2004).

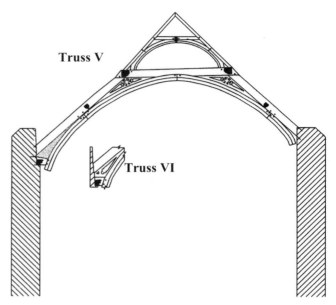

a: Archdeacon of Exeter's House, Exeter, Devon
1414-40d

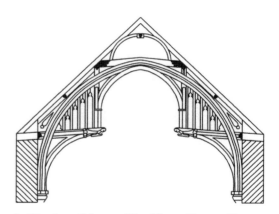

b: The Law Library, The Close, Exeter, Devon

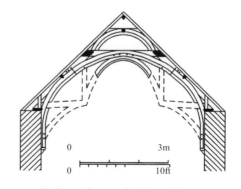

c: Cadhay, Ottery St Mary, Devon

Fig 5.36: Three of the 'Exeter Group' roofs

(Redrawn by John Walker based on Blaylock 2004, 176; Wood 1965, 317; and Henderson et al 1995)

Fig 5.37: Archdeacon of Exeter's House, Exeter, Devon
1414-40d

Fig 5.38: Exeter Guildhall , Exeter, Devon
*c.*1467-9 (documentary)

Fig 5.39: The Law Library, The Close, Exeter, Devon

A plainer 15th century arch-braced roof over Annuellers Hall in South Street was destroyed in the Exeter Blitz of 1943. The surviving back wall shows something of the method of construction in what was clearly a smart polite building. The stone wall was built up to the level of the springing of the window arches. There is a distinct horizontal break at this point. There are large stone pads directly above this line under the positions of the trusses. The roof was then erected in vernacular jointed cruck fashion, the cruck posts carved as the lower parts of the arch bracing. When the roof was finished the upper wall was built up around the arch-braced posts producing the slots visible today. From the other side it is clear to see that the inferior upper rubble walling was built up around already existing principal and common rafters.

Other roofs over lower-status ranges of the canons' houses in Exeter Cathedral Close and in gentry mansions illustrate jointed cruck construction in the grandest of 15th century houses.

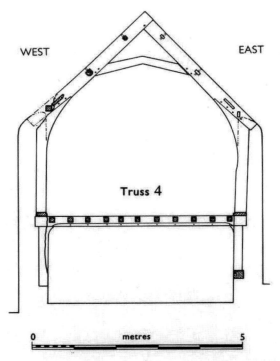

Fig 5.40: Solar crosswing of Prowse, Sandford, Devon

However there are a couple of details that still distinguish the polite from the vernacular. This can be illustrated by comparing the roofs of the solar crosswing at Prowse in Sandford (polite) (Fig 5.40) with the detached chamber block at Elley in Colebrooke (vernacular) (Fig 5.41). Both are essentially similar. Their first floor beams are supported on jowled posts set into the side walls and the roof is carried on side-pegged jointed crucks built on top of the cross-beams. Both have butt purlins, mortice-and-tenoned collars etc. However Elley has a ridge, whereas Prowse does not. Prowse also has a square-set lower purlin in the form of a false wall plate with the face of the wall built up to the base of it.

Fig 5.41: Detached chamber block, Elley, Colebrooke, Devon

110

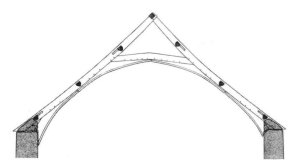

Fig 5.42: Hall truss, 38 North St, Exeter, Devon
probably early 16th C

38 North Street, Exeter, was a merchant's hall house, probably from the early 16th century. It was demolished in 1972, but recorded by the author for Exeter Museums Archaeological Field Unit (Exeter Archaeology archives) (Beecham 1990, 104). The hall trusses were A-frames which sat on top of stone side walls which were then cobbed up to the underside of the common rafters and to the lower purlin (Fig 5.42). They carried three sets of chamfered butt purlins and a large diagonal ridge. They were fully arch-braced and each bay contained two sets of curving windbraces, the upper pair inverted. A remarkably similar roof over the hall of the small gentry mansion of Hams Barton in Chudleigh, only 5-6km from Exeter, has no ridge.

Late 16th and 17th Century Roofs

As the 16th century proceeded fewer ornamental roofs were built. New houses were built without open halls and the fashion for plaster ceilings was established. Roof carpentry was generally less prominent in all but the most utilitarian buildings. Essentially the polite tradition had all but died out by the late 16th century. Some wagon roofs might date from the 17th century, but plastered roofs were the fashion in churches too. Just about all the domestic roofs from this time can be regarded as vernacular. Certainly they all had ridges. In the larger towns most roofs were plain-collared A-frames by c.1600, whilst the jointed cruck or the raised cruck maintained their popularity in the smaller towns and countryside.

One phenomenon that might be regarded as the last expression of the Devonian polite tradition is the series of common rafter roofs built in some of the grandest early 17th century houses in the county. They were simple structures with collars and curving arch braces since they were designed to provide an uninterrupted barrel vault for an ostentatious display of ornamental plasterwork. There are two such first floor rooms in Richard Reynell's Forde House in Newton Abbot, built in 1605. Talaton Farm, Talaton was expensively refurbished in 1623 by William St Pole (according to a date-plaque). A barrel-vaulted common rafter roof was built over the new principal chamber, but it would seem that the money ran out because it has never been ceiled.

Back in the prevailing vernacular tradition, the inner room end of Cullacott in Werrington, Cornwall, was extended to a two-bay parlour with chamber above in 1579 according to the date-plaque. The new roof is carried on a raised cruck truss with a fully-halved, dovetail-shaped, lap-jointed collar (Fig 5.43). This revival of an archaic form was a serious improvement since it held the collar so much tighter than the mortice-and-tenon joint, which relied solely on one or two green-oak pegs. The revived medieval technique seems to have begun in Cornwall where several examples are known from the second half of the 16th century. There is the odd use of the technique in Devon roofs from the late medieval period, as for instance in the late 15th - early 16th century hall roof at Higher Uppacott in Poundsgate, Widecombe, but from 1600 onward it was generally adopted in both jointed cruck and A-frame roofs. There must be hundreds of examples from the 17th century including a variety of collar shapes from the dovetail proper to fishtails and other variants.

The earliest dated example from Devon proper comes from the so-called Manor House, Cullompton, actually a merchant's house built for

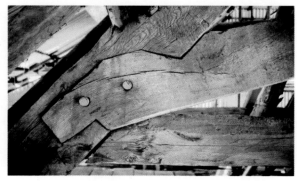

Fig 5.43: Dovetail-shaped lap-jointed collar
Parlour chamber, Cullacott, Werrington, Cornwall
1579

Fig 5.44: Manor House, Cullompton, Devon
1603

Thomas Trock in 1603 (Fig 5.44). Here such collars are in A-frame trusses in a roof which must surely include the latest example of curving windbraces. Just outside the town, but in the same parish, is (or was) Hackland Farm. According to a plaque on the hall chimney shaft it was massively rebuilt in 1605 and had similar lap-jointed collars on side-pegged jointed crucks. They occur in gentry houses where they were invisible behind plaster, such as Hayes Barton in East Budleigh (date-plaque of 1627) with jointed crucks, or Chaffcombe

Manor in Down St Mary (dendro-dated 1670-4d, VA36, 84) with A-frames. They are exposed to view in 17th century farm buildings, as for instance in the cider house at Middle Mackham in Clayhidon or the barn at Uphay just outside Axminster.

Butt purlins had effectively (but not entirely) died out by c.1600, whilst trenched purlins continued in widespread employment. However many 17th century roofs employ threaded purlins, in which the holes cut into the trusses

a: House - A-frames

b: Barn - jointed crucks

Fig 5.45: Pound Farm, Luppitt, Devon - house & barn
both built 1675-80s d

are the full size of the purlins. Commonly the lengths of purlins are simply scarfed together within the truss. Another 17th century develop-ment is that the common rafters are often not coupled, but individually pegged onto the ridge. Also, since the roofs were not to be seen, they were often built of irregular waney timbers. At Pound Farm, Luppitt, both house and barn were built together (dendro-dated *c*.1675-80s d^2) with A-frames in the house and jointed crucks in the barn (Fig 5.45). These are the latest dated examples of fully halved dovetail-shaped lap-jointed collars. In such examples from the second half of the 17th century, the fixing pegs were often augmented by iron spikes. Also, at Pound Farm, Luppitt, the trenched purlins were spiked to the principals.

Another unexpected revival from around the third quarter of the 17th century was the face-pegged jointed cruck with slip tenons as at Clannaborough in Throwleigh. However, it is clear that the jointed cruck was in general de-cline through the 17th century and particularly so in the second half. A-frame trusses were gradually becoming the standard form. Whilst the principals stay engaged at the apex with notched or unnotched mortice-and-tenon joints held by pegs, the collars evolved to simple laps onto the face of the principals where they are fixed by pegs and wrought iron spikes (Fig 5.46). The earliest use of such plain lap-jointed collars is the roof of Exeter Customs House (1680), which is also the earliest dated use of pine roof timbers in Devon (although the pegs are oak).

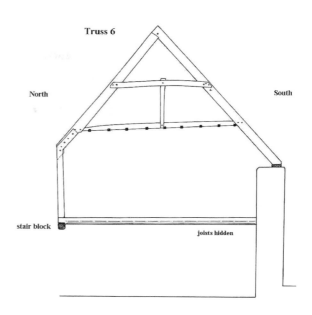

Fig 5.47: Higher Bonehill, Widecombe, Devon
early 18th C

An early 18th century roof at Higher Bonehill in Widecombe is typical of this late utilitarian car-pentry. It is carried on plain A-frame trusses (Fig 5.47). The bases of the principals sit on axial timber spreader plates, buried in the walls since the final cobbing up. In this case it is not known whether they are birdsmouthed over the inner edge of the plates or are tenoned into the top of them. At the apex the principals are joined by a notched mortice-and-tenon joint secured by a single peg. These trusses have slightly cambered unhalved lap-jointed collars fixed to the principals by an oak peg and a wrought iron spike each side. The principals and collars have carpen-ters' assembly marks in the form of chiselled Roman numerals but the trusses were not raised in order. Truss 6, for in-stance is numbered V, whilst the adjacent Truss 5, is numbered III. There are no purlins or ridge. The relatively close-set trusses were designed for stout thatching battens – the first vernacular Devon roof truly sans purlin and sans ridge. The rear (northern) principal of

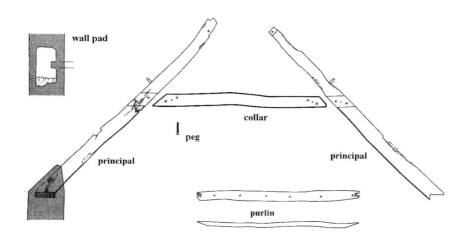

Fig 5.46: Roof of disused farmhouse at East Week, South Tawton, Devon

Fig 5.48: 28 South Street, Great Torrington, Devon
1701

Truss 6 descends into the stairblock so it has a supporting post (resting on a first floor cross-beam, itself on an axial timber across the stair-block opening) (Fig 5.47). The post has an angled head following the pitch of the foot of the principal. The head of the post and base of the principal are halved and lapped together and held tight by three pegs and two spikes creating a bastard form of jointed cruck. A second lower collar is a rather flimsy timber spiked onto the principals and supported in the centre by an upright timber hanging from the main collar. This arrangement is original and designed to carry the first floor ceiling joists.

The End of the Tradition

The tiebeam truss appears in houses as early as 1605, e.g. at the Walronds in Cullompton. It was popular in higher-status houses to accommodate servant accommodation or storerooms within the roof space. The early 17th century examples were simple adaptations of the vernacular A-frame form. Nearly a hundred years later, in 1701, a smart and urbane brick house was built at 28 South Street, Great Torrington. It, too, had attic rooms in the roof space, but the construction of the tiebeam truss roof was of a type that might be found in houses of similar status and appearance anywhere in southern England at the time (Fig 5.48). It incorporates features which do not come out of the local repertoire. For instance, it has staggered butt purlins, no ridge and the original common rafters are short lengths which are mortice and tenoned into the main purlins (the structure somewhat like beams and joists in a floor).

However it is interesting to note that the principals curve down onto the tiebeams in a somewhat cruck-like fashion. The basic design was presumably taken from a printed pattern book. The strong historic identity of the Devon vernacular was over, carrying on in debased (but still sometimes interesting) forms in farm buildings and lower-status housing.

Footnotes

[1] It was recorded by Michael Laithwaite.

[2] Unpublished results of the Devon Dendrochronology Project, Part 2. The results have been passed to Keystone Historic Buildings Consultants by Cathy Groves of the University of Sheffield Dendrochronology Laboratory.

[3] Called a 'crown stud' in CBA Glossary (Alcock et al 1996, G5). There are at least another three examples of such an arrangement in Devon, including a probably later one close by at Clifford Barton in the adjoining parish of Dunsford.

[4] One such roof has been recorded in detail following a natural disaster – see Westcott 1992, *passim.*

[5] Margaret Wood identified the group as five roofs (1965, pp.316-8.). Another was discovered in the 1980s. There is not the space here to discuss these roofs or their precise dating but they and their wider context is assessed in some detail in Stuart Blaylock's monograph on Bowhill 2004, 176-185.

[6] Blaylock 2004 references all the earlier publications of these roofs.

by Robert Hook

(Unless stated otherwise, all illustrations are by the editor)

In recent years a number of large scale dendrochronological surveys have been carried out with a view to gaining a better understanding of the development of particular building techniques and types, rather than seeing the dating of individual buildings as an end in itself. Moreover, such surveys can enable valuable information to be obtained from buildings which may not in themselves be of more than local significance. Examples of systematic surveys of this kind have included the Leverhulme Cruck Project and the Royal Commission on the Historical Monuments of England's surveys of the medieval houses of Kent and of the medieval roofs of the north of England. The latter survey began in 1989 and, in the early stages, attention was concentrated on what has been termed the 'Truncated Principal Trusses Project', although this has since broadened out into a wider survey of other medieval roof types of the region.

Early Collar Purlin and Side Purlin Roofs in the North of England

The earliest collar purlin roof in the north of England of which the author is aware is the Knights Templars' hall at Foulbridge, Snainton, North Yorkshire (Figs 6.1 & 6.2), dated by dendrochronology to 1288d (VA15, 68) (RCHME 1987, 15-17). This was an aisled hall with double tiebeams and four-way braced crownposts, two to the collar purlin and two to the collar. Another early collar purlin roof is to be found at Baxby Manor, Husthwaite, near Thirsk, North Yorkshire, recently dated by dendrochronology to 1308d (see Fig 7.1). This too was an aisled structure, but with a base cruck truss in the hall. As at Foulbridge, the trusses have four-way arch-braced crownposts (Harrison and Hutton 1984, 23). Of similar date, but towards the lower end of the social scale is Lady Row, 60-72 Goodramgate, York, built in 1316 (RCHME 1981, 143-45). The Row was built on the edge

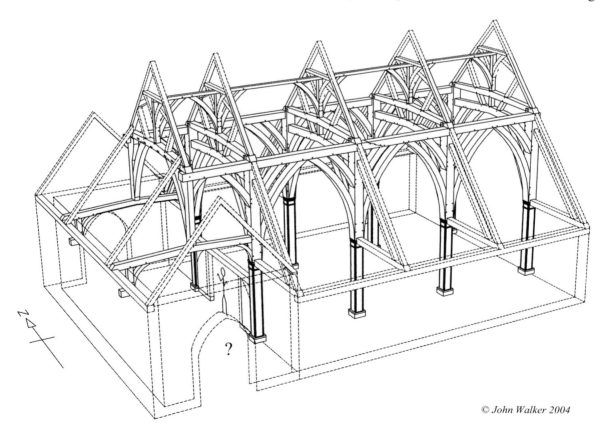

© John Walker 2004

Fig 6.1: Reconstruction and possible interpretation of Foulbridge Hall, Snainton, North Yorkshire
1288d

Fig 6.2: Foulbridge Hall today looking west
The aisles have been removed and the crownpost roof has been lowered, converting the crownposts to king-posts, with the collar purlin becoming a ridgepiece

Fig 6.4: Jowled crownpost in the Merchant Adventurers' Hall, York
1358-60

of the churchyard of Holy Trinity and provided a number of one-up, one-down tenements. The crownposts of the roof of Lady Row are two-way arch braced up to the collar purlin. There are no braces up to the collars but it has two braces down to the tiebeam (Fig 6.3).

Until the mid 14th century, the majority of Yorkshire crownposts were straight and of relatively slight scantling. Around that time crown-posts with heavily double jowled or expanded heads clasping the collar purlin made their appearance in the north of England - the Merchant Adventurers' Hall, York, of 1358-60 being the

earliest example identified to date (Fig 6.4). Thereafter the jowled/expanded head became the standard form in Yorkshire and it is also found as far north as Carlisle, Cumbria, where a number of trusses survive in the city's former Guildhall (dated to 1392-7d, VA25, 43) (Fig 6.5).

The majority of these trusses are two-way arch braced, the crownpost being attached to the collar by tenons on the jowled/expanded heads of the posts rather than by braces. Nearly all the northern crownposts identified are braced downwards to the tiebeams, and in most cases

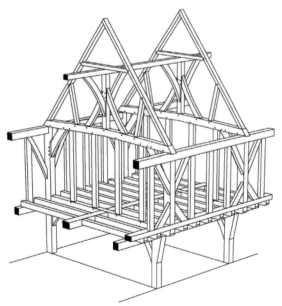

Fig 6.3: One bay of Lady Row,
60-72 Goodramgate, York
1316

Fig 6.5: Crownpost with expanded head clasping the collar purlin in north crosswing of Carlisle Guildhall, Cumbria. The roof has been lowered as at Foulbridge Hall, converting the crownposts to kingposts.
1392-7d

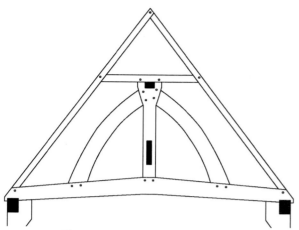

Fig 6.6: 16-22 Coney Street, York
(Redrawn from RCHME 1981)

the upper ends of the braces are tenoned into the angled faces of the jowls (Fig 6.6). A major exception appears to be Lancashire, where two examples of straight crownposts of heavy scantling have been identified, both of which are four-way arch braced. These are Morley's Hall, Wigan (dated 1463d by dendrochronology (unpublished)), and the Dutton Chapel of St Wilfrid's, Ribchester (dated to the late 14th or early 15th century on stylistic grounds).

After the introduction of the collar purlin, the next major development in roof structures was the appearance of roofs combining both collar purlins and side purlins. Roofs of this type are known to have been built in the south of England in the mid to late 13th century, examples including the nave of Chichester Cathedral, Sussex (Fig 6.7) and the chapel of the Bishop's Palace, also at Chichester. The earliest example of a northern collar and side purlin roof identified by the RCHME survey is 12-15 Newgate, York (Fig 6.8). The building, which is all that remains of a row of tenements built on the edge of St Samson's churchyard, has been dated by documentary sources to 1337 (RCHME 1981, 171). The collar purlin of the roof of this building is supported by two-way arch-braced plain crownposts (as at Lady Row (Fig 6.3)), and the side purlins by raked struts with jowled heads. By the middle of the following century this combination of crownpost and raked-purlin struts was commonly used in the roofs of York townhouses, a good example of that period being found in 28-32 Coppergate (one of the few buildings that failed to date by dendrochronology) (Fig 6.9).

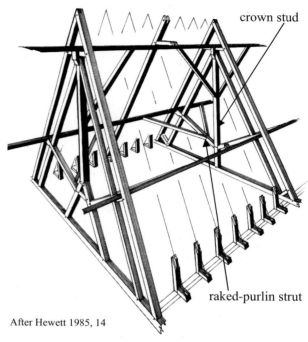

crown stud

raked-purlin strut

After Hewett 1985, 14

Fig 6.7: Late 13th century roof over nave of Chichester Cathedral, Sussex. A crown stud rises to a collar which carries a collar purlin and raked-purlin struts to side purlins
*c.*1272-1307d (VA23, 54)

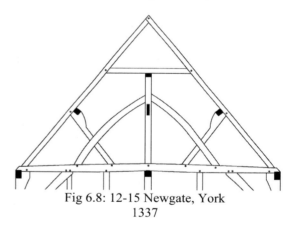

Fig 6.8: 12-15 Newgate, York
1337

(Redrawn from RCHME 1981)

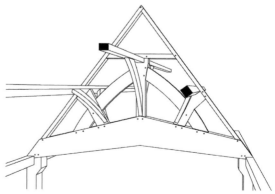

Fig 6.9: Open truss of rear range of
28-32 Coppergate, York

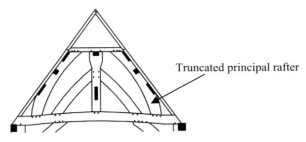

Truncated principal rafter

1a: Merchant Adventurers' Hall, York
1358-60

Type 1
This type has crownpost, truncated principals, collar purlin and side purlins.

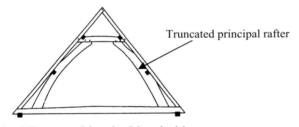

Truncated principal rafter

2a: 79 Low Petergate, York [i]

Type 2
This type similar to Type 1 but no crownpost, the collar purlin being clasped between double collars. Also this type often has no windbraces or other longitudinal bracing.

Truncated principal rafter

3a: 23 Stonegate, York
- late 16th C [i]

3b: 49 Goodramgate, York
- mid 16th C [i]

Type 3
This type has truncated principals supporting the side purlins and no collar purlin. It usually has no windbraces or other longitudinal bracing.

Truncated principal rafter

4a: 7 Eastgate, Lincoln, Lincolnshire
*c.*1500 [ii]

Type 4
This type has side purlins clasped by a collar plus often, but not always, a lower set of side purlins supported by the truncated principals. It usually has no windbraces or other longitudinal bracing.

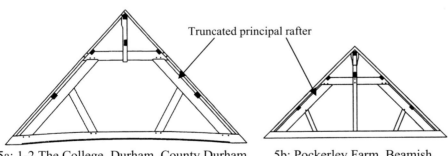

Truncated principal rafter

5a: 1-2 The College, Durham, County Durham
1531-2d (VA23, 59) [iii]

5b: Pockerley Farm, Beamish,
Northumberland
- 1441-2d

Type 5[1]
This type has a kingpost and ridgepiece with side purlins clasped by a collar plus often, but not always, a lower set of side purlins supported by the truncated principals. It usually has longitudinal arch bracing rising up from the kingpost to the ridgepiece.

Fig 6.10: Types of truncated principal rafter trusses

([i]   Redrawn from RCHME 1981
 [ii]   Redrawn from Jones et al 1990, 60
 [iii]   Redrawn from VAG Spring 1991, 15 - the kingpost may be later, converting this from a Type 4 to Type 5)

Truncated Principal Rafter Trusses[1]

This type appears to be predominantly northern in its distribution and is relatively widespread in the counties east of the Pennines, although one example has been identified in Peterborough from archive sources and another has been found even further south in West Tytherley, Hampshire (see page 56 & Figs 3.17 & 6.13). The element which distinguishes truncated principal rafter trusses is the presence of a pair of principal rafters which terminate at a collar, the purpose of which is to support one or more rows of side purlins. The name *truncated principal* was settled upon because these rafters stop short of the apex of the roof, rather than meeting at it. The Oxford English Dictionary defines truncated as 'cut short (actually or apparently); having a part cut off, or of such a form as if a part were cut off'. When the Royal Commission came across trusses of this type during its survey of the City of York it gave them the name *kerb principals,* while others have referred to them as *short principals.* Both these terms were considered but rejected as not being sufficiently descriptive. The use of the word kerb in this context was felt to be inappropriate in that it describes neither the form nor the purpose of the rafters. The adjective short was also ruled out on the grounds that it suggests that the principals are of 'small longitudinal extent', which is not always true, and because it does not imply that the rafters do not meet at the apex, whereas the term *truncated* does.

Truncated principal trusses divide into a number of sub-types, these being as follows (Fig 6.10):

1. trusses with truncated principals supporting side purlins, and a collar purlin supported by a crownpost;

2. trusses with truncated principals supporting side purlins, and a collar purlin supported by a lower collar rather than a crownpost;

3. trusses with truncated principals supporting side purlins, but no collar purlin;

4. trusses with side purlins clasped by a collar (often also with a lower row of purlins supported by the truncated principals);

5. trusses with side purlins, truncated principals and with a ridgepiece supported by a kingpost (in most cases the kingpost rests on the collar).

In all cases there is a common rafter pair which is tenoned into the tiebeam, joined to the collar, and meeting at the apex of the roof. For convenience, these sub-types will be referred to as types 1 to 5 in the text that follows, although it is not suggested that this method of classification should be generally adopted.

The earliest dated example of a truncated principal truss so far identified in England is that at Church Farm, West Tytherley, Hampshire of 1334/5d (Fig 6.13). Apart from this, all the other dated examples are in northern England, the earliest of which so far is in the Merchant Adventurers' Hall, York (Fig 6.11), a building

a: Main truss - Type 1 truncated principal rafter truss   b: Intermediate truss - Type 2 truncated principal rafter truss

Fig 6.11: Roof of Merchant Adventurers' Hall, York with alternating type 1 & 2 trusses
1358-60

which has been dated by both dendrochronology and documentary sources. In this instance dendrochronology was commissioned with a view to checking the accuracy of this method of survey. In the event, the correlation between the estimated felling date obtained by tree-ring dating and the documentary date was close - the samples taken give a felling date between the years 1358-1387 (VA23, 60), while the documentary sources show that work started in June 1357, with the majority of the timber being bought in 1358 (RCHME 1981, 82-88). This suggests it was built 1358-60.

The hall, which consists of two parallel roofs (Fig 7.10), has both side and collar purlins. The main trusses have both crownpost and truncated principals (type 1) (Fig 6.11a), while the intermediate trusses have truncated principals, but no crownpost (type 2) (Fig 6.11b). In the case of the latter, the collar purlin is held in place by being clasped between a pair of collars. In both types of truss the truncated principals support a single row of side purlins, these being trenched into the back of the principals and overlaid by the common rafters.

The type 1 truss, with its crownpost and truncated principals, appears to have become reasonably common in Yorkshire, with a number of examples of late 14th and of 15th century date having been identified. These include 27 Market Place, Ripon, North Yorkshire (dated to the late 14th century on stylistic grounds); Sharlston Hall, Sharlston, West Yorkshire (late 14th/early 15th century on stylistic evidence); Cad Beeston, Leeds, West Yorkshire (1421d unpublished); and the three western bays of St Anthony's Hall, York (1435-59d, VA41, 101 and 1453 by documentary evidence (RCHME 1981, 91-93)) (Fig 7.20).

All the type 1 trusses mentioned above have crownposts with double jowled heads. It is not clear when the jowled head, which is characteristic of the northern crownpost, first made its appearance. As already stated, the late 13th and early 14th century northern collar purlin roofs tend to have straight and very plain crownposts. Indeed, the trusses in the Merchant Adventurers' Hall are the earliest so far identified that have the pronounced jowl, as well as being the earliest example of the use of the truncated principal truss.

A number of other methods of supporting the side purlins of composite collar purlin and side purlin roofs were adopted, although none of these was as popular as the raked-purlin strut with a jowled head. At 51 Fleetgate, Barton upon Humber in North Lincolnshire (dated to the mid 15th century on stylistic evidence), heavy scantling principal rafters were used to support a single row of butt purlins. More unusual still was the solution adopted at Lake View Farm, Ferrensby, North Yorkshire, where the curved braces from crownpost down to the tiebeam were enlarged so as to be able to carry the side purlins (dated to the 15th century on stylistic evidence).

The type 2 truss seems to make its appearance at the same time as the type 1, the earliest example identified so far being the intermediate trusses at the Merchant Adventurers' Hall, York. Other buildings with type 2 trusses include: Sexhow Hall, Sexhow, North Yorkshire (dated to c.1400, on stylistic grounds) (Fig 7.9a); the Banqueting House, Cawood Castle, North Yorkshire (1426-51, on documentary evidence (information provided by York Archaeological Trust)); the Gate House, Bolton Percy, North Yorkshire (1501d, VA19, 45); and the open truss of Barley Hall, Coffee Yard, York (15th or early 16th century[2]) (Fig 6.12). The type 2 truss appears to have been most popular in North Yorkshire, and to have been employed from the mid 14th century to the early 16th century. In some cases this is the only type of internal truss to be utilised, while in others it is used in conjunction with type 1 trusses (as at the Merchant Adventurers' Hall) or with trusses which have crownposts and queenposts.

Fig 6.12: Type 2 truncated principal rafter truss
Barley Hall, Coffee Yard, York
15th/early 16th C

The type 3 truss is, essentially, the type 2 truss without its collar purlin. This truss seems to have made its appearance in the early 15th century, and appears to be part of a general move towards abandoning collar purlins in favour of side purlins. Examples of this type of truss were found at Tom Brown's House, 114 High Street, Yarm, North Yorkshire (dated 1444-5d, VA23, 59), and the Unicorn Inn, Richmond, North Yorkshire (dated to the mid 15th century, on stylistic grounds). A variant on the type 3 truss has been found with a crown strut rising from tiebeam to collar, examples of which are at Shandy Hall, Coxwold, North Yorkshire, and the Manor House, Skelton, also in North Yorkshire.

The most common of the five sub-types, and the one with the widest geographical distribution, was the type 4 truss. This type differs from the type 3 in that the upper rank of side purlins is clasped between the collar and the common rafters. It is very common in County Durham and North Yorkshire, and a number have been found as far south as Lincoln, but the earliest found so far is a single example in Hampshire at Church Farm, West Tytherley dated to 1334/5d (VA38, 128) (Fig 6.13). Other examples include the roofs of the transept and choir of Durham Cathedral (dendrochronology gave a felling date of 1458d (VA23, 59), while documentary research found that the previous roof was destroyed by fire in 1459) (Fig 6.14); a building in H.M. Prison, Durham (1464-6d, VA23, 59); Crook Hall, Durham (1467-8d, VA23, 59) (Fig 6.15); the east wing

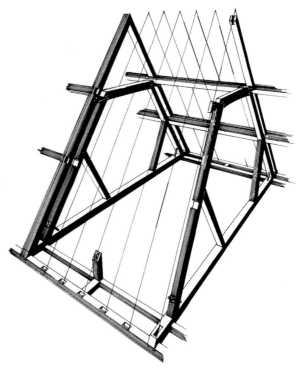

Fig 6.14: Type 4 truncated principal rafter roof over Choir of Durham Cathedral, County Durham

(After Hewett 1985, 70)

of Seaton Holme, Easington, County Durham (c.1479d, unpublished); the Dominican Friary, Beverley, East Yorkshire, built following a fire which destroyed the previous building on the site in 1449 (Miller et al 1982, 48-51); 11 Minster Yard, Lincoln (1488-1523d, VA23, 60, and

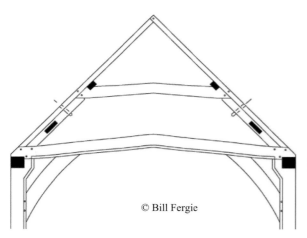

© Bill Fergie

Fig 6.13: Type 4 truncated principal rafter roof truss at Church Farm, West Tytherley, Hampshire 1334/5d

Fig 6.15: Type 4 truncated principal rafter roof at Crook Hall, Durham, County Durham 1467-8d

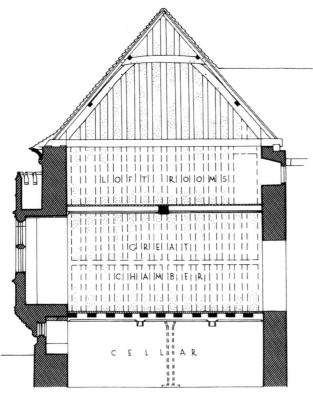

Fig 6.16: Type 4 truncated principal rafter roof truss in Street Range of 11 Minster Yard, Lincoln, Lincolnshire

(© Jones et al 1984, 57)

1485-1506, on documentary evidence (Jones, Major and Varley 1984, 51-63)) (Fig 6.16); and the Bishop's House, 13 Eastgate, Lincoln (*c.*1510d, VA23, 60). The evidence suggests that in northern England this type of roof made its appearance sometime around the middle of the 15th century, and that it became increasingly common in the second half of the century. Once established, the type 4 truss continued in use for around two hundred years in the north. A number of 17th century examples have been found in both Yorkshire and County Durham, including one built from imported pine, rather than oak, in the former shipbuilding town of Whitby.

The type 5 truss is, in effect, a variant of the type 4 truss, the difference being that it has a ridgepiece as well as side purlins, the ridgepiece being supported by a kingpost. The earliest and most elaborate example of this type was found in a bastle house at Pockerley Farm, Beamish in County Durham (dated to 1441-2d, unpublished) (Figs 6.10.5b & 6.17).[1]

The kingposts at Pockerley have heads which are fully jowled on both sides, but some kingposts are jowled on one side only, as at 1-2 The

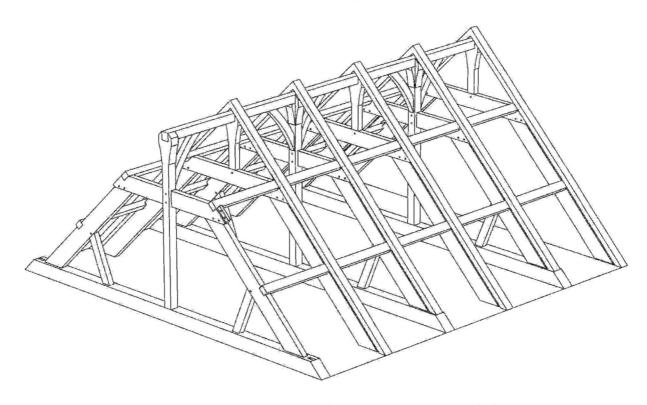

Fig 6.17: Type 5 truncated principal rafter roof at Pockerley Farm, Beamish, County Durham
1441-2d

122

Fig 6.18: Type 5 with kingpost 1-2 The College, Durham, County Durham
1531-2d

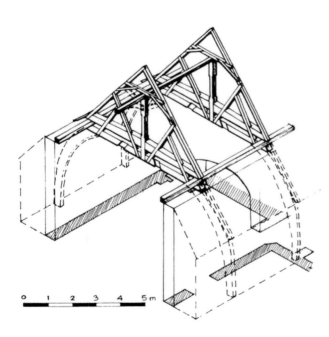

Fig 6.19: Reconstruction of open hall of Canons' Garth,
Helmsley, North Yorkshire
early 14th C

(© Harrison & Hutton 1984, 23)

College, Durham (Figs 6.10.5a and 6.18). The single jowl is a detail of construction that is found in a number of 15th and early 16th century kingposts in Newcastle upon Tyne. Good examples of kingpost trusses of this type are to be found at the former Dove's Warehouse, 35 The Close, Newcastle upon Tyne (dated to *c*.1514d, VA22, 41).

Conclusions

Distribution maps tell us only what we know, but the spaces on them act as a guide as to where to look. As more work is undertaken the picture changes incrementally.

Few early roofs survive or have yet been recognised: extant examples include Foulbridge Hall, Snainton, North Yorkshire, a former preceptory of the Knights Templar (1288d) (Fig 6.1) - and Canons' Garth, Helmsley, North Yorkshire, early 14th century (stylistic) (Fig 6.19), both with crownposts. Crownposts are now known to have a wide distribution – ubiquitous in York and found all over the region reaching as far north as Carlisle. Arch-braced collar trusses are equally ubiquitous, both in date and distribution.

There appears to be more elaborate ornamentation (such as moulding) on the western side of the Pennines. Examples such as Vale Royal Abbey, Winsford, Cheshire, late 15th century (stylistic) or Sutton Hall, Sutton Weaver, Macclesfield, Cheshire, 1490s, are comparable with buildings of similar dates in the south of England.

Crownposts, kingposts and truncated principals are all present at an early stage. The Merchant Adventurers' Hall, York, 1358-60, with its combination of crownpost and truncated principal (Fig 6.11), indicates that earlier examples may well have existed in northern England.

The truncated principal truss makes its appearance in northern England in the middle of the 14th century, providing an alternative to the raked-purlin struts as a means of supporting side purlins.

In the century that followed, truncated principals were used in a number of collar and side purlin roofs, the majority being in buildings in the City of York, although one has been found at Hutton Rudby in the north of the county and others as far west as the manor houses of Sharlston Hall in Sharlston and Cad Beeston in Leeds, both in West Yorkshire.

By the middle of the 15th century builders had started making trusses which had truncated principals supporting one or more rows of side purlins, but which had dispensed with the collar purlin. The type 3, 4 and 5 trusses all seem to make their appearance in domestic structures around this time, although it is possible that roofs with truncated principals but without collar purlins were in use in barns before the end of the previous century. These trusses, like the collar purlin roof, are found mainly in the lowlands of the North of England, and are present in both towns and rural areas. However, unlike the collar purlin, all the examples identified by the survey are on the east side of the Pennines, with particularly large concentrations in and around the cities of Durham and York. A large number of surviving examples are found in buildings connected with the church, including a friary, a deanery, a rectory, a grange and a number of parish churches. As with the collar purlin roof, no rural examples were found in houses of less than gentry status.

Different types of roof structure can indicate a social hierarchy, not a date progression, as at the Old Vicarage, Tadcaster, North Yorkshire, 1474d (VA26, 50) where raked-purlin struts, truncated principals and arch-braced trusses are all exactly contemporary. This magnesian limestone building consists of a north crosswing with, to the south, an open hall, crosspassage, service room with chamber above and then a kitchen open to the roof. The dais and low-end hall trusses are truncated principals, the open trusses of the hall and crosswing are arch braced, and the truss dividing the service bay from the kitchen has raked-purlin struts.

Footnotes

[1] **Note by editor.** At the end of 2008, nearly 6 months after this paper was read at the EHBG Day School, Martin Roberts published his paper '*A preliminary Roof Typology for the North East of England c.1200-1700*', in VA39. This includes distribution maps and detailed discussion of the different historic roof types in north-east England, and provides the first published results from the RCHME Truncated Principal Trusses Project on truncated principal rafter roofs. Roberts also suggests a five type classification of these roofs; the first four types being the same as proposed in this paper by Robert Hook. However he limits his Type 5 to roofs that have a short kingpost rising from the collar to a ridgepiece with a single side purlin each side supported by the truncated principal rafter - basically a Type 2 roof with a kingpost and ridgepiece but without a collar purlin. Because the roofs over both Pockerley Farm, Beamish and 1-2 The College, Durham have two side purlins each side, the upper one clasped by the collar (Figs 6.10.5a & b, 6.17 & 6.18), Roberts defines these roof respectively as Type 4 with modifications and as Type 4 with kingpost (Roberts M 2008, 46-47). However these two roofs are conceptually different from Type 4 as both have ridgepieces and kingposts. For this reason Hook's wider classification above has greater merit.

[2] According to the Barley Hall guide book the hall gave two different dendrochronology dates, the first group felled 1425-51, the second 1515, and says it is 'likely that the hall was originally built in the 1430s and altered or rebuilt about 1515' (Knightly 1999, 4).

7 ROOFS IN YORKSHIRE TIMBER-FRAMED BUILDINGS BEFORE *c.*1560

By Barry Harrison, Yorkshire Vernacular Buildings Study Group

(Unless stated otherwise, all drawings are by the YVBSG)

This paper is based on drawings and reports made by the Yorkshire Vernacular Buildings Study Group (YVBSG), together with published work by other organisations and individuals, notably the inventories and regional studies by RCHME. A total of 226 roofs have been identified in timber-framed buildings of the pre-Elizabethan period in Yorkshire, of which 74 are in York and 21 in six other large towns. Others are located in the southern Pennine valleys and foothills/coal measures (75) and in the southern and central Vale of York (44). The remainder are widely scattered over the county and generally confined to buildings of manorial status or above (Fig 7.2). Only 30 roofs have been tree-ring dated of which 15 are in the South and West Yorkshire uplands and 9 in the central and southern Vale of York. There is however a fairly clear chronological sequence of roof-types which allows many other roofs to be approximately dated.

The numbers may seem small for such a huge area but it has to be remembered that the whole of the north-east and north-west of the county, together with the northern Vale of York, lie in a well-defined zone characterised by cruck construction (Figs 1.2 & 7.3). Only in the southern Pennine valleys and foothills is there much intermixing with box-frame types. Limited tree-ring dating (19 examples, 15 of them in South Yorkshire) shows that crucks (excluding base-crucks) can be as early as 1475 but as late as 1670 and there are no clear structural changes which would allow us to posit an approximate chronology for the rest. Cruck buildings have therefore been excluded from this study.

Early Timber-Framed Buildings

There are a surprising number of buildings using early carpentry techniques – scissor bracing, passing braces, duplication of rafters, square-section members, lap joints etc. About fourteen examples are known, of which half a dozen are from the City of York and the rest mostly located in the lowland Vales of York and Pickering. The earliest are the great barn at Whiston, near Rotherham, South Yorkshire (Fig 1.31), tree-ring dated to 1233-52d (VA33, 117), and the Knights Templars' Foulbridge Hall, Snainton, North Yorkshire, dated 1288d (VA15, 68) (Fig 6.1). Base-crucks have been recorded at the Canons' Garth, Helmsley (Fig 6.19), and at Baxby Manor near Thirsk, the latter dated to 1308d (VA25, 43) (Fig 7.1), both in North Yorkshire.

Common Rafter Types

Crownpost Roofs

About seventy examples of this form are known in the county. Nearly fifty are located in York and ten more in other large urban centres as far north as Whitby. Surprisingly, there are only eleven rural examples, mostly in the southern Vale of York and associated with large houses of manorial or prebendal status.

The crownpost forms go well back into the 13th century and they are a feature of several of the early buildings mentioned above. Thus Baxby Manor (1308d) has crownposts above the base crucks, with three-way bracing. The common rafters above the trusses are duplicated (Fig 7.1). In simple common rafter roofs, the crownpost form appears at Lady Row,

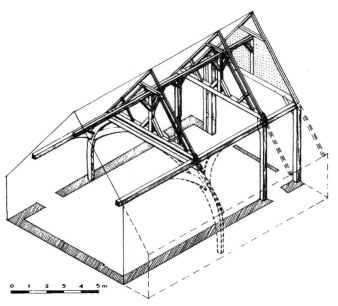

Fig 7.1: Baxby Manor, Husthwaite, Thirsk,
North Yorkshire
1308d

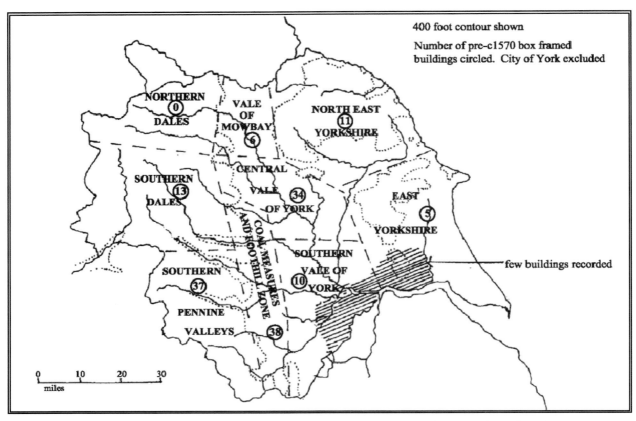

Fig 7.2: Regions of Yorkshire showing the number of box-framed buildings in each region

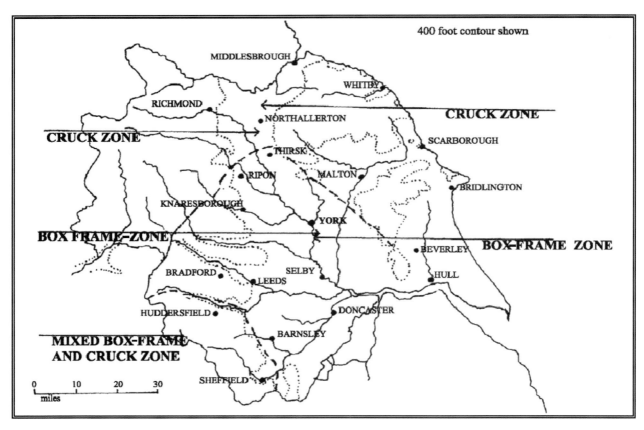

Fig 7.3: Yorkshire: Cruck, box-frame and mixed zones

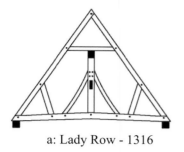 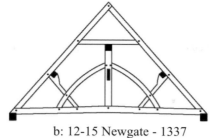 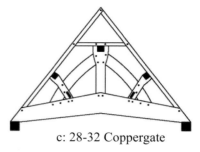

| a: Lady Row - 1316 | b: 12-15 Newgate - 1337 | c: 28-32 Coppergate |

Fig 7.4: Development of crownpost roofs in York

(Redrawn from RCHME 1981)

Goodramgate, York, built in 1316 (Figs 7.4a & 6.3) and another row in Newgate built in 1337 (RCHME 1981, 143-145 & 171) (Fig 7.4b). The latter is more fully developed with side purlins supported by struts from the tiebeams crossing the downward struts from the crownposts, a decorative "X" formation which becomes general in the 15th and early 16th centuries. In about a dozen cases there are "X" struts but no side purlins. The form of the crownpost roof is much the same from Tickhill in the far south to Whitby in the far north of the county. With hardly any tree-ring dates it is difficult to provide a more exact chronology on the basis of roof structure alone. Crownposts in Yorkshire rarely have mouldings or other decoration. The form of the crownpost develops from a thin post with the collar purlin sitting on top, to a much thicker post with a handsome jowled head clasping the collar purlin, which first appears in the mid 14th century. In its heyday, a century or so later, the jowled head is a prominent element in a fine decorative display in closed trusses and particularly in gable ends (Fig 7.4c, 28-32 Coppergate). One particular oddity, confined almost exclusively to York, is the use of flying braces rising from the feet of the raking struts to the side purlins, a strange-looking confection the like of which I have not seen elsewhere (Figs 7.5 & 7.6). These braces have been found in thirteen York roofs and, apart from the Merchant Adventurers' Hall of 1358-60, the next earliest is thought to be of c.1400 (Bowes Morrell House, Walmgate) and the latest early 16th century (RCHME 1981, lxx). Only two crownpost roofs, both in rural situations, have been recorded as "sooted": Baxby Manor, Husthwaite, North Yorkshire (a base cruck) (Fig 7.1), and a late 14th century house at 4 Walseker Lane, Woodall, South Yorkshire, just inside the border with Nottinghamshire (Ryder 1987). Whether there is sooting in any of the roofs in York is not apparent from the published RCHME inventories.

flying brace

Fig 7.5: Scotton Old Hall, Scotton,
near Knaresborough, NorthYorkshire
Note "flying braces"

Fig 7.6: Example of "flying braces"
at 41-43 Goodramgate, York
late 15th/early 16th C

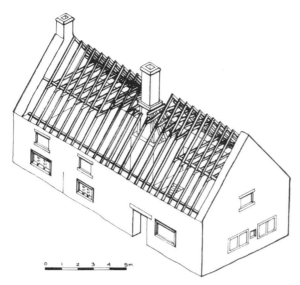

Fig 7.7: Common rafters with collars & later inserted side purlins at Rose Cottage, Clint, near Harrogate, North Yorkshire

Simple Common Rafter Roofs

Roofs composed of pairs of trussed common rafters with collars, but without purlins, are associated with small linear houses, for the most part in the countryside of the central and southern Vale of York. Some of these are of post-medieval date, but about two dozen examples are thought to have been built no later than the mid-16th century. Most of these have heavily smoke-encrusted roofs, the soot often extending the whole length of the building, even when the end or ends were floored over. An unpublished survey by the author of early/mid 16th century probate inventories for a number of villages in the central Vale of York, suggest that single-storey houses with a ground-floor solar were particularly common in the area. A number of such houses have been recorded by the YVBSG, the earliest example of which, a miniature aisled hall at Long Marston, is thought to be of c.1300. An unusually complete (un-aisled) example has been recorded by the Group at Rose Cottage, Clint, an isolated farmhouse in the lower reaches of the Forest of Knaresborough (Fig 7.7). This has a roof of simple trussed rafters, originally hipped at both ends. The roof is smoke-blackened throughout (including the laths between the rafters), even though there is evidence for an upper room at one end. The smoke seems to have escaped from an opening just below the eaves, possibly the upper part of the hall window, where the wallplate is blackened on the underside. Alternatively this opening may have been a smoke

vent from a chamber above a floored hall. In the hall below there was a low stone fireback behind the crosspassage which was later built up into a stone wall (at ground-floor level only) and surmounted by a timber firehood. The outer walls of the house were rebuilt in stone in the 17th century. A few such houses are clearly the precursors of the "Vale of York" houses of the later 16th and early 17th centuries (Harrison & Hutton 1984, 30-31). These are linear buildings of two storeys with a single aisle at the rear. Home Farm and Oak View, both in Scriven, near Knaresborough, North Yorkshire, have storeyed ends but sooting throughout the roof. Oak View has been tree-ring dated to 1516+d (VA12, 40).

Truncated Principal Rafter Roofs (or Kerb-Principal Roofs)

This type of roof has attracted a good deal of attention in recent years. It seems to be a particularly common type in the North-East, where crownposts and other common forms are rare. Seventeen examples have been tree-ring dated to the period c.1440 to 1570, all of them from a manorial or ecclesiastical context, and it is suggested that this type of roof may have been common in Yorkshire and Lincolnshire as well (Roberts M 2008). In Yorkshire such roofs do in fact have identical features - truncated principal rafters (also called short or kerb principals) running up to a collar, the upper side purlins being clasped between the collar and the common rafters and the lower side purlin clasped between the truncated principal and the common rafters (Figs 7.8 & 7.9).

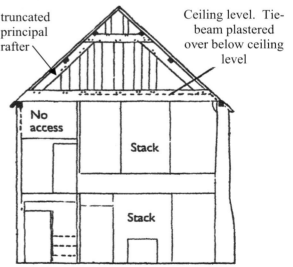

Fig 7.8: Kirkness Cottage, Briggate, Knaresborough, North Yorkshire

128

Thirty such roofs have been recorded in the county and, as in Durham, most of them are associated with prestigious buildings. These include the three great Guildhalls of York: the Merchant Adventurers' Hall (1358-60) (Fig 7.10), the Merchant Taylors' Hall (c.1400) and the three western bays of St. Anthony's Hall

(1435-59d, VA41, 101). In the countryside the form is also associated with houses of manorial status, widely scattered over the central lowlands and ranging in date, by typological analysis, from the mid-14th to mid-16th centuries. One such house, Cad Beeston at Holbeck, Leeds, has an unlisted tree-ring date of 1421 (Michelmore 1991). A few of the earlier examples include crownposts supporting collar purlins, as in the Merchant Adventurers' Hall at York (Fig 7.10), Cad Beeston, Leeds and 4 Walseker Lane, Woodall in the far south of South Yorkshire (Ryder 1987). A few other examples in York, at Sexhow Hall, Sexhow, North Yorkshire (Figs 7.9a & 7.11) and in Blackburn's Yard, Whitby, North Yorkshire have (or have had) no crownpost but just a col-

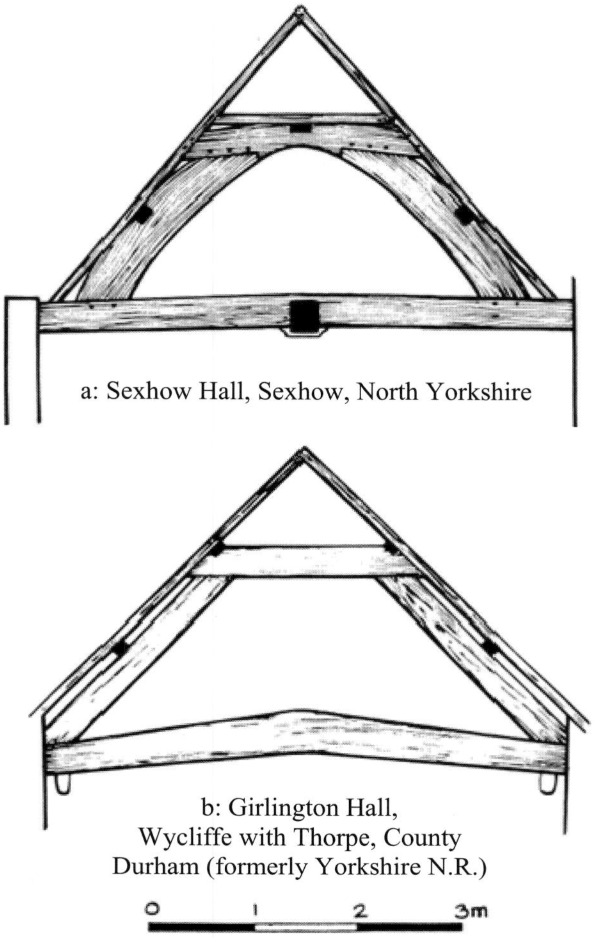

a: Sexhow Hall, Sexhow, North Yorkshire

b: Girlington Hall,
Wycliffe with Thorpe, County
Durham (formerly Yorkshire N.R.)

Fig 7.9: Examples of truncated principal rafter roofs
in Yorkshire

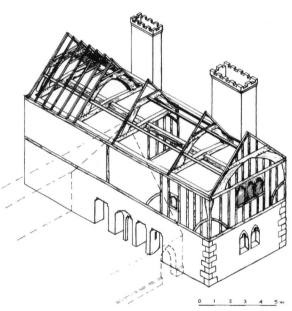

Fig 7.11: Sexhow Hall, Sexhow, North Yorkshire

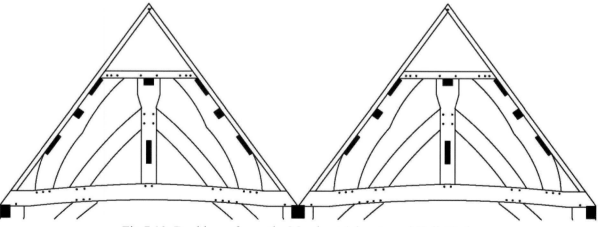

Fig 7.10: Double roof over the Merchant Adventurers' Hall, York
1358-60

lar purlin resting in a trench in the collar. Quite a high proportion of truncated principal rafter roofs are located in towns. A couple were urban manors or vicarages (in Helmsley and Tadcaster), but most were probably merchants' houses. Seven have been recorded in York (excluding the Guildhalls), three in Ripon and one each in Knaresborough, Yarm, Whitby and Guisborough. Those in York, excluding the Guildhalls, are attributed to the 16th century (RCHME 1981, lxxii) but a few elsewhere are undoubtedly earlier: the fine cusped truncated principals at 27 Market Place, Ripon, are thought to be of 14th century date, while the roof of 114 High Street, Yarm, North Yorkshire (formerly Cleveland) has been dated to 1444/5d (VA23, 59). As in Durham, this roof-type seems to continue into the late 16th or even the early 17th centuries. Later examples, towards the west of the county, sometimes have a king-post set on the collar, as at St. Agnes House, Ripon *c.*1542-1573d (VA38,115) (Fig 7. 12).

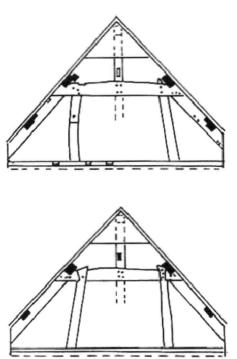

Fig 7.12: St Agnes House, Ripon, North Yorkshire
*c.*1542-1573d

The small number of examples makes it difficult to generalise as to why this form of roof was occasionally preferred to the crownpost type before *c.*1500. Of 26 examples where the position of truncated principles has been established, three were over Guildhalls in York,

seven were over domestic halls, nine over solars, five over attics and two over barns. Those located over domestic halls tend to be of early date (14th/early 15th centuries) while those over solars seem to be of a rather later date, usually appearing in an added cross wing, as at Sharlston Hall, Sharlston near Wakefield (Giles 1986, 5). Attic roofs of this kind are only found in towns and they are generally attributed to the 16th century. It would seem that the truncated principal form satisfied a number of different needs at different times: first for a wide and spacious unaisled hall; later for an aesthetically pleasing solar and finally for unhindered commercial storage space. For the last function, the form was continued in Yorkshire towns well into the 17th century and thus beyond the scope of this survey.

The Raked-Purlin Strut Roof

In this type of roof a single pair of side purlins are supported by raking struts running from tiebeam to common rafter (Fig 7.13). Such roofs are the dominant form for smaller houses in both town and country between the mid-16th and mid-17th centuries over much of the Vale of York and, to a lesser extent, the southern Pennine Foothills. However, some 25 examples can be dated with some confidence to an earlier

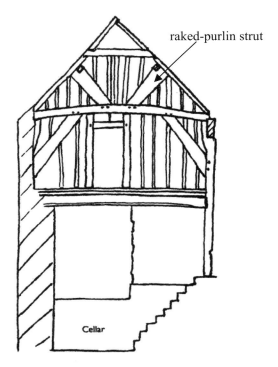

Fig 7.13: Clasped side purlins with raked-purlin struts
Longley Old Hall, near Huddersfield,
West Yorkshire

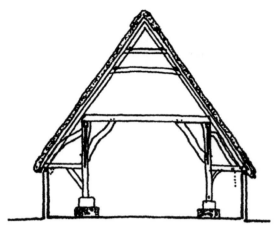

Fig 7.14: Tithe Barn, Easington in Holderness, East Yorkshire

north of York, some of these houses were certainly longhouses in origin and often converted to the central lobby-entry plan in the 17th century (Harrison 1991).

In a few large barn roofs, requiring at least two sets of purlins, the side purlins are supported on collars between the rafters above the tiebeam, without the use of raking struts (Fig 7.14). Timber-framed barns at Easington and Cottingham, both near Humberside and both of uncertain date, have this type of roof. A domestic example of *c.*1500 has recently been recorded in a large town house, now a public house, in Beverley (YVBSG Report 1,783).

period. Of these nine are in York and eleven in the Coal Measures and Pennine Valley areas of South and West Yorkshire. The earliest tree-ring dates are at Netherhall Barn, Dalton (near Huddersfield) (1453d, VA39, 128), Houndhill Barn, Barnsley (1486-95d, VA21, 44) and Netherfold Farmhouse, Thorpe Common near Rotherham (1494/5d, VA12, 40). In the south-western uplands the form disappears early, seemingly superseded by the kingpost (Ryder 1978), but it spread rapidly throughout the lowlands of the Vale of York in the late 16th and early 17th century, where it is closely associated with the standard "Vale of York" timber-framed house, numerous examples of which have been recorded between Northallerton in the north and Selby in the south (Harrison & Hutton 1984). On the east side of the Vale,

Principal Rafter Types

Kingpost Roofs

The kingpost roof is far and away the most dominant type in south-western Yorkshire, from the southern Dales to the Derbyshire boundary. Since it is also very common in eastern Lancashire and Cheshire, it is often regarded as the archetypal Pennine roof. In various forms it persists until the 18th century. A few examples are also known on the western side of the Vale of York, notably on the Magnesian Limestone belt just east of the Coal Measures. Although few have been tree-ring dated, the medieval examples can be recognised by a number of features, notably the use of "A" (Fig 7.15b) or "I" strutting (vertical struts from the tiebeam to principals as in Fig 7.17) in

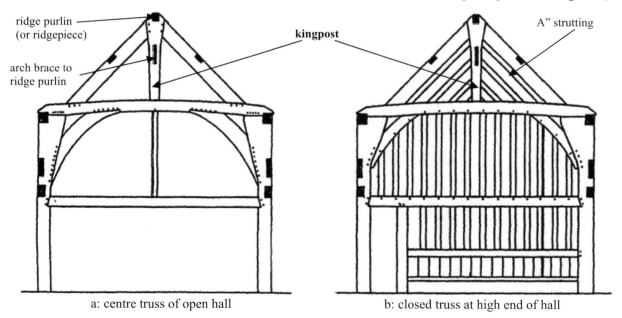

a: centre truss of open hall

b: closed truss at high end of hall

Fig 7.15: Kingposts at Low Hollin, Hebden Bridge, near Halifax, West Yorkshire

Fig 7.16: Example of 'V' strutting
176 Leeds Road, Lofthouse, West Yorkshire

closed trusses. A few examples with the, generally later, "V" strutting are thought to belong to the first half of the 16th century (Fig 7.16). Over sixty examples, arguably constructed before the middle decades of the 16th century, have been recorded – all but five of them in rural locations. They are the most well-known of all northern roof-types not least because they often occur in quite large houses of cross-wing plan ("H" or "T") and, in some cases, with aisled halls. These houses are particularly associated with the minor gentry and emergent yeoman clothiers who prospered during the first phase of the woollen cloth boom between the 1470s and the mid-16th century (Giles 1986). They were built throughout with timbers of

Fig 7.17: Solar wing of Smithills Hall,
Bolton, Greater Manchester (formerly Lancashire)

heavy scantling, providing a good show in closed trusses, and particularly on gable-ends. Ornamentation, both external and internal, was generally kept to a minimum, except in a few houses with an arch-braced truss over the hall (see below). Even windbracing is very rare. Roofs were of relatively shallow pitch and covered with heavy sandstone flags.

The kingpost roof seems to emerge quite suddenly and at a relatively late date. The half-dozen examples which have been tree-ring dated fall between 1475 and 1536+. They are thought to have succeeded earlier common forms, at least in South Yorkshire (Ryder 1978), yet the kingpost form was undoubtedly known from a much earlier date: the magnificent kingpost roof (with cusped principals) in Long Preston parish church (Ribblesdale) belongs to a rebuilding in the Decorated style of the late 14th century, as does the solar wing truss at Smithills Hall near Bolton, Greater Manchester (formerly Lancashire) (Fig 7.17). In its fully developed form, the kingpost had a heavily jowled head clasping a square-set ridge purlin, with upward bracing from kingpost to ridge (Fig 7.17). One, or occasionally two, sets of side purlins are trenched into the backs of the principals. The form was popular with the builders of the new "Pennine Perpendicular" churches of the period, where there was often no division between nave and chancel, the kingpost trusses running from one end of the church to the other, as at Kildwick and Bingley, both in the Aire Valley. One apparently local variation, found in four aisled barns in the Lower Wharfedale and Airedale area, together with the parish church of Addingham in the same district, is the use of sharply-cranked principals which engage with the tiebeams well inside the line of the posts below (Fig 7.18). This form

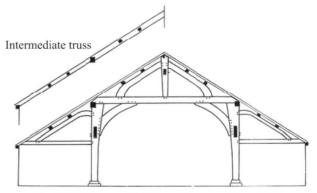

Intermediate truss

Fig 7.18: Weston Hall Barn, Lower Wharfedale, North Yorkshire

may have been influenced by cruck construction and in one or two cases former cruck members may have been used.

The Arch-Braced Collar Truss

The most decorative roofs in Yorkshire are those with an arch-braced truss over the hall or, less frequently, the solar. In common rafter roofs they occur only in York, where they are associated with buildings of high social status. There are eight examples in the City, half of which are associated with major institutional buildings: the Bedern Hall (mid-14th century) (Fig 7.19), Merchant Tailors' Hall (*c.*1400), the six eastern bays of Saint Anthony's Hall (1435-59d, VA41, 101) (Fig 7.20) and Saint William's College (*c.*1465). The rest are in the larger halls hidden behind, and subsequently amalgamated with, the front buildings. None are identical in form

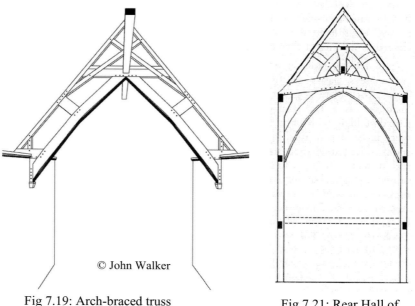

© John Walker

Fig 7.19: Arch-braced truss
Bedern Hall, York
mid-14th C

Fig 7.21: Rear Hall of
35 The Shambles, York

(after RCHME 1981)

but, with the exception of the earliest, Bedern Hall, the braces are pegged to principal rafters carrying butt purlins which facilitate windbracing of the roof (Fig 7.20b). The desire for display is also demonstrated in a couple of three-storey halls where the tiebeams are set at a great height. Here huge arch braces ran up through two storeys to meet in a pointed arch just beneath the centre of the tiebeam. This form was used in two well-known houses: 35-36 The Shambles (The Margaret Clitherow House) (Fig 7.21) and Barley Hall, 2 Coffee Yard, Stonegate (Fig 6.12) (RCHME 1981, 217-218 & 232).

bays of truncated principals beyond, looking west
both roofs 1435-59d

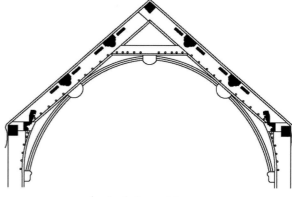

b: Arch-braced truss
1435-59d

(redrawn by John Walker from RCHME drawing)

Fig 7.20: Great Hall of St. Anthony's Hall, York

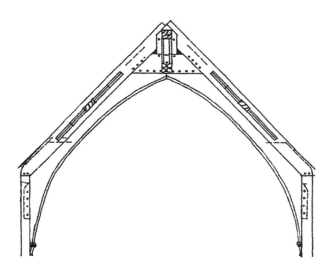

Fig 7.22: Arch-braced truss
Fold Farm, Kettlewell, Wharfedale,
North Yorkshire

Arch-braced trusses of a rather different type are found in the uplands and foothills of West Yorkshire, where there are half a dozen examples, together with a single outlier in nearby Wharfedale (Fig 7.22). They generally date from the late 15th or early 16th centuries and four of them share a quite distinctive form: long braces attached to wall posts and principal rafters and meeting at a yoke on which stands a very short kingpost into which the principal rafters are set. The overall impression is very cruck-like but they make a fine display of carpentry with elegant chamfering and occasional carved corbels and decorative rosettes etc., notably at Horbury Hall near Wakefield and Fold Farm, Grassington in Wharfedale. The other trusses in these houses are of standard kingpost type. There are also a couple of good examples at Tadcaster on the west side of the Vale of York: the Old Vicarage (1474d VA26, 50) with arch braces over both hall and solar, and over the solar at The Ark Museum (the hall range has been demolished). The form became quite popular in parish churches all over Yorkshire, particularly for chancel roofs; good examples can be seen at Gisburn in Bowland, near the Lancashire border and at Bolton Percy in the central Vale of York.

A couple of arch-braced roofs lack both collar and saddle but have a large triangular block between the tops of the principals, the latter clasping the ridge on top (Rawthorpe Old Hall, Dalton near Huddersfield, and Kirby Hall, Ouseburn, in the western Vale of York) (Fig 7.23). Although medieval examples of the arch-braced roof are quite thin on the ground, it reappears in a modified form in the upper chambers of new stone-built houses in the late 16th/ early 17th centuries, particularly in the southern Pennine valleys.

Simple Principal Rafter Roofs

As we have seen, simple A-frames bearing one or two sets of butt or threaded purlins, were associated with arch-braced collar trusses in both York and West Yorkshire. Towards the middle of the 16th century arch-braced trusses over halls were abandoned in the rapidly proliferating two-storey stone buildings of the textile districts and simple kingpost construction became the norm. In York and the east, however, timber-framed construction remained the norm until the middle decades of the 17th century and with it various types of common rafter and truncated principal roofs. However, principal rafter roofs with butt or threaded side purlins (but without ridge-purlins) gradually began to appear, particularly in higher-status buildings. About a dozen examples are thought to belong to the 16th century or earlier. In a few cases there is an attempt to provide the visual display of the closed kingpost truss with V-struts. At St. John's House, Knaresborough (thought to be c.1520) and the somewhat later Wakeman's House in Ripon, there are fine gable displays but the kingpost has been reduced to a mere ornamental strut, the principal rafters being

Fig 7.23: Example of large triangular block between the top of the principals in the false hammer beam roof of the Chapel at Calverley Hall, Leeds
1485-95d (VA14, 61)

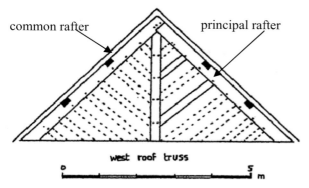

common rafter | principal rafter

west roof truss

0 ——————————— 5 m

Fig 7.24: Manor Farm, Morton-on-Swale,
near Thirsk, North Yorkshire
late 16th C

halved or tenoned together at the apex and carrying no ridge purlin. Examples include the late 16th century Manor Farm, Morton-on-Swale, North Yorkshire (Fig 7.24). The only dated examples of simple principal rafter roofs are at 41 Yorkersgate, Malton (1469d, VA39, 114) and the so-called tithe barn at Nether Poppleton near York (1542/3d VA30, 126) (Fig 7.25). Until recently an excellent through-purlin roof (now almost entirely collapsed) could be seen over a range of early/mid 16th century buildings at Watton Priory near Beverley in the East Riding of Yorkshire (Fig 7.26).

Fig 7.26: Through-purlin roof over
Watton Priory, near Beverley,
East Riding of Yorkshire
early/mid 16th C

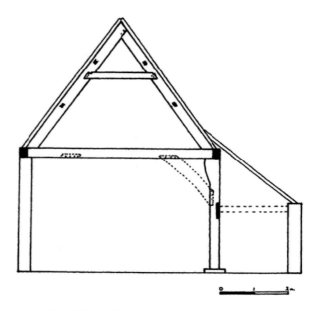

Fig 7.25: Nether Poppleton Barn, near York
1542/3d

Conclusion

Yorkshire is a huge county and the number of recorded pre-Elizabethan timber-framed houses is very small except in York itself, and largely confined to the textile areas of the south-west, to parts of the central and southern Vale of York and to a few of the larger towns. Partly this is due to the predominance of cruck-construction in the north and east while in the Dales there was certainly a "great rebuilding" in the 17th century, which swept away practically everything which had gone before. Although the numbers recorded have increased hugely in recent times, there are likely to be far more timber-framed buildings than we know about, a proportion of which are likely to be of medieval date. Being, however, for the most part encased in brick or stone, they tend to be discovered more by accident than by design! Nevertheless enough recording has now been done in most areas of the historic county to allow some tentative classifications and distributions to be attempted.

Note

Copies of all the YVBSG drawings are held by the Yorkshire Archaeological Society and by English Heritage.

8   QUEENPOST ROOFS IN EAST ANGLIA

by Philip Aitkens
(Unless stated otherwise, all drawings are by the author)

In the 14th century the main roof type in East Anglia was the crownpost, but in the late 14th century a very distinctive type of side-purlin roof emerged in north Suffolk and south Norfolk - a queenpost roof with queenposts that had jowled heads clasping a square-set side purlin, all topped by a collar, creating a roof type that looked like an aisled hall rising above the tie-beams (Fig 8.1). This East Anglian queenpost roof continued to be built into at least the late 16th century in north Suffolk and south Norfolk, with possibly a few being built on into the first half of the 17th century. It was constructed over medieval open hall houses, over 16th century transitional sub-medieval two storey houses with chimney stacks, over barns and over two storey public buildings such as guildhalls and hunting lodges. It never completely replaced the crownpost in north East Anglia, and provided an alternative roof type first to the crownpost in the 15th and 16th centuries and then, for a while, to the new clasped side purlin roof that replaced the crownpost in the 16th century. However this is not a simple homogeneous roof type. Most examples are single-tier roofs with a single side purlin on each side of the roof (Fig 8.1), of which there are at least three variants. In addition there are two-tier versions with two tiers of purlins, of which there are a whole set of different subgroups combining a lower tier of queenposts with virtually every other roof type for the second tier (Figs 8.2 & 8.16).

Location

More than 250 East Anglian jowled queenpost roofs have been discovered in Suffolk, most of which are in the north east of the county, north of the Gipping Divide (see p140); they are absent from south, central and west Suffolk (Fig 8.3). This roof continues up into south east Norfolk, though we have no clear idea of the numbers there as, unlike Suffolk, roof types were not systematically noted in the 1980's Accelerated Resurvey of listed buildings in Norfolk. Also the area with a large number of queenposts - the Rural District of Depwade containing Harleston and Diss and now part of the modern South Norfolk District Council - was resurveyed before the Accelerated Resurvey and lacks even the detail of the later lists. The map at Figure 8.4, largely based on work by Stephen Heywood, gives an indication of the distribution of East Anglian queenpost roofs within Norfolk. They are mainly concentrated to the south of Norwich. It should be emphasised that the absence of East Anglian jowled queenpost roofs from south, central and west Suffolk is not due to a lack of surviving medieval and 16th century roofs; large numbers of historic roofs survive in these areas, mostly with coupled rafters, crownposts, or clasped or butt side purlins. Examples of the jowled East Anglian queenpost are relatively rare outside Suffolk and Norfolk – Essex has identified about three examples as mentioned by David

Fig 8.1: Single-tier queenpost roof
Wisteria Cottage, Hacheston, Suffolk
a transitional high end stack house of 1541
(photo by John Walker)

Fig 8.2: A two-tier queenpost roof at
Park Farm, Somerleyton, Suffolk
(photo by John Walker)

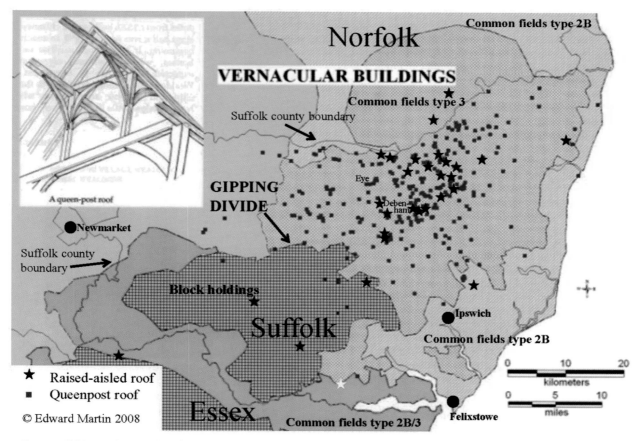

Common fields type 2B - number of common fields very variable and an individual's strips tend to be clustered in the vicinity of the holder's house

Common fields type 3 - common fields a minority part of the farmland and had largely disappeared by 16th century (For more information on field types see Martin & Satchell 2008, 20-25)

Gipping Divide - For a description of the Gipping Divide and its significance see page 140 below

Fig 8.3: Distribution of raised-aisled halls and queenpost roofs in Suffolk and types of historic fields

Fig 8.4: Location of some of Norfolk's queenpost roofs
Based mainly on Stephen Heywood's article (Heywood 2002) in Stenning & Andrews eds 2002
The buildings marked with a star at Denton and Harleston are raised-aisled halls

Stenning (two of which are at Figs 2.29 & 2.30) – and there is a small group in Cambridgeshire in the area to the west of Mildenhall in Suffolk. However there is one very distant outlier in Durham at Elvethall Manor, a two-tier version with a lower tier of jowled queenposts with square-set purlins and an upper tier of side purlins, set at the angle of the roof, clasped between the rafter and a raked-purlin strut rising from the collar. Martin Roberts suggested this may date to the late 14th century (Roberts M 2008, 32). Also, as David Stenning mentions in his paper, probably the earliest version of this roof is that over the Warden's Hall, Merton College, Oxford built in 1299-1300, another two-tier version with a crownpost forming the upper tier (Fig 2.26).

Most of the East Anglian jowled queenposts are very plain (Figs 8.1 & 8.2), including most of those over open halls. However there are a few examples where the queenposts were moulded, looking like crownposts with capitals, bases and a moulded shaft. These occur both over open halls, such as Mill Farm Cottage, Bedfield, Suffolk (Fig 8.5) and the early 15th century Messuage Farmhouse, Kenton, Suffolk (Fig 8.6), and occasionally over 16th century two storey buildings such as the sub-medieval house called 'The Guildhall' in Wrentham, Suffolk, a two storey house with its chimney stack at the high end of the hall (Fig 8.7).

Fig 8.6: Decorated queenpost on centre truss of open hall at Messuage Farmhouse, Kenton, Suffolk early 15th C

© John Walker

Fig 8.5: Centre truss of open hall of Mill Farm Cottage, Bedfield, Suffolk 15th C

Fig 8.7: Decorated queenpost on centre truss of two storey house 'The Guildhall', Wrentham, Suffolk 16th C

Origins

Despite the early two-tier roof of 1299-1300 at Merton College, jowled queenpost roofs did not appear in East Anglia until the late 14th century. The raised-aisled hall must have been their East Anglian grandparent (Fig 8.8). Raised-aisled halls are aisled halls which have the centre truss of the open hall raised up on to a dropped tie-beam in order to clear the open hall of arcade posts. The greatest concentration of them in England is in north east Suffolk and south Norfolk, in the same area as the jowled queenpost roofs (Fig 8.3). The two overlap in date in north Suffolk and south Norfolk – raised-aisled halls being built in the 14th to early 15th century with jowled queenposts appearing in the late 14th century and continuing until at least the late 16th century. The raised-aisled halls were relatively high status buildings whereas the jowled queenpost roofs extended much further down the social scale.

Many conventional aisled halls in Suffolk were converted to raised-aisled halls by inserting a dropped tiebeam in the centre truss of the open hall to carry the arcade posts, thus removing the these posts from the centre of the open hall (Fig 8.9). These conversions may have given added encouragement to the birth of the queenpost roof, though Essex also converted many conventional aisled halls into raised-aisles without being encouraged to build queenpost roofs.

Fig 8.9: Low Barn Cottage, Thorndon, Suffolk
An aisled hall converted to a raised-aisled hall in the 15th C

The position and height of the dropped tiebeam supporting the arcade posts of a raised-aisled hall vary from being well below the wall plates (Fig 8.8) to just below them as at The Hermitage, Frostenden, Suffolk (Fig 8.10). In the latter group the roof over the centre truss is very similar to a queenpost roof and on occasions it raises the question: at what point does a raised-aisle become a queenpost roof? It is clearly a raised-aisled hall when there are full height arcade posts in the hall's closed trusses, as at The Hermitage, Frostenden, or when the dropped tiebeam is well below the wall plates, as at Choppins Hill, Coddenham, Suffolk (Fig 8.8) and Baythorne Hall, Birdbrook, Essex (Fig 2.24b). But it is much less clear for houses like

Fig 8.8: Choppins Hill, Coddenham, Suffolk
A raised-aisled hall built about 1390

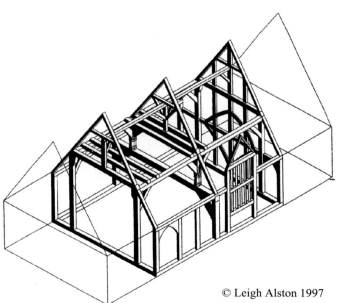

© Leigh Alston 1997

Fig 8.10: Reconstruction of the raised-aisled hall
The Hermitage, Frostenden, Suffolk viewed from NE
14th C

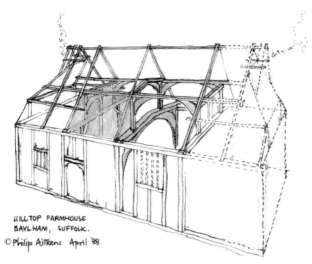

Fig 8.11: Reconstruction of Hilltop Farmhouse, Baylham, Suffolk. The two braces rising to the left from the posts on the central open truss have been omitted for clarity.

Hilltop Farmhouse, Baylham, Suffolk (Fig 8.11) which has queenposts on the closed trusses and, unlike The Hermitage, has no full-height arcade posts in these trusses. However it is clearly a queenpost roof when there is no dropped tiebeam and all the tiebeams are in normal assembly; it is not a raised-aisled roof as mistakenly described in the CBA Glossary (Alcock et al 1996, G16 & Fig F1B)[1].

Most raised-aisled halls in East Anglia have crownpost roofs above the nave and there is a small but important subgroup of two-tier jowled queenpost roofs in Suffolk and Norfolk which have a crownpost on top of a pair of queenposts. Therefore these belong with both roof types. It is also the clearest descendant of the high-class raised-aisled halls (Fig 8.16a).

The main late-medieval roof type in most of East Anglia was the crownpost, which was replaced by clasped and butt side purlins in the 16th century. The jowled queenpost in north East Anglia co-existed alongside all these roof types in the 15th and 16th centuries, providing an alternative roof form. This is demonstrated by a recent study of the timber-framed buildings of New Buckenham in south Norfolk by the Norfolk Historic Buildings Group. This shows there was a battle between roof types even in the centre of medieval queenpost country as the study found coupled rafter roofs, side purlins, crownposts and queenposts all existing side by side (Longcroft 2005).

The raised-aisled halls and queenpost roofs in Suffolk are north of what is called the Gipping Divide, a term coined by Edward Martin. In their study of East Anglian historic fields and landscape, Edward Martin and Max Satchell found there was a distinctive difference north and south of the River Gipping in the pattern of medieval fields, in the soil and in the shape and lay of the land (Fig 8.3) (Martin & Satchell 2008). Interestingly, looking back a little further, they found that Scandinavian place-names in East Anglia occur mainly to the north of the Gipping Divide, suggesting this was the effective boundary between the English south and the Scandinavian-influenced north. However Edward Martin warns that the true answer could be more complicated. He said that *"the distribution pattern of objectives associated with the Anglian folk in the Early Anglo-Saxon period was mainly to the north of the Divide, suggesting that the area to the south of it may originally have been controlled by the Saxons allied to the 'East Saxons' of Essex. More than this, the Divide is also very similar to the postulated Late Iron Age boundary between the Trinovantes (south) and the Iceni (north) tribes"* (Martin E 2008). Today the Gipping Divide equates more or less with the A14 road running across Suffolk from Felixstowe to Newmarket.

There are also a number of cultural differences north and south of the Divide, one of which is in historic carpentry. Not only are the raised-aisled halls and queenpost roofs mainly found north of the Gipping Divide, but there are differences north of the Divide compared with the south in the form of the passing braces in 13th and 14th century aisled halls; in the shape of wall braces used in 15th to 17th century houses and barns; in the form of the 16th and 17th century clasped side-purlin roofs (as described by David Stenning); in the early date - from at least the mid-15th century - when the exterior of the timber frame started to be covered in daub plaster north of the Divide; and in the very high incidences north of the Divide in the 16th and 17th centuries of sub-medieval two-storey houses with the chimney stack at the high end of the hall. In fact East Anglia north of the Gipping Divide probably has the highest concentration of high-end stack sub-medieval houses in England.

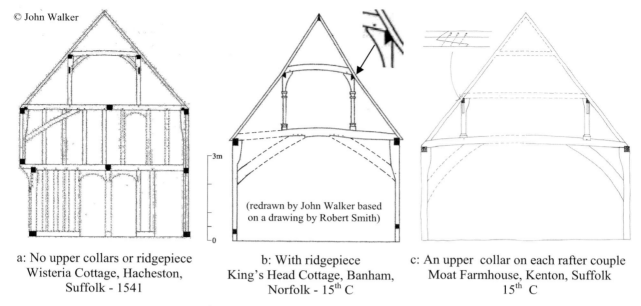

a: No upper collars or ridgepiece
Wisteria Cottage, Hacheston,
Suffolk - 1541

b: With ridgepiece
King's Head Cottage, Banham,
Norfolk - 15th C

(redrawn by John Walker based
on a drawing by Robert Smith)

c: An upper collar on each rafter couple
Moat Farmhouse, Kenton, Suffolk
15th C

Fig 8.12: Types of single-tier queenposts

Types of queenpost roofs

Single-Tier Queenposts

The single-tier jowled queenpost roof came in at least three variations (Fig 8.12). The simplest, and the one found all over north east Suffolk and south Norfolk, has two jowled queenposts sitting on the tiebeam of the principal trusses, each supporting a square-set purlin with a collar above them, and common rafters with no collars as in Figures 8.1 and 8.12a. Other roofs, such as King's Head Cottage, Banham, Norfolk (Fig 8.12b), have a ridgepiece which in profile can be narrow, triangular or square, or some hybrid of these shapes. The third variation has coupled rafters with an upper collar about one-third of the way down the roof on every rafter couple and widely spaced queenposts, such as at Moat Farmhouse, Kenton, Suffolk (Fig 8.12c). However no queenpost roof has so far been found with both collars and a ridgepiece. The collars are more likely to be found in Suffolk, and the ridgepiece is the more popular type in Norfolk and the northern part of east Suffolk.

Each carpentry workshop would have had favourite variations of this roof type, which would have evolved from one generation to the next. For a bigger and more successful workshop the sphere of influence would be greater. It is clear that some Suffolk workshops favoured collars, probably influenced by a previous 14th century generation who exclusively

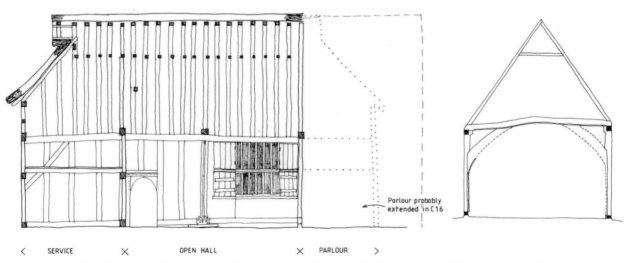

Parlour probably
extended in C16

< SERVICE   ×   OPEN HALL   ×   PARLOUR   >

Fig 8.13: Coupled rafter roof over Upper Spring Cottage, Coddenham, Suffolk - an open hall house
15th C

used collar rafter roofs without queenposts. Immediately north of Ipswich there are few queenpost roofs; here the favourite medieval roof was the simple collar rafter roof without any purlins (Fig 8.13). But to the north of these, particularly around Eye and Debenham, queenposts roofs with common rafters with high collars are found (Fig 8.5). It seems likely that the popularity of these collar rafter couples above Ipswich influenced their use over queenposts further north in Suffolk.

This raises the question: was there also a group of Norfolk carpenters who inherited a collarless ridgepiece tradition from their 14th century forefathers? In the absence of surviving 14th century vernacular roofs in Norfolk we must look at church roofs. There was a developing tradition in Norfolk of daring principal trusses either lacking collars, or with a collar just below the ridge (Fig 8.14). Purlins tenoned into the principal rafters carried the common rafters. There were no collars on the common rafters, and the roofs have survived without them, whether or not they had hammerbeams or tiebeams.

One important characteristic distinguishing the collared queenpost roofs from the other two single-tier types is that the collared roofs are likely to have widely-spaced queenposts. These support purlins which are less than half-way up the roof slope. The other two types - those with

Fig 8.14: Nave roof of St Mary Magdalen,
Pulham St. Mary, Norfolk
15th C
(from Brandon 1849, plate XXVII)

Fig 8.15: Queenpost roof of barn at Crows Hall, Debenham, Suffolk
1478d
note the fractured tiebeam.

142

a ridgepiece and those without collars or ridgepiece - have taller queenposts supporting purlins about half-way up the roof slope. The shape of the square-set purlins varies on all types from being square or with a deep-and-narrow profile (Fig 8.5), to like those over the King's Head Cottage, Banham, Norfolk (Fig 8.12b); also all types may or may not be splayed on the back to follow the roof pitch to the point where they are triangular (Fig 8.12c). The deep-and-narrow purlins tend to occur on the queenpost roofs with a ridgepiece, but are not confined to this type of queenpost roof. Larger 16th century roofs in Suffolk could continue to have big square-set purlins, notably over barns.

Two-tier queenposts (Fig 8.16)

Wide buildings presented problems when built with a single-tier queenpost roof. In the more southerly parts of East Anglia, barns on large farms would have been aisled in the 15th century. Instead, John Framlingham of Crows Hall, Debenham, Suffolk chose in 1478d (VA42 forthcoming) to build his barn with a very wide span (8.5m (28ft)) using queenpost trusses (Fig 8.15). Like a similar roof at Badley Hall, Badley, Suffolk, the tiebeams were unable to cope with such a load and repairs and extra support was needed for the tiebeams. In some other wide queenpost roofs the span of the purlins was too great and the roof broke its back in other ways. Again and again, these roofs

a: Two-tier queenpost roof with crownpost - Buck's Hall, Rishangles, Suffolk 15th C

© Mark Barnard 1995

b: Two-tier queenpost roof with kingpost and ridgepeice at Poplar Farmhouse, Oakley, Suffolk late 15th C
(Redrawn from sketch by Sylvia Colman)

c: Two-tier queenpost roof with clasped side purlins in barn at Eye, Suffolk. This design marks the decline of the queenpost tradition mid 16th C

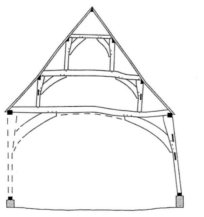

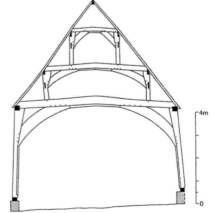

d: Two tiers of queenposts over Dairy Farm Barn, Newton Flotman, Norfolk 15th C
(after Robert Smith)

Fig 8.16: Types of two-tier queenpost roofs

143

have failed because the designer over-reached himself.

The solution was to build a second tier of purlins and a few barns with a wide span were given two tiers of purlins with the upper tier of purlins propped by a second set of queenposts - a greatly improved design for large roofs. Examples include the barn at Dairy Farm, Newton Flotman, Norfolk (Fig 8.16d) and a similar one at Rook Hall, Eye, Suffolk, which may be earlier (and better) than the 1478d barn at Debenham. This, very sensible, upper tier was used again in the 16th century for another massive barn at Roydon Hall, Creeting St. Peter, Suffolk and also at the barn at Park Farm, Somerleyton, Suffolk (Fig 8.2).

Two-tier queenpost roofs gave medieval carpenters great opportunities for innovation which they seized with alacrity (Fig 8.16). In addition to an upper tier of queenposts, they built queenpost roofs where the upper tier was a crownpost as at Buck's Hall, Rishangles, Suffolk (Fig 8.16a), was a kingpost as at Poplar Farmhouse, Oakley, Suffolk (Fig 8.16b) or was a pair of clasped side purlins as at a barn at Eye, Suffolk (Fig 8.16c).

Of these, probably one of the most important subgroups is those with a kingpost sitting on the collar above the queenposts and supporting a ridgepiece (Fig 8.16b). A number are concentrated in and around the town of Eye in Suffolk. The Honour of Eye was a powerful medieval administrative unit, which may partly explain the special character of the architecture in this area. Most two-tier examples around Eye are late 15th century or c.1500 - one or two are dated by documents - and they were used mainly over guildhalls and wide open halls. At The Old Vicarage, Hoxne, Suffolk, four miles to the north east of Eye, is an extraordinary roof of about 1500 with closely-spaced trusses employing queenposts, arch-braced collarbeams, and long or short kingposts in turn. There could well have been hammerbeams as well but we cannot be sure as the lower parts of some trusses are missing. The Guildhall at Eye was built on land purchased in 1495. The incomplete roof has queenposts at each truss, and there were probably kingposts above on alternate trusses to support a ridgepiece. A few two-tier queenpost roofs with kingposts were built

elsewhere in East Anglia and there may be one at Riverside Farm, Forncett St Mary, Norfolk, tree-ring dated to 1645d, but the published information is insufficient to be certain that it has jowled queenposts (Longcroft 2009, 127).

As outlined above, virtually every other roof type has been combined with queenposts in the two-tier roofs, including a few composite roofs combining queenposts with full crownpost, the crownposts rising from the tiebeam as at Park Farmhouse, Hoxne, Suffolk and 22 Castle Street, Eye, Suffolk (Fig 8.17), rather than rising from the collar as at Buck's Hall, Rishangles, Suffolk (Fig 8.16a).

Fig 8.17: No 22 Castle Street, Eye, Suffolk
a town house combining queenposts
and full height crownposts
early 16th C

Dating Queenpost Roofs

The plainness of queenpost roofs makes them very difficult to date, and relatively few have been tree-ring dated. A tree-ring date for the barn at Wingfield College, Wingfield, Suffolk of 1527d (VA30, 88) was earlier than expected (Fig 8.18), although its roof closely resembles that of 1478d at Crows Hall (Fig 8.15). Both are single-tier queenposts roofs, the former with a ridgepiece, the latter without one. Wingfield was funded by Charles Brandon, Duke of Suffolk, before the College's dissolution. It would be interesting to determine whether queenpost-roofed barns developed as early as those over houses. However this seems unlikely given the strong tradition of aisled barns in East Anglia.

Summary

Queenpost roofs consisting of jowled queen-posts with square-set purlins and a collar above the purlins are not completely unique to north East Anglia but it has the highest concentration of such roofs in the country. They look like an aisled building set on the tiebeams and are sometimes mistakenly called a raised-aisled roof. They are not; they are a queenpost roof, but to distinguish them from other queenpost roofs which are unjowled, have the purlins set to the plane of the roof and are not topped by a collar, it is suggested that they are called East Anglian queenpost roofs, in the same way that medieval open-hall houses with recessed fronts are called Wealden Houses even though they are found over a much wider area (Fig 1.38).

What is perhaps surprising is the sheer variety in this roof form in the relatively small area of north East Anglia. Probably no other roof type has this level of innovation, even when looking across the whole country. Because of these variations, care needs to be taken when recording East Anglian queenpost roofs as today houses often have a ceiling above the side purlins, making it difficult or impossible to see if there are collars, crownposts, ridgepieces, etc above the collar over the queenposts of the principle trusses. To improve our knowledge of the distribution of these different queenpost roofs, published drawings of queenpost roofs showing no features above the collar need to indicate if the upper part of the roof was visible to the recorder.

later insertions

later insertions

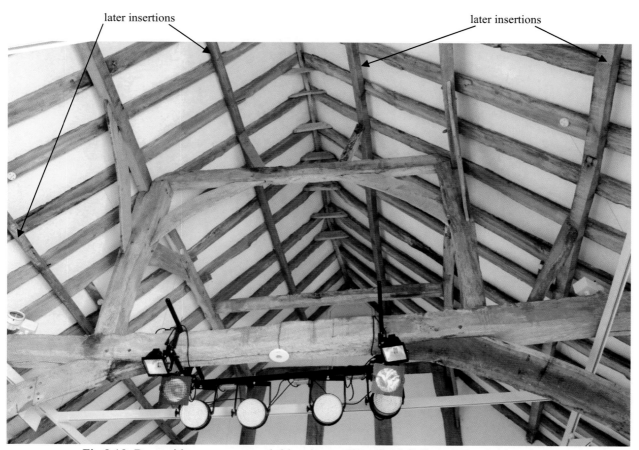

Fig 8.18: Barn with queenposts and ridgepiece at Wingfield College, Wingfield, Suffolk
1527d

(photo by John Walker)

Footnote

[1] **Note by Editor.** The CBA Glossary does not include a definition of a raised-aisled hall. It does include an entry for a 'raised aisle truss' which it defines as one which 'has a complete aisled structure standing on a tiebeam', and illustrates this with a drawing of the centre truss of Lewknor Church Farm, Oxfordshire as shown opposite in Fig 8.19 (Alcock et al 1996, G16 & Fig 1B). However, this is a two-tier queenpost roof with an upper tier of clasped side purlins (Figs 8.19 & 8.20).

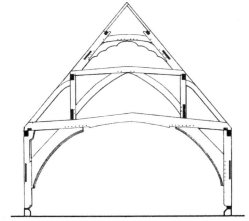

Fig 8.19: Centre truss of Lewknor Church Farm, Oxfordshire
1350/1d (VA21, 47)

(redrawn from Mercer 1975, 194)

Fig 8.20: Roof of Lewknor Church Farm, Oxfordshire
1350/1d (VA21, 47)

(Picture by John Walker)

9 GLOSSARY

By John Walker

(Unless stated otherwise, all drawings are by the author)
(* indicates that the text in " " is taken from the *CBA Illustrated Glossary,* Alcock, Barley, Dixon & Meeson 1996.
SMALL CAPITALS indicate cross-references to entries in this Glossary.)

A-frame: See TRUSS

aisle*: "The side compartment of a house, hall or barn, separated from the main body of the building by an ARCADE." See Fig 9.1.

aisled hall: A house with an open hall and side aisles separated from the central nave by an ARCADE. See Fig 9.1.

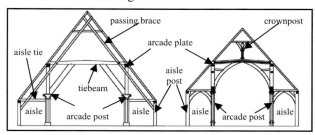

Fig 9.1: Aisled buildings

arcade*: "Division in a building consisting of a row of posts"/columns "and its superstructure, between the nave or central space of an aisled building and its AISLES." See Fig 9.1.

arcade plate*: "Plate set along the tops of ARCADE POSTS in an aisled building." See Fig 9.1.

arcade post*: "One of the posts in an ARCADE" which supports an ARCADE PLATE. See Fig 9.1.

arch brace: Timber rising up from a post to a horizontal timber such as a TIEBEAM, COLLAR, mid-rail or WALL PLATE. Also called an *up-brace* or *head brace*. See Fig 9.2.

ashlar piece*: "Vertical timber forming a triangle between the rafter and the inner face of the wall" or with a horizontal timber such as a COLLAR. Also called an *ashlar post*. See Fig 9.3b.

assembly: See Fig 9.2.

a. normal assembly: Method of construction in which the TIEBEAM sits on top of the WALL PLATES as in Fig 9.6 and in the CLOSED TRUSS in Fig 9.2.

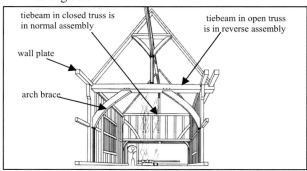

Fig 9.2: Normal & reverse assembly tiebeams at Brick House, Debden, Essex, a wealden house

b. reverse assembly: Method of construction where the WALL PLATES rest on top of the TIE-BEAM, i.e. the tiebeam is under the wall plates, as for the tiebeam in the OPEN TRUSS in the foreground of Fig 9.2.

base cruck*: "A CRUCK whose BLADES reach only as high as the first transverse member ..... excluding those, as in Figs 3.4 & 3.5c, with blades terminating in an apparently 'cut-off' fashion above the COLLAR"

There are four main variants of base cruck construction, as shown in Fig 9.3:

a: a double TIEBEAM clasps the ARCADE PLATE,

b: a single TIEBEAM in REVERSE ASSEMBLY, i.e. under the ARCADE PLATES,

c: a single TIEBEAM on top of the ARCADE PLATES in NORMAL ASSEMBLY,

d: various hybrids with only one full TIEBEAM which is on top of the ARCADE PLATES.

The first two can be assembled on the ground and reared like a TRUE CRUCK, but for the third and fourth, with their tiebeam in normal assembly, each blade has to be erected separately, the plates then fitted on top of the blades before laying the tiebeam on top of these plates as in a BOX-FRAMED building. There are substantial numbers of both 'reared' and 'box-framed' base crucks; further research is needed to determine which is in the majority.

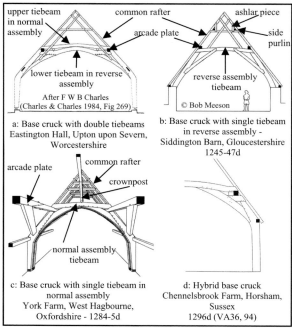

Fig 9.3: Base crucks

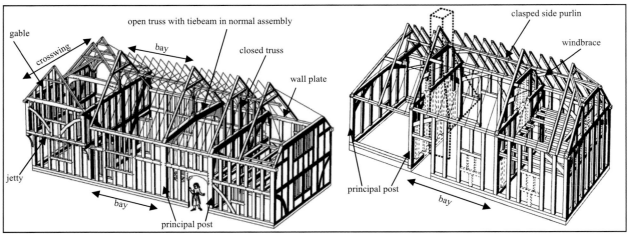

a: Box-framed building with crownpost roof
Valley Farm, Flatford, Suffolk
15th C

b: Box-framed building with side purlin roof
also called *post & truss construction* (not recommended)
Wynters Cottage, Magdalen Laver, Essex
16th C

Fig 9.4: Box-framing

bay: The area of a timber-framed building between TRUSSES. See Figs 9.4a & b.

bent principals: See PRINCIPAL RAFTER WITH CURVED OR BENT FEET.

block: See YOKE & Fig 9.26a.

box-framing*: "Form of construction in which the roof trusses are carried on a frame composed of posts, TIEBEAMS and WALL PLATES." See Fig 9.4. Box-framed buildings with SIDE-PURLIN roofs, as in Fig 9.4b, are sometimes referred to as of *'post and truss construction'* - not recommended as the framing of a building is not dependent on whether it has a CROWNPOST or SIDE-PURLIN roof. There is no change to the frame when, as happened with many historic buildings, the crownpost roof was replaced with a side-purlin roof.

closed truss: See TRUSS CLOSED

collar*: "A transverse timber connecting rafters or CRUCK BLADES at a point above their feet and below the apex of the roof." See Figs 9.5, 9.6, 9.7, 9.8 & 9.10.

collar plate*: "Plate resting on COLLARS", i.e. the plate is on top of the collars. See Fig 4.7.

collar purlin: A longitudinal timber set square to the ground which passes under the middle of, and supports, the COLLARS of COMMON RAFTERS. Usually, but not always, supported by a CROWNPOST or KING STRUT. See Figs 9.6 & 9.10.

collar rafter roof: A roof consisting entirely of pairs of COMMON RAFTERS linked by a COLLAR, and with no PURLINS.

common rafters*: "Rafters of uniform size regularly spaced along the length of a roof, or intermediate rafters between PRINCIPAL RAFTERS; a pair of common rafters is a *rafter couple*." See Figs 9.6, 9.11a, 9.21b & 9.23.

common rafter roof: A roof consisting of COMMON RAFTERS of uniform scantling, that is of uniform size, without any PRINCIPAL RAFTERS. Also called *coupled rafter roofs* or *trussed rafter roofs*.

crosswing*: "Section of house roofed at right angles to the adjacent main range, usually the hall." See Figs 9.4a, 9.9 & 9.17b.

crown strut*: "An upright timber similar to a CROWNPOST, but not supporting a plate" or PURLIN. See Fig 9.5.

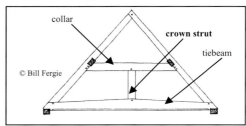

Fig 9.5: Example of crown strut
1 King Street, Odiham, Hampshire
1447d

crownpost*: "The upright timber standing on a TIEBEAM or occasionally a COLLAR, supporting the COLLAR PURLIN (also sometimes called a *crown plate*) and not rising beyond a collar." See Fig 9.6.

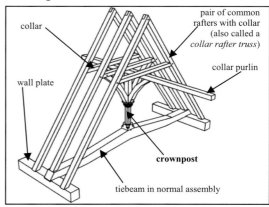

Fig 9.6: Crownpost

148

cruck*: See Figs 9.7 & 9.8.

  a: true cruck - Fig 9.7 - "consists of a pair of timbers (blades) straight or curved, serving as the PRINCIPAL RAFTERS of a roof, and stretching to a point at or close to the apex of the roof from a level well down the side walls."

  b: jointed cruck - Fig 9.8 - "is a cruck truss whose blades are composed of two pieces of timber joined near the wall head in a variety of ways" as shown in Fig 5.11.

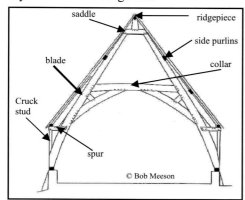

Fig 9.7: True cruck
Leigh Court Barn, Worcestershire
*c.*1344d

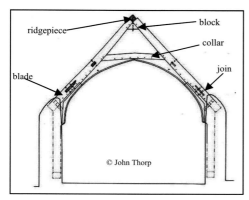

Fig 9.8: Jointed cruck
Cleavanger, Nymet Rowland, Devon
1396-1400d

cruck blade*: "One of the two principal timbers of a cruck truss." See Fig 9.7 & 9.8.

diminished principal rafter*: "In a roof with CLASPED SIDE PURLINS, it is a PRINCIPAL RAFTER cut back above the side purlin to the depth of a COMMON RAFTER." See Figs 9.18 & 9.19.

double arch-braced truss*: See entries for TRUSS and for WAGON ROOF.

gable: The triangular top section between the TIEBEAM and the rafters of an exterior side wall with a pitched roof. See Figs 9.4a & 9.9.

gablet*: "A small gable above a roof hip." Fig 9.9.

hammer beam roof truss: A roof truss where the centre of the 'tiebeam' is cut out; the ends of the 'tiebeam' are called *hammer beams* which support vertical posts called *HAMMER POSTS*. See Figs 2.35a & b and 4.22.

Fig 9.9: Example of gable, gablet, jetty and crosswing on Valley Farm, Flatford, Suffolk

hammer post*: "A vertical timber resting on a hammer beam and forming a triangle between it and a PRINCIPAL RAFTER." See Figs 2.35a & b.

hammer beam: false*: A false hammer beam is a "transverse timber resembling a hammer beam but without a HAMMER POST above; instead, it is braced to a PRINCIPAL RAFTER or a COLLAR." See Figs 1.19 & 2.35c.

jetty*: "Cantilevered overhang of one storey (Fig 9.9), or of a GABLE, over the storey below it."

jowl*: "Expansion of the inner face of the top of a wall post to accommodate housings for the WALL PLATE and TIEBEAM". See Fig 9.20. Also the expansion at the top of
  a. a CROWNPOST - see Fig 2.10;
  b. a KINGPOST - see Figs 6.17 & 7.15;
  c. an 'EAST ANGLIAN' QUEENPOST - see Fig 9.14.

kerb piece*: Another name for a TRUNCATED PRINCIPAL RAFTER.

king strut*: "A vertical timber standing on a COLLAR or TIEBEAM and rising to the apex of a roof without a RIDGEPIECE." See Fig 9.10. A king strut sometimes supports a COLLAR PURLIN as shown in Fig 9.10.

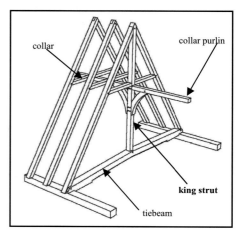

Fig 9.10: King strut

149

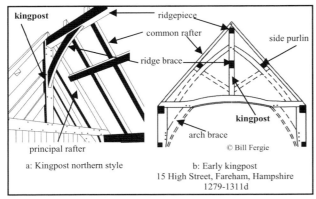

Fig 9.11: Kingposts

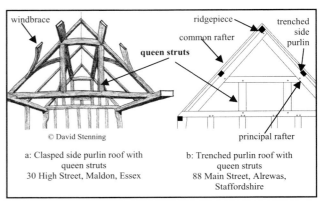

Fig 9.13: Examples of queen struts

kingpost*: "An upright timber standing on a TIE-BEAM or COLLAR and rising to the apex of a roof to support a RIDGEPIECE - see Fig 9.11; where there is no ridgepiece, it should be called a KING STRUT" as in Fig 9.10.

knee brace*: "A very short brace (bracket) between post and TIEBEAM, or post and WALL PLATE", or between a post and a square-set PURLIN - see Fig 2.14. "Similar timbers used horizontally (normally between wall plates and tiebeams) are corner braces"; also called *angle ties*.

normal assembly*: See ASSEMBLY.

notched lap joint: A lap joint with a notch cut into one side to prevent withdrawal. See Fig 9.12.

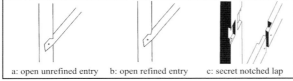

Fig 9.12: Types of notched lap joints

open truss: See TRUSS OPEN.

passing brace*: "A long and usually straight timber, halved across other timbers, especially running from a wall post or aisle post across the TIEBEAM to the opposing rafter." See Fig 9.1.

post and truss: See BOX-FRAMING & Fig 9.4b.

principal post*: "A vertical timber, usually substantial, and usually forming part of the main framework" of a truss. See Fig 9.4.

principal rafter*: "An inclined timber in a roof truss supporting a PURLIN." Principal rafters are usually of a larger scantling, that is size, than the COMMON RAFTERS.

principal rafter with curved or bent feet*: A PRINCIPAL RAFTER "which has its lower end curved". See Fig 5.48.

principal rafter, tiebeam & collar truss: See TRUSS.

purlin: Longitudinal timber giving support to the COMMON RAFTERS in a roof. SIDE PURLINS are usually set in the plane of the roof, but are

sometimes set square, as in 'EAST ANGLIAN' QUEENPOST ROOFS. COLLAR PURLINS are set square.

purlins: staggered*: "PURLINS set out on different alignments in adjacent BAYS." See Fig 5.48.

queen struts*: "Paired struts framed between TIE-BEAM and COLLAR, and not supporting a longitudinal timber." See Fig 9.13. These can be found in all types of SIDE-PURLIN roofs that have a TIEBEAM and COLLAR: i.e. in roofs with:
a. CLASPED SIDE PURLINS (Fig 9.13a),
b. BUTT & THREADED PURLINS (Fig 9.21) &
c. TRENCHED PURLINS (Fig 9.13b).

queenposts*: "Paired posts set on a TIEBEAM and directly supporting plates or PURLINS." Variants include:

a: 'East Anglian' queenpost roofs: Queenposts with jowled tops, or front UP-STANDS, clasping a square-set SIDE PURLIN and tenoned into a COLLAR on top of the PURLINS, creating a roof looking like an AISLED HALL rising above the TIEBEAMS. (But just as a pair of CRUCK BLADES raised on to a tiebeam are called BENT PRINCIPALS or PRINCIPALS WITH CURVED FEET, these are queenposts not AR-CADE POSTS.) Chapter 8 suggests these be called *'East Anglian' queenposts* as the highest concentration is in this region. See Fig 9.14.

b: Two-tier 'East Anglian' queenpost roofs: Two-tier roof, the lower tier of 'EAST AN-GLIAN' QUEENPOSTS with square-set SIDE PURLINS, while the upper tier can be virtually any other roof type (see Chapter 8), including

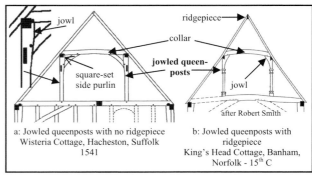

Fig 9.14: Single-tier 'East Anglian' queenposts

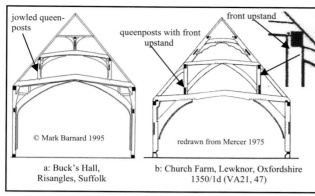

a: Buck's Hall,
Risangles, Suffolk

b: Church Farm, Lewknor, Oxfordshire
1350/1d (VA21, 47)

Fig 9.15: Two-tier 'East Anglian' style queenpost roofs

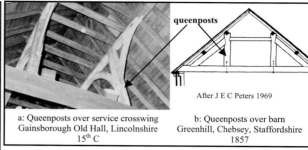

a: Queenposts over service crosswing
Gainsborough Old Hall, Lincolnshire
15th C

b: Queenposts over barn
Greenhill, Chebsey, Staffordshire
1857

Fig 9.16: Queenposts with no collar and unjowled

another set of jowled 'EAST ANGLIAN' QUEEN-POSTS. The CBA Glossary mistakenly classi-fies these as raised-aisle trusses; they are two-tier queenpost roofs. See Fig 9.15.

c: *queenposts (no collar & unjowled)*:
These differ from 'EAST ANGLIAN' QUEENPOST ROOFS (Figs 9.14 & 9.15) as the queenposts are unjowled and there is no COLLAR above them. See Fig 9.16. Usually, but not always, the SIDE PURLINS in these roofs are set in the plane of the roof, not square-set. For some, each rafter couple has a COLLAR and the queenposts act like a pair of CROWNPOSTS (Fig 9.16a).

rafter brace*: "Rafter running obliquely across a series of COMMON RAFTERS." See Fig 1.10.

rafters: common: See COMMON RAFTERS.

raised-aisled hall: An AISLED HALL with the AR-CADE POSTS in the centre truss of the open hall raised up on to a dropped tiebeam. The dropped tiebeam can be set low down the aisle posts as in Fig 9.17a, or immediately under the WALL PLATES in REVERSE ASSEMBLY as in Fig 9.17b. In both types there will normally be full height ARCADE POSTS in other trusses in the building as in Fig 9.17b. Where there are no

full height arcade posts it may be a QUEENPOST roof building. See Chapter 8 for further discus-sion.

raked-purlin strut: A RAKING STRUT which direct-ly supports a SIDE PURLIN. There is no agreed term to distinguish this type from a raking strut which does not support a side purlin. In Chap-ter 3 this strut supporting a side purlin is de-scribed as a 'raking queenpost', a very clear and unambiguous description, but one the CBA Glossary dislikes as a 'post' is defined as a vertical timber. Elsewhere in this publication a raking strut supporting a purlin is called a raked-purlin strut. See Fig 9.18.

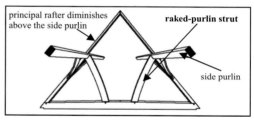

Fig 9.18: Raked-purlin strut

raking struts*: "Paired struts, straight or curved, set at an angle to the TIEBEAM and framed into the PRINCIPAL RAFTER" and which do not sup-port SIDE PURLINS. See Fig 9.19 overleaf.

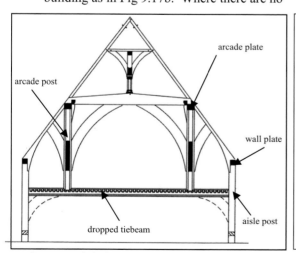

a: Centre truss of raised-aisled hall with dropped tiebeam well below
wall plates.
Baythorne Hall, Birdbrook, Essex
1341/2d

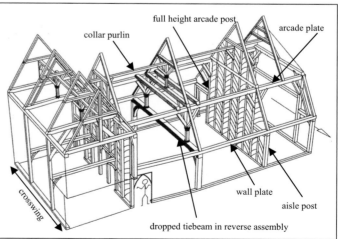

b: Raised-aisled hall with centre truss having a dropped tiebeam in reverse assembly
(that is immediately under the wall plates), with full arcade posts in the closed trusses.
Wymondleybury, Little Wymondley, Hertfordshire
1378/9d (VA37, 107)

Fig 9.17: Raised-aisled halls

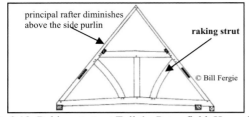

Fig 9.19: Raking struts at Tully's, Petersfield, Hampshire 1442d

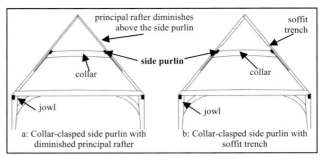

a: Collar-clasped side purlin with diminished principal rafter
b: Collar-clasped side purlin with soffit trench

Fig 9.22: Collar-clasped side purlins

reverse assembly: See ASSEMBLY & Fig 9.2.

ridgepiece*: "General term for the longitudinal timber at the apex of a roof (the term 'Ridge' alone is not recommended). The angle at which the ridgepiece is set may be indicated by the terms *ridge purlin* (set diamond-wise) and *ridge plate* (set square). Very thin ridgepieces, set upright, are sometimes termed *ridge planks"* or *ridge boards.*

saddle*: See YOKE & Fig 9.26b.

sans purlin roof: A COMMON RAFTER ROOF without any PURLINS. The common rafter couples may, or may not, have COLLARS. See Fig 9.20.

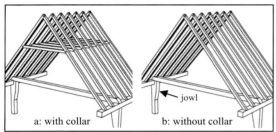

a: with collar   b: without collar

Fig 9.20: Sans purlin roofs
(uniform scantling roofs without purlins)

scissor brace*: Crossing braces which are not parallel to the rafters and which are "halved or lapped across each other, tying pairs of rafters together". See Figs 2.8, 4.6 & 7.19.

side purlins: A longitudinal timber running down the side of the rafters giving support to the COMMON RAFTERS and situated between the WALL PLATE and the ridge. There can be one or more on each side of the roof. Side purlins can be back, butt, clasped, threaded or trenched:

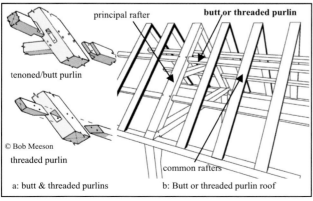

a: butt & threaded purlins   b: Butt or threaded purlin roof

Fig 9.21: Butt/tenoned and threaded side purlin roofs

a: back side purlin*: A side purlin "carried on the back of the PRINCIPAL RAFTER."

b: butt side purlin: A side purlin which is tenoned into the PRINCIPAL RAFTER. Also called a *tenoned purlin.* See Figs 9.21a & b.

c: clasped side purlin*: Side purlin "supported by a COLLAR (Fig 9.22), QUEENPOST or RAKING STRUT (Fig 9.18) and resting against the soffit of a PRINCIPAL RAFTER." Figs 9.22a & b illustrate collar-clasped side purlins. In 9.22a the principal rafter diminishes above the side purlin. In 9.22b a trench is cut into the soffit of the principal rafter immediately above the side purlin - the shape of which varies - to allow the side purlin to be fitted.

d: threaded side purlin*: A side purlin which "passes through a hole in a PRINCIPAL RAFTER and is usually scarfed at that point." It can be difficult to tell the difference between a butt purlin and a threaded purlin if close inspection is not possible. See Fig 9.21a.

e: trenched side purlin*: A purlin which "sits in a trench across the back of a PRINCIPAL RAFTER." See Fig 9.23.

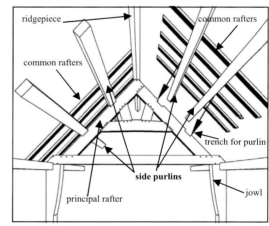

Fig 9.23: Exploded drawing of trenched side purlin roof

soulace*: Brace, usually straight, "from rafter to COLLAR in a COMMON RAFTER ROOF". See Figs 2.12, 3.8 & 4.5.

spur or cruck spur*: "Short piece of timber halved across a CRUCK BLADE, either carrying a WALL PLATE or attached to the cruck stud." See Fig 9.7.

tension brace*: "A brace running from a vertical to a lower horizontal timber." Also called a *down brace* or *foot brace*. See Fig 9.24.

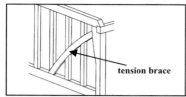

Fig 9.24: Tension brace
also called *down brace* or *foot brace*

tiebeam*: "Main transverse timber connecting the tops of walls or ARCADE POSTS and ARCADE PLATES - see Fig 9.1, 9.2, 9.3 & 9.6; also the main transverse timber of a CRUCK truss."

true cruck*: See CRUCK & Fig 9.7.

truncated principal rafter*: "A short PRINCIPAL RAFTER running between TIEBEAM and COLLAR", and often carrying a SIDE PURLIN on its back. See Fig 9.25. Also called a *kerb piece* or *kerb principal*. There are a number of different types as set out in Fig 6.10.

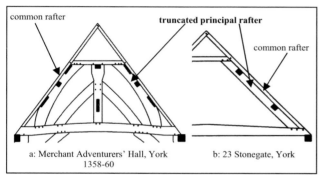

a: Merchant Adventurers' Hall, York 1358-60   b: 23 Stonegate, York

Fig 9.25: Truncated principal rafter roofs

truss: A combination of timbers constructed at BAY intervals which form a rigid cross-frame consisting of a pair of PRINCIPAL POSTS supporting WALL PLATES, a TIEBEAM or COLLAR, and a pair of rafters. See Fig 9.4a.
Some of the different types of trusses are:
a: A-frame truss: a truss with PRINCIPAL RAFTERS where the TIEBEAM is replaced by a COLLAR. Sometimes the JOWL on the principal post extends up to the principal rafter - see Figs 2.43 & 2.44.
b: arch-braced collar truss: A truss consisting of a pair of PRINCIPAL RAFTERS and a COLLAR with ARCH BRACES rising from the rafters up to the collar. See Figs 4.18a & b.
c: double arch-braced truss*: "A truss in which two pairs of ARCH BRACES form a continuous curve from the wall heads or below to meet in the centre of the collar." See Fig 5.14.
d: principal rafter, tiebeam & collar truss: A truss consisting of a pair of PRINCIPAL RAFTERS with a COLLAR, sitting on a TIEBEAM, and carrying SIDE PURLINS. The side purlins on these

trusses can be BACK, BUTT (Fig 9.21b), CLASPED (Fig 9.22), THREADED (Fig 9.21) or TRENCHED (Figs 9.13b & 9.23), and the trusses can have any type of struts - QUEEN STRUTS, CROWN STRUT, RAKING STRUTS or no struts.
e: truss closed*: "A truss in which spaces between timbers are filled, as between rooms and at the end of a building." See Figs 9.2 & 9.4a.
f: truss open*: "A truss in which spaces are left open, as in the centre of a hall of two bays or in an undivided building such as a barn." See Fig 9.4a.

trussed rafter roof: See COMMON RAFTER ROOF.

upstand: Where a post supporting a plate is wider than the plate and extends up either behind or in front of the post. The part extending up the side of the plate is called an 'upstand'. A front upstand is where the upstand is on the interior side of the plate and acts like a JOWL - see Fig 9.15b. A rear upstand is where the upstand is on the exterior side of the plate - see Fig 1.8.

wagon roof*: "Consists of a close-set series of DOUBLE ARCH BRACED TRUSSES (generally of COMMON RAFTER form), giving the appearance of a barrel vault." See Fig 5.14.

wall plate*: "Longitudinal timber, set square to the ground on top of a wall frame or a masonry wall, on which the roof trusses rest." See Figs 9.2 & 9.4a.

wealden house*: "Type of medieval house, concentrated in but not confined to the Weald, with an open hall in the middle and a two storeyed BAY at each end, roofed in line. The upper floors of the end bays are JETTIED to the front and the eaves are continuous, so the hall roof projects in front of its wall and is carried on a flying WALL PLATE." See Fig 1.38.

windbrace*: "A brace in the plane of a roof, usually tying together a PRINCIPAL RAFTER and a SIDE PURLIN or RIDGEPIECE." See Fig 9.13a.

yoke*: "Short timber linking two pieces of timber, e.g. the apex of CRUCK BLADES" - see Fig 9.26c. This contrasts with two other methods of linking cruck apexes:
a: the **Block*,** "a small piece of timber occupying the angle between two other timbers, eg in a cruck apex" - see Fig 9.26a, and
b: a **Saddle*,** "a short timber set on top of two CRUCK BLADES" - see Fig 9.26b.

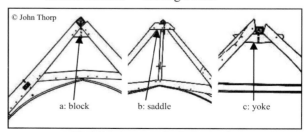

a: block   b: saddle   c: yoke

Fig 9.26: Apex methods for crucks

10   BIBLIOGRAPHY

Addyman P V & Hall R A 1991, *Urban structures and defence. Lloyds Bank, Pavement and other sites, with a survey of defences north-east of the Ouse*, York Archaeological Trust / Council for British Archaeology

Alcock N W 1966, A Devon farm: Bury Barton, Lapford, *Transactions of the Devonshire Association*, **98**, 105-131

Alcock N W 1968, Devonshire farmhouses – Part I, *Transactions of the Devonshire Association*, **100**, 13-28

Alcock N W 1972, Devon farmhouses – Part 1V, *Transactions of the Devonshire Association*, **104**, 35-56

Alcock N W 1981, *Cruck construction: an introduction and catalogue*, CBA Research Report **42**

Alcock N W 1982, The hall of the Knights Templar at Temple Balsall, West Midlands, *Med. Arch.* **26**, 155-58

Alcock N W 1997, A response to: cruck distribution: a social explanation by Eric Mercer, *Vernacular Architecture* **28**, 92-93.

Alcock N W 2006, The origin of crucks: Innocence or naiveté? A response, *Vernacular Architecture* **37**, 51-53

Alcock N W 2007, A rejoinder, *Vernacular Architecture* **38**, 11-14

Alcock N W 2008, F Épaud, De la Charpente Romane à la charpente Gothique en Normandie. Évolution des techniques et des structures de charpenterie aux XIIe-XIIIe siècles (2007), Review in *Med. Arch.* **52**, 448-449

Alcock N W 2010, The distribution and dating of wealden houses, *Vernacular Architecture* **41**, 37-44.

Alcock N W & Barley M W 1972, Medieval roofs with base crucks and short principals, *Antiq. J.* **52**, 132-68

Alcock N W, Barley M W, Dixon P W, & Meeson R A 1996, *Recording Timber-Framed Buildings; An Illustrated Glassary*, Council for British Archaeology Practical Handbook No 5 (Revised Edition)

Alcock N W & Meeson R A 1997, *150 High Street, Henley in Arden*, Rep. No. 97/06, unpublished client report

Alcock N W & Meeson R A 1999, *Mancetter Manor, Warwickshire*, Rep. No. 99/15, unpublished client report

Alcock N W & Meeson R A 2007, Baddesley Clinton: architectural responses to social circumstances, *Antiq. J.* **87**, 295-345

Alcock N W & Meeson R A 2009, Radiocarbon dating of a reused cruck blade from Warwickshire and its implications for the typology of cruck construction, *Vernacular Architecture* **40**, 96-102

Alcock N W, Meeson R A & Meeson E J 2007, *Polesworth Abbey Gatehouse: a documentary history and an historic building analysis*, Report 0706, Warwickshire Museum Field Services

Alcock N W & Walsh D 1993, Architecture at Cowdery's Down: a reconsideration, *Archaeol. J.* **150**, 403-409

Alcock N W & Woodfield C T P 1996, Social pretensions in architecture and ancestry: Hall House, Sawbridge, Warwickshire and the Andrewe family, *Antiq. J.* **76**, 51-72

Aldsworth F 2007, An early 15th-century barn at Charlton Court, Steyning, West Sussex, *Sussex Archaeological Collections* **145**, 153-79

Alston Leigh 1997, The Hermitage, Frostenden, *Eavesdropper-the Newsletter of the Suffolk Historic Buildings Group* **10** Autumn 1997, 13-14

Andrews D D, Gibson A & Tyres I 1997, Netteswellbury, Harlow, The Monks Barn, *Essex Archaeology and History* **28**, 234-7

Arnold A J, Laxton R R & Litton C D 2002, *Tree-ring analysis of timbers from 8 Vicars' Close, Lichfield, Staffordshire*, Centre for Archaeology Rep No 16/2002

Aston M, Austin D & Dyer C eds 1989, *The rural settlements of medieval England*, Oxford

Bailey John 2002, The development of carpentry in Bedfordshire, 1200-1550, in Stenning D F & Andrews D D eds 2002, 55-67

Barnard Mark 1995, drawing in note by Gosling Jane 1995, Visit to Debenham, *Eavesdropper-the Newsletter of the Suffolk Historic Buildings Group* **5** December 1995, 5-6

Beecham P Ed 1990, *Devon Buildings*, Devon Books

Beresford G 1975, *The medieval clay-land village: excavations at Goltho and Barton Blount*, Society for Medieval Archaeology Monograph **6**, London

Beresford G 1987, *Goltho: the development of an early medieval manor c.850-1150*, London, HMSO

Blair J 1987, The 12th-century Bishop's Palace at Hereford, *Med. Arch.* **31**, 59-72

Blaylock S R 1987, *Observations at the Bishop's Palace, Exeter*, Exeter Museums Archaeological Field Unit Report 87.03

Blaylock S R 2004, *Bowhill: The archaeological study of a building under repair in Exeter, Devon, 1977-95*, English Heritage monograph

Bonney H 1964, Balle's Palace, Salisbury, *Wiltshire Archaeology and Natural Hist Mag*, **59**, 155-67

Brandon R & J A 1849, *Open Timber Roofs of the*

Middle Ages, London

Bridge M 2008, The tree-ring dating of timbers from the 'Old Stables', Bishops Waltham Palace, Hampshire, *Oxford Dendrochronological Laboratory Report 2008/26*

Brigham T, Goodburn D & Tyers I with Dillon J 1995, A Roman timber building on the Southwark Waterfront, London, *Archaeol. J.* **152**, 1-72.

Brooke C 1969, *From Alfred to Henry III: 871-1272,* London

Brown S & M & Tyers I 2010, Manor Farm, Norfolk, *Norfolk Historic Buildings Group Newsletter* **19** Spring 2010, 8-11

Chapelot J & Fossier R 1985, *The village and house in the middle ages*, London

Charles F W B 1967, *Medieval cruck building and its derivatives*, Society for Medieval Archaeology Monograph **2**

Charles F W B 1971, The Guesten Hall roof, Worcester Cathedral, *Trans Ancient Monuments Soc* **18**, 49-63.

Charles F W B 1974, The timber-framed buildings of Coventry: 169 Spon Street, *Trans. Birmingham & Warwickshire Archaeol. Soc.* **86**, 113-131

Charles F W B 1997, *The great barn of Bredon: its fire and reconstruction*, Oxford

Charles F W B & Charles M 1984, *Conservation of timber buildings*, London

Colman S & Barnard M 1999, Raised-aisled halls and queen-post roofs, in Dymond & Martin 1999, 180-1

Cordingley R A 1961, British historical roof-types and their members, *Trans Ancient Monuments Soc* **9** New Series, 73-131

Courtenay L T 1984, The Westminster Hall roof and its 14th-century sources, *Journal of the Society of Architectural Historians* **43**, No 4, December, 295-309

Cox J & Thorp J R L 2001, *Devon Thatch*, Devon Books

Crook J 2002, Bishops and base crucks: fourteenth-century timber halls in England and their carpentry, in Meirion-Jones G, Impey E & Jones M eds 2002, 89-100

Currie C R J 1983, A Romanesque roof at Odda's Chapel, Deerhurst, Gloucestershire, *Antiq. J.* **63** pt 1, 58-63

Currie C R J 1988, Time and chance: modelling the attrition of old houses, *Vernacular Architecture* **19**, 1-9

Currie C R J 1990a, Time and chance: a reply to comments, *Vernacular Architecture* **21**, 5-9

Currie C R J 1990b, Gazetteer of archaic roofs in Herefordshire and Worcestershire churches, *Vernacular Architecture* **21**, 18-32

Currie C R J 1992, Larger medieval houses in the Vale of White Horse, *Oxoniensa* **57**, 81-244

Davis Beth 2002, Cambridgeshire: a cross roads for traditional building, in Stenning D F & Andrews D D eds 2002, 31-39

Dixon P 1982, How Saxon is the Saxon house?, in Drury P J ed 1982, 275-87

Dixon P 2002, The reconstruction of the buildings, in Losco-Bradley S & Kinsley G 2002, 89-99

Drinkwater N 1964, The Old Deanery, Salisbury, *Antiq. J.* **44** pt 1, 41-59

Drury P J ed 1982, *Structural reconstruction*, BAR British Series **110**

Dyer C 1989, *Standards of living in the later middle ages*, Cambridge

Dymond D & Martin E 1999, *An historic atlas of Suffolk*, Suffolk County Council, Lavenham 3rd Edition

Épaud Frédéric 2007, *De la Charpente Romane à la Charpente Gothique en Normandie*, Caen

Epaud F & Bernard V 2008, L'évolution des charpentes d'églises du Val d'Oise, du xie au xxe siecle, *Revue archéologique du centre de la France* **47**, 7-12

Fletcher J M & Spokes P S 1964, The origin and development of crown-post roofs, *Med. Arch.* **8**, 152-183

Giles Colum 1986, *Rural houses of West Yorkshire*, RCHME

Gilman P 1991, The Golden Fleece, Brook Street, South Weald, *Essex Archaeology and History* **22**, 76-86

Green H J M 1982, The origins and development of cruck construction in eastern England, in Drury P J ed 1982, 87-99

Gray P J 1990, Dating buildings in the Weald, in Warren 1990, 47-60

Greenslade M W ed 1990, *Victoria history of the County of Stafford 14*, Oxford

Harding J M 1980, Medieval vernacular roof trusses in Surrey, *Vernacular Architecture* **11**, 11.39-11.42

Harding J M 1993, Timber-framed early buildings in Surrey: a pattern for development, *c.*1300-1650, *Transactions of the Ancient Monuments Society* **37**, 117-145.

Harris R 2007, Dating the museum's buildings by tree-ring analysis, *Weald and Downland Open Air Museum House Magazine*, **spring 2007**, 31

Harrison Barry 1991, Longhouses in the Vale of York, *Vernacular Architecture* **22,** 31-39

Harrison Barry & Hutton Barbara 1984, *Vernacular Houses of North Yorkshire and Cleveland*, Edinburgh, John Donald

Henderson C G, Matthews A J & Parker R W 1995, *Archaeological evaluations of the Presentation of Mary convent school buildings, Palace Gate, Exeter*, Exeter Museums Archaeological Field Unit Report 95.05

Hewett Cecil 1974, *English cathedral carpentry*,

London, Wayland

Hewett C A 1980, *English historic carpentry*, Chichester, Phillimore

Hewett C A 1982, *Church carpentry*, Chichester, Phillimore

Hewett C A 1985, *English cathedral and monastic carpentry,* Chichester, Phillimore

Heywood Stephen 2002, Timber-framing in Norfolk, in Stenning D F & Andrews D D eds 2002, 47-50

Higham R & Barker P 1992, *Timber castles*, London

Hill N 2005, On the origin of crucks: an Innocent notion, *Vernacular Architecture* **36**, 1-14

Hill N 2007, New ideas revisited, *Vernacular Architecture* **38**, 8-10

Hill N & Miles D 2001, The Royal George, Cottingham, Northamptonshire: an early cruck building, *Vernacular Architecture* **32**, 62-67

Hoffsummer Patrick ed 2009, *Roof frames from the 11th to the 19th Century*, Bropols, Belgium

Hussey G 2003, Drawings of the Aisled Barn, Abbey Farm, Snape, *Eavesdropper-Newsletter of Suffolk Historic Buildings Group* **23**, 16-17

James S, Marshall A & Millett M 1984, An early medieval building tradition, *Archaeol. J.* **141**, 182-215

Jennings N 1997, Earthfast crucks in Cumbria, *Vernacular Architecture* **28**, 97-8

Jones S R 1977, West Bromwich Manor-house, *Trans. S. Staffordshire Archaeol. Hist. Soc.* **17** for 1975-76, 1-63

Jones Stanley, Major Kathleen & Varley Joan 1984, *The survey of ancient houses in Lincoln: I Priorygate to Pottergate*, Lincoln Civic Trust

Jones Stanley, Major Kathleen & Varley Joan 1990, *The survey of ancient houses in Lincoln: III Houses in Eastgate, Priorygate and James Street*, Lincoln Civic Trust

Knightly Charles 1999, *Barley Hall York,* Barley Hall Trust

Lewis E 1985, Excavations in Bishop's Waltham, 1967-78, *Proceedings of the Hampshire Field Club and Archaeological Society* **41**, 81-126

Lewis E, Roberts E & Roberts K 1988, *Medieval hall houses of the Winchester Area*, Winchester City Museums

Longcroft Adam Ed 2005, *The historic buildings of New Buckenham*, Journal of Norfolk Historic Buildings Group **2**

Longcroft Adam Ed 2009, *The Tacolneston project*, Journal of Norfolk Historic Buildings Group **4**

Losco-Bradley S & Kinsley G 2002, *Catholme: an Anglo-Saxon settlement on the Trent gravels in Staffordshire*, Nottingham Studies in Archaeology **3**

McDermott Mark 2006, The Somerset dendrochronology project: Summary of results, *Vernacular Architecture* **37**, 77-83

Martin David & Barbara 2006, *Farm Buildings of the Weald 1450-1750*, Kings Lynn, Heritage Marketing & Publications

Martin Edward 2008, The making of the East Anglian landscape, *Essex Historic Buildings Group Newsletter* **7**, 3-6

Martin Edward & Satchell Max 2008, *Wheare most inclosures be - East Anglian Fields: History, Morphology and Management*, East Anglian Archaeology Report **124**

Meeson R A 1971, Fourth report of excavations at Tamworth, Staffs., 1968 – some timber-framed and other buildings in Church Street, *Trans. S. Staffordshire Archaeol. Hist. Soc.* **12**, 5-8

Meeson R A 1983a, Plank-walled building techniques and the church of St. Lawrence, Rushton Spencer, *Vernacular Architecture* **14**, 29-35

Meeson R A 1983b, The timber frame of the hall at Tamworth Castle, Staffordshire, and its context, *Archaeol. J.* **140**, 329-340

Meeson R A 2001, Archaeological evidence and analysis: a case study from Staffordshire, *Vernacular Architecture* **32**, 1-15

Meeson R A 2002a, Time and place: medieval carpentry in Staffordshire, in Stenning D F & Andrews D D eds 2002, 110-122

Meeson R A 2002b, *119-122 Upper Spon Street, Coventry*, Rep. No. 02/18, unpublished client report

Meeson R A 2009, Wren, Pearce and St Mary's: Ingestre parish church and its roofs, *Trans. S. Staffordshire Archaeol. Hist. Soc.* **43**, 101-125

Meeson R A & Kirkham A 1993, 6 Market Street, Tamworth: a timber-framed building of 1695 and its context, *Trans. S. Staffordshire Archaeol. Hist. Soc.* **33** for 1991-92, 42-48

Meeson R A & Kirkham A 1995, Two medieval buildings in Horninglow Street, Burton-upon-Trent, *Trans. S. Staffordshire Archaeol. Hist. Soc.* **34** for 1992-93, 21-34

Meirion-Jones G, Impey E & Jones M eds 2002, *The seigneurial residence in western Europe AD c.800-1600*, BAR International Series **1088**

Mercer Eric 1975, *English vernacular houses*, London, HMSO

Mercer E 1990, Time and chance: a timely rejoinder, *Vernacular Architecture* **21**, 1-3

Mercer E 1996, Cruck distribution: a social explanation, *Vernacular Architecture* **27**, 1-2

Mercer E 1998, Cruck distribution – a brief note, *Vernacular Architecture* **29**, 57

Mercer E 2003, *English architecture to 1900: the Shropshire experience,* Logaston

Michelmore D J H 1991, Medieval houses in the Manor of Wakefield and Honour of Pontefract, *Yorkshire Archaeological Society 1991 (programme for study tour)*

Miles D 1997, Analysis of an archaic roof at Wistanstow, Shropshire, *Vernacular Architecture* **28**, 105-6

Miles D, Bridge M and Roberts E 2008, List 202: Hampshire dendrochronolgy project – phase 14, *Vernacular Architecture* **39**, 135-7

Miles D and Roberts E 2005, List 167; Hampshire dendrochronology project – phase 11, *Vernacular Architecture* **36**, 96-8

Miles D, Worthington M J, Groves C, 1999, *Tree-ring analysis of the nave roof, west door, and parish chest from the church of St Mary, Kempley, Gloucestershire,* Ancient Monuments Laboratory Rep 36/99, English Heritage

Miller K, Robinson J, English B and Hall I 1982, *Beverley, an archaeological and architectural study*, RCHME, HMSO

Millett M & James S 1983, Excavations at Cowdery's Down, Basingstoke, Hampshire 1978-81, *Archaeol. J.* **140**, 151-279

Milne G 1992, *Timber building techniques in London c.900-1400,* London

Milner J 1839 3rd. edn, *History and survey of the antiquities of Winchester*

Moran M 1985, Padmore, Onnibury, Shropshire, *Archaeol. J.* **142**, 340-60

Moran M 2003, *Vernacular buildings of Shropshire*, Logaston

Morley B M 1985, The nave roof of the Church of St Mary, Kempley, Gloucestershire, *Antiq. J.* **65** pt 1, 101-111

Morriss R K 2000, *The archaeology of buildings*, Stroud

Munby J, Sparks M and Tatton-Brown T 1983, Crown-post and king-strut roofs in south-east England, *Med Arch* **27**, 123-135

Oswald A 1962-3, The excavation of a thirteenth-century wooden building at Weoley Castle, Birmingham, 1960-61, *Med. Arch.* **6-7**, 109-134

Pearson S 1994, *The medieval houses of Kent: an historical analysis*, London, HMSO

Pearson S, Barnwell P S & Adams A T 1994, *A gazetteer of medieval houses in Kent,* London, HMSO

Penoyre Jane 2005, *Traditional houses of Somerset*, Somerset Books

Peters J E C 1969, *The development of farm buildings in western lowland Staffordshire up to 1800,* Manchester, MUP

Rackham O, Blair W J & Munby J T 1978, The thirteenth-century roofs and floor of the Blackfriars Priory at Gloucester, *Med. Arch.* **22**, 105-122

Rahtz P 1976, Buildings and rural settlement, in Wilson D M ed 1976, 49-98

Rahtz P 1979, *The Saxon and medieval palaces at Cheddar: excavations 1960-62*, BAR. British Series **65** 1979

Rahtz P & Watts L 1997, *St Mary's Church, Deerhurst, Gloucestershire,* Society of Antiquaries Research Report **55**

Roberts E 1998, The rediscovery of two major monastic buildings at Wherwell, *Proceedings of the Hampshire Field Club and Archaeological Society* **53**, 137-54

Roberts E 2003, *Hampshire houses 1250-1700: their dating and development*, Hampshire County Council

Roberts E 2005, The late-medieval remodelling of early roofs, *Vernacular Architecture* **36**, 66-8

Roberts E, Bans J-C and P, and Smith P, 1996, A thirteenth-century king-post roof at Winchester, *Vernacular Architecture* **27**, 65-68

Roberts Martin 2008, A preliminary roof typology for the North East of England, *Vernacular Architecture* **39**, 27-49

RCHME 1968 Royal Commission on Historic Monuments (England), *West Cambridgeshire*, London, HMSO

RCHME 1981 Royal Commission on Historic Monuments (England), *City of York: Vol 5 The central area*, HMSO

RCHME 1986 Royal Commission on Historic Monuments (England), *Rural houses of West Yorkshire 1400-1830*, London, HMSO

RCHME 1987 Royal Commission on Historic Monuments (England), *Houses of the North York Moors*, London, HMSO

Ryder P F 1978, *Timber framed buildings in South Yorkshire,* South Yorkshire County Council Archaeology Monograph **1**

Ryder P F 1987, Five South Yorkshire timber framed houses, *Yorkshire Archaeology J.* **59**, 51-82

Ryder Peter 2002, Timber-framing in South Yorkshire: confluence or confusion, in Stenning D F & Andrews D D eds 2002, 123-129

Smith C 2008, *A survey of the barn at West Court, Binsted, Hampshire*, Unpublished thesis, Hampshire Record Office: 52AO8/1.

Smith J T 1958, Medieval roofs: a classification, *Archaeol. J.* **115**, 111-49

Smith J T 1964, Cruck construction: a survey of the problems, *Med. Arch.* **8**, 119-51

Smith J T 1992, *English houses 1200-1800: The Hertfordshire evidence*, London, HMSO

Smith J T 2004, The origins and early development of the coupled rafter roof, *Sonderdruck aus Alles unter einem Dach,* Petersberg, 305-315

Smith P 1966, Footnote, in Roberts *et al.* 1996

Smith P 1988, *Houses of the Welsh countryside* 2nd edn., London HMSO

Smith P 1990, Time and chance: a reply, *Vernacular Architecture* **21**, 4-5

Stenning D F 1997, Wakes Colne, Normans Farm, *Essex Archaeology and History* **28**, 240-43

Stenning D F 2003, Small aisled halls in Essex, *Vernacular Architecture* **34**, 1-19

Stenning D F & Andrews D D eds 2002, *Regional variation in timber-framed building in England down to 1550*, 2nd ed, Chelmsford, Essex County Council

Taylor H M 1978, *Anglo-Saxon architecture 3,* Cambridge

Tringham N J 1990, The Cathedral and the Close, in Greenslade M W ed 1990

VAG 1991, *Vernacular Architecture Group spring conference programme 1991 – County Durham*

VAG 2008, *Vernacular Architecture Group Spring Conference Programme 2008 - Devon*

Vyner B ed 1994, *Building on the past: papers celebrating 150 years of the Royal Archaeological Institute*, London

Walker John 1996, A 13th/14th century roof at Bradwell Hall, Bradwell-on-Sea, Essex, *Essex Archaeology and History* **27**, 325-329

Walker J 1999, Late-twelfth and early-thirteenth-century aisled buildings: a comparison, *Vernacular Architecture* **30**, 21-53

Warren J ed 1990, *Wealden buildings: Studies in the timber-framed tradition of building in Kent, Sussex and Surrey*, Wealden Buildings Study Group

Warren W T 1899, *St. Cross Hospital, near Winchester*, Winchester

Watkins A 1918-20, Three early timber halls in the city of Hereford, *Woolhope Club Transactions*, 165-70

Westcott K 1992, The spire and roofs of Hatherleigh Church: Investigations following the storm damage of 1990, *Proceedings of the Devon Archaeological Society,* **50**, 61-89

Wilson D M ed 1976, *The archaeology of Anglo-Saxon England*, London

Wood M 1966, *The English medieval house,* London, Phoenix

Wrathmell S 1989a, *Domestic settlement 2: medieval peasant farmsteads*, York University Archaeological Publications **8**

Wrathmell S 1989b, Peasant houses, farmsteads and villages in north-east England, in Aston M, Austin D & Dyer C eds 1989, 247-259

Wrathmell S 1994, Rural settlements in medieval England: perspectives and perceptions, in Vyner B ed 1994, 189-190

Yeomans D T 1999, Early carpenters' manuals, 1592-1820, in Yeomans D T ed 1999, 189-209

Yeomans D T ed 1999, *The development of timber as a structural material*, Studies in the History of Civil Engineering **8**, Aldershot

11 INDEX OF BUILDINGS ILLUSTRATED

Buildings are indexed by Country, County, Parish or Town, and building name followed by Fig No.

BELGIUM
Liège, Sainte-Croix: 1.35

ENGLAND
Cambridgeshire
Croxton, Croxton Manor House: 1.25
Ely, Three Blackbirds: 2.5

Cornwall
Werrington, Cullacott: 5.32, 5.43

County Durham
Durham, Cathedral Choir: 6.14
    1-2 The College: 6.10.5a, 6.18
    Crook Hall: 6.15
Wycliffe with Thorpe, Girlington Hall: 7.9b

Cumbria
Carlisle Guildhall: 6.5
Kendal, Preston Patrick Hall: 1.36

Devon
Abbotsham, Shamlands, Barn: 5.10
Bratton Clovelly, Chimsworthy: 5.16
Brentor, East Liddaton: 5.11c
Bridford, Old Rectory: 5.7, 5.8, 5.9
Chagford, Higher Horselake: 5.17
Cheriton Bishop,
    Old Cheriton Rectory: 5.12, 5.13
Churchstow, Leigh Barton: back cover
Coldridge, Leigh Barton: 5.18
    Lower Chilverton: 5.33
Colebrooke, Elley: 5.41
Cornwood, Fardel, Domestic chapel: 5.4
Cotleigh, South Wood: 5.2b, 5.30
Cullompton, Langford Court: 5.11a
    Manor House: 5.44
Exeter
   Archdeacon of Exeter's House: 5.36a, 5.37
   Bishop's Palace: 5.3
   Cathedral roof: 5.24
   Exeter Guildhall: 5.38
   38 North St: 5.42
   The Close, The Law Library: 5.36b, 5.39
Great Torrington, 28 South Street: 5.48
Halberton, Moorstone Barton: 5.20, 5.21
Kentisbeare, Woodbarton: 5.23
Lapford, Bury Barton: 5.26, 5.28
Luppit, Pound Farm: 5.45
    St Mary: 5.14
Lustleigh, Old Rectory: 5.35
Morchard Bishop, Rudge: 5.25, 5.27
Nymet Rowland, Cleavanger: 5.29, 9.8
Ottery St Mary, Cadhay: 5.36b
Rose Ash, South Yarde: 5.11b, 5.34
Sandford, Prowse, house: 5.31;

Sandford, Prowse, solar crosswing: 5.40
Sherford: Keynedon Barton: 1.30
South Tawton, East Week: 5.46
Stockland, Townsend: 5.6
Tawstock, Fishleigh Barton: 5.5
Totnes, Dartington Hall Gatehouse: 5.19
Uplowman, Uplowman Court: 5.22
Widecombe, Higher Bonehill: 5.47
Witheridge, Pilliven: 5.15
Zeal Monachorum, Hayne: 5.2a

East Yorkshire
Beverley, Watton Priory: 7.26
Easington in Holderness, Tithe Barn: 7.14

Essex
Aldham, Ford Street, Wash Farm: 2.30
Aveley, Bretts Farm: 2.38
Billericay, Red Lion: 2.36c
Birdbrook, Baythorne Hall: 2.24b, 9.17a
Bradwell, Bradwell Hall: 2.4
Brentwood, 60-64 High Street: 2.19
Clavering, The Bury: 1.1a
Coggeshall, White Hart: 2.29
Colchester, High St, The George: 2.13b
Cressing Temple, Barley Barn: 2.3
    Barns: page 162
Debden, Brick House: 9.2
Fobbing, Copeland House: 2.44, 2.45
Fyfield, Fyfield Hall: 1.10, 2.1
Gestingthorpe, Hill Farm: 2.42
Great Bardfield, Gobions: 2.21
Great Dunmow, Shingle Hall: 2.13c
Great Easton, The Bell: 2.31
Great Maplestead, Hosdens: 2.43
Great Sampford, River Green House: 2.13a
Halstead, Bourchiers Chantry: 1.19, 2.35c
Heybridge, Heybridge Hall: 2.9
Little Chesterford, Old Cottage: 2.18
Little Waltham: 2.20
Littlebury, Catmere End, Graves Farm: 2.17
Magdalen Laver, Wynters Cottage: 9.4b
Maldon, 30 High Street: 2.46, 9.13a
Netteswellbury, Monks Barn: 2.32
Newport, Monks Barn: 2.13d
Roydon Church: 4.3
Saffron Walden, Ancient House: 2.35a
    Freswell House: 2.15a
Southminster, Sheepcote Farmhouse: 2.52
South Weald, Golden Fleece: 2.37
Stebbing, Tweed Cottage: 2.7
Terling, Ringers: 2.8
Thaxted, Horham Hall: 2.34
Wakes Colne, Normans Farmhouse: 2.16
Wethersfield, Great Codham Hall: 2.11
    The Stables: 2.49

Willingale, Shellow Cross Farmhouse: 2.51
Wimbish, Tiptofts: cover, 1.3c, 2.6, 2.10, 2.24a

Gloucestershire
Derehurst, Odda's Chapel: 4.2
Gloucester, Blackfriars: 4.6
Kempley, St Mary's Church: 4.4
Siddington, Siddington Barn: 1.9, 4.12a, 9.3b
Tewkesbury, 81-82 Barton St: 4.17

Greater Manchester
Bolton, Smithills Hall: 1.37;
      Solar wing: cover, 7.17

Hampshire
Andover, The Angel: 3.24b
Bishop's Waltham Palace,
    Lodging Range: 3.15a; stables 3.12c
Boarhunt: 3.18
Burgate, Lilac Cottage: 3.20
East Meon, Forge Sound: 3.9
    The Court House: 3.14
Fareham, 15 High Street: 3.12b, 9.11b
Hannington, Tan-y-Bryn: 3.5b, 3.5d
Kimpton Manor: 3.15b
Kingsclere, The Swan: 3.24c
Littleton, The Manor: 3.21b, 3.24d
Lymington, 26-7 High Street: 3.24a
Michelmersh Manor Farm: 3.8
Monk Sherborne, Priory Farm: 3.26
North Warnborough,
    Shepherd's Cottage: 3.23a
Odiham, 1 King Street: 3.21a, 9.5
    Manisty Cottage: 3.23b
    The Old Pest House: 3.21c
Petersfield, Tully's: 3.21d, 9.19
Ringwood, Poulner, Water Ditch Farm: 3.5a
Romsey Abbey: 3.10
South Stoneham, Shamblehurst Manor: 3.21e
Tichborne, Park View: 3.4, 3.5c
Titchfield, Abbey Barn: 3.13
    Place House Cottage: back cover
    The Jetty: 3.23c
West Tytherley, Church Farm: 3.17, 6.13
Wherwell Abbey: 3.11
Winchester, 35 High Street: 3.16
    St. Cross Hospital,
        The Brethren's Hall: 3.25

Herefordshire
Hereford, Bishop's Palace: 4.8b

Hertfordshire
Little Hadham, Clintons: 1.24
Little Wymondley, Wymondleybury: 9.17b
St Michael, Westwick Cottage: 1.8

Kent
Canterbury
    Guest Hall of St Augustine's Abbey: 1.14

Chiddingstone, Bayleaf: 1.38c
Harrietsham, Old Bell Farm: 1.38b

Lancashire
Bolton, Smithills Hall: 1.37;
      Solar wing: cover, 7.17

Lincolnshire
Gainsborough Old Hall: 9.16a
Lincoln, Cathedral: 4.7
    7 Eastgate: 6.10.4a
    11 Minster Yard: 6.16

Norfolk
Banham, King's Head Cottage: 8.12b, 9.14b
Denton, Lodge Farm: 2.28
Hales, Hales Hall Farmhouse: 2.33
Kings Lynn, No 3 King Street: 2.22
Newton Flotman, Dairy Farm Barn: 8.16d
Pulham Market, Manor Farm: 2.50
Pulham St. Mary, St Mary Magdalen: 8.14
Thetford, Thetford Priory, Abbey Farm: 2.23
Wacton, White House: 2.25

Northamptonshire
Cottingham, Royal George: 1.12

Northumberland
Beamish, Pockerley Farm: 6.10.5b, 6.17

North Yorkshire
Briggate, Kirkness Cottage: 7.8
Clint, Rose Cottage: 7.7
Helmsley, Canons' Garth: 6.19
Husthwaite, Baxby Manor: 7.1
Kettlewell, Fold Farm: 7.22
Lower Wharfedale, Weston Hall Barn: 7.18
Morton-on-Swale, Manor Farm: 7.24
Nether Poppleton, Barn: 7.25
Ripon, St Agnes House: 7.12
Scotton, Scotton Old Hall: 7.5
Sexhow, Sexhow Hall: 7.9a, 7.11
Snainton, Foulbridge Hall: 6.1, 6.2
York,
    Barley Hall: 6.12
    Bedern Hall: 7.19
    16-22 Coney Street: 6.6
    28-32 Coppergate: 6.9, 7.4c
    41-43 Goodramgate: 7.6
    49 Goodramgate: 6.10.3b
    60-72 Goodramgate, Lady Row: 6.3, 7.4a
    79 Low Petergate: 6.10.2a
    Merchant Adventurers' Hall: 1.34, 6.4,
        6.10.1a, 6.11, 7.10, 9.25a
    12-15 Newgate: 6.8, 7.4b
    St. Anthony's Hall: 7.20
    35 The Shambles: 7.21
    23 Stonegate: 6.10.3a, 9.25b
    50 Stonegate: 1.6
    111 Walmgate: 1.32, 1.33

Oxfordshire
Harwell, Lime Tree House: 1.16b
Lewknor Church Farm: 8.19, 8.20, 9.15b
Oxford, Merton College, Warden's Hall: 2.26
West Hagbourne, York Farm: 1.15, 9.3c

Shropshire
Astley Abbotts, Colemore Farm: 4.18e
Great Binnal: 4.19
Bedstone Manor: 4.15c
Donington Church: 4.22
Longnor, Moat House: 4.18b
Much Wenlock, 15 High Street: 4.11d
Newport Guildhall: 4.18d
Onibury, Padmore: 4.18c
Shrewsbury, Rigg's Hall: 4.26
Stokesay Castle: 4.15a
Upton Magna, Cruck Cottage: 4.12b
Wistanstow, Holy Trinity: 4.5

Somerset
Glastonbury Abbey Barn: 1.29
Wells Cathedral: Nave: 1.27; north aisle 1.11
Taunton, Fore St, The Tudor Tavern: 1.28

South Yorkshire
Whiston, Whiston Barn: 1.31

Staffordshire
Alrewas, 88 Main Street: 4.20c, 9.13b
Burton upon Trent, Horninglow Street: 4.16d
Burton upon Trent, Burton Abbey,
Abbot's House, Solar: 4.25
Catholme, Anglo-Saxon Building AS29: 4.2
Chebsey, Greenhill: 9.16b
Handsacre Hall: 4.11b
Ingestre Church: 4.24
Lichfield, 8 Vicars' Close: 4.20a
Longdon, Hill Top: 4.15b
Mavesyn Ridware Gatehouse: 4.16e
Rushton Spencer Church: 4.16a
Tamworth, 44-45 Church Street: 4.23c
West Bromwich Manor House: 1.16a, 4.11a

Suffolk
Baylham, Hilltop Farmhouse: 8.11
Bedfield, Mill Farm Cottage: 8.5
Brundish, The Woodlands: 1.5
Bures St Mary: 2.14c
Bury St Edmunds, The Guildhall: 2.40
62 Whiting Street: 2.36b
Coddenham, Choppins Hill: 8.8
Upper Spring Cottage: 8.13
Debenham, Crows Hall: 8.15
Eye, 22 Castle Street: 8.17
barn: 8.16c
Flatford, Valley Farm: 2.13e, 9.4a, 9.9
Framsden, Framsden Hall: 2.41
Fressingfield, Church Farm Stables: 2.12
Frostenden, The Hermitage: 8.10

Hacheston, Wisteria Cottage: 8.1, 8.12a, 9.14a
Hadleigh, 33 George St: 1.1b
Hundon, Thatchers: 1.38d
Ipswich, Ancient House: 2.35b
Clothiers' Hall: 2.39
Kenton, Messuage Farmhouse: 8.6
Moat Farmhouse: 8.12c
Layham, Marks Cottage: 2.48
Oakley, Poplar Farmhouse: 8.16b
Preston St. Mary, Swift Manor: 2.14b
Rishangles, Buck's Hall: 8.16a, 9.15a
Saxtead: 2.14a
Snape, Abbey Barn: 2.2
Somerleyton, Park Farm: 8.2
Stoke By Clare, Cellarers Hall: 2.36a
Thorndon, Low Barn Cottage: 8.9
Wenhaston, Railway Terraces: 2.15c
Wingfield, Wingfield College, barn: 8.18
Wrentham, 'The Guildhall': 8.7

Sussex
Chichester, Cathedral: 6.7
St. Mary's Hospital: front page
Horsham, Chennelsbrook Farm: 9.3d

Warwickshire
Baddesley Clinton: 4.20b, 4.20d, 4.23b
Coventry, 169 Spon Street: 4.16f
Henley-in-Arden, Heritage Centre: 4.16c
Knowle, Guild House: 1.1c
Mancetter Manor, House: 4.11c;
Crosswing 4.16b
Stratford upon Avon,
Masons Court: 1.38a
Anne Hathaway's Cottage: 4.15d
Temple Balsall: 4.8a

West Midlands
Temple Balsall: 4.8a

West Yorkshire
Hebden Bridge, Low Hollin: 7.15
Huddersfield, Longley Old Hall: 7.13
Leeds, Calverley Hall, Chapel: 7.23
Lofthouse, 176 Leeds Road: 7.16

Wiltshire
Salisbury, 62 The Close: back cover

Worcestershire
Bredon Barn: 4.9b
Leigh Court Barn: 4.9a, 9.7
Longdon, Upton upon Severn,
Eastington Hall: 4.10, 9.3a
Worcester, Guesten Hall roof: 4.18a

FRANCE
Normandy, Champagne-sur-Oise: 3.12a
Gisors, Chapelle Saint-Laurent des Vaux:
1.17

The Essex Historic Buildings Group

The Group was formed in 1983 by a varied collection of professionals and amateurs keen to see more work published on the lesser buildings of Essex for all to see and comment on. They were a mix of people with many interests, covering buildings, materials, documents, landscape or just an inquisitive mind. EHBG has published a continuing series of booklets, a manual on recording a building, holds an annual day school, and provides Sunday guiding at the Cressing Temple barns near Witham, Essex. The Group holds evening meetings about every six weeks, usually in Chelmsford, where local, national and internationally known speakers are invited to talk to the Group. In addition occasional visits are arranged to timber-framed buildings.

New members are always welcome; the only qualification is to have an interest in historic buildings, their use, setting or documented history. For more details see the Group's website www.ehbg.co.uk or email info@ehbg.org.uk

Barns at Cressing Temple, Essex